HISTORICAL DICTIONARIES OF PEOPLES AND CULTURES

Jon Woronoff, Series Editor

Kurds, by Michael M. Gunter, 2004. *Out of print. See No. 8.*
Inuit, by Pamela R. Stern, 2004.
Druzes, by Samy Swayd, 2006.
Southeast Asian Massif, by Jean Michaud, 2006.
Berbers (Imazighen), by Hsain Ilahiane, 2006.
Tamils, by Vijaya Ramaswamy, 2007.
Gypsies, 2nd ed., by Donald Kenrick, 2007.
Kurds, 2nd ed., by Michael M. Gunter, 2011.
Jews, by Alan Unterman, 2011.
Catalans, by Helena Buffery and Elisenda Marcer, 2011.
Australian Aborigines, by Mitchell Rolls and Murray Johnson, 2011.

REFERENCE
Library Use Only

Historical Dictionary of Australian Aborigines

Mitchell Rolls
Murray Johnson

Introduction by Henry Reynolds

*Historical Dictionaries of
Peoples and Cultures, No. 11*

The Scarecrow Press, Inc.
Lanham • Toronto • Plymouth, UK
2011

REF
DU
123.4
.R65
2011

Published by Scarecrow Press, Inc.
A wholly owned subsidiary of The Rowman & Littlefield Publishing Group, Inc.
4501 Forbes Boulevard, Suite 200, Lanham, Maryland 20706
http://www.scarecrowpress.com

Estover Road, Plymouth PL6 7PY, United Kingdom

Copyright © 2011 by Mitchell Rolls and Murray Johnson

All rights reserved. No part of this book may be reproduced in any form or by any electronic or mechanical means, including information storage and retrieval systems, without written permission from the publisher, except by a reviewer who may quote passages in a review.

British Library Cataloguing in Publication Information Available

Library of Congress Cataloging-in-Publication Data

Rolls, Mitchell, 1960-
  Historical dictionary of Australian Aborigines / Mitchell Rolls, Murray Johnson ; introduction by Henry Reynolds.
    p. cm. — (Historical dictionaries of peoples and cultures ; no. 11)
  Includes bibliographical references.
  ISBN 978-0-8108-5997-5 (cloth : alk. paper) — ISBN 978-0-8108-7475-6 (ebook)
  1. Aboriginal Australians—History—Dictionaries. 2. Aboriginal Australians—Dictionaries. I. Johnson, Murray, 1956- II. Title.
  DU123.4.R65 2011
  305.89'915003—dc22
                                                            2010037785

∞™ The paper used in this publication meets the minimum requirements of American National Standard for Information Sciences—Permanence of Paper for Printed Library Materials, ANSI/NISO Z39.48-1992.

Printed in the United States of America

Contents

Editor's Foreword *Jon Woronoff*	vii
Acknowledgments	ix
Note on Orthography	xi
Acronyms and Abbreviations	xiii
Maps	
Australian Aboriginal Tribes	xv
Australia	xvi
Chronology	xix
Introduction	1
THE DICTIONARY	9
Bibliography	185
About the Authors	213

Editor's Foreword

Of the various people examined in this series, few have felt the effects of European colonization to the same extent as the Australian Aborigines. Yet, when the Aboriginal people first set foot on this vast continent, perhaps 60,000 years ago, they were in the vanguard of human cultural development. By 35,000 years ago, they had spread throughout the land, occupying and adapting to a host of environmental conditions, ranging from sub-antarctic tundra in the south to tropical rainforest in the north and arid desert in the interior. Not surprisingly, this ensured that Aboriginal culture itself diversified widely, although without exception, all aspects of life were intrinsically linked to the territory of each particular group.

From 1788, however, the world of the Aboriginal people began to collapse when the British laid claim to Australia. Frontier conflict, introduced disease, loss of land, and the depletion of natural resources, all contributed to their dramatic demographic collapse. By the late 19th century, it appeared the Aborigines were destined to become extinct, which to some extent accounts for the confused British-Australian official policies that wavered between assimilation and segregation. But the Aboriginal people did not die out as expected; indeed, their resistance gradually strengthened, and although they remain today as a minority group within the broader Australian community, they have achieved considerable gains. Australian Aborigines today have full citizenship and political rights, and many groups have seen the return of their traditional land. Yet while Aboriginal art, literature, and other aspects of culture are increasingly respected by their fellow Australians, Aboriginal people still face numerous social and economic barriers to further advancement, and their overall circumstances remain far from satisfactory.

The *Historical Dictionary of Australian Aborigines* deals with all these issues, which has been a difficult task. The Aborigines are not a united community, and their lived experiences have differed widely throughout Australia. Nonetheless, through the chronology and introduction, it is possible to gain a clear understanding of these people, the effects of European colonization, and how they have managed to accomplish a cultural renaissance. More exacting details are then accessible through the many dictionary entries, which focus on the history, economy, society, and culture of the Aboriginal past and present. The entries also include significant people, places, institutions, concepts, and traditions. Fortunately, Aboriginal issues have increasingly gained significance in recent decades, and the bibliography includes an impressive array of books and articles.

This volume was written by two academics, Mitchell Rolls and Murray Johnson. Dr. Rolls is senior lecturer and codirector of the Riawunna Centre for Aboriginal Studies at the University of Tasmania, with his major research focus being cultural identity, race, and representation. Dr. Johnson has taught Australian and Aboriginal history at the University of Queensland, the Australian National University, and is also now at the Riawunna Centre for Aboriginal Studies. The introduction was produced by the eminent historian, Professor Henry Reynolds, who holds an honorary position at the University of Tasmania. All three have published extensively in their particular fields. Between them, they tell the story of a people who, despite being the subject of continuous research and scrutiny, deserve to be better known.

Jon Woronoff
Series Editor

Acknowledgments

Producing a dictionary is a complex task, and the authors are grateful for the invaluable assistance of those who helped and whose interest sustained our efforts. Three research assistants contributed prompt, thorough, and cheerful support. Helena Kajlich's assistance at the initial stage was instrumental. In the latter stages and at short notice, Nick Brodie undertook the tasks of drafting the chronology and painstakingly checking the bibliography. Pauline Marsh assisted as a researcher and with administrative matters. We thank Simon Barnard for producing the map and responding patiently to the many amendments we requested. Henry Reynolds wrote the introduction for us, assisted in drafting the bibliography, and read through the entries with care. We are grateful for his advice. The dictionary would not have been completed but for Murray Johnson's agreeing to be a coauthor at a late stage in the project. We thank Jon Woronoff, the series editor, for his interest in this project, patience, and advice. Queries, and they were multiple, were always promptly answered. We owe many heartfelt thanks to Lyn McGaurr, whose meticulous editing of our manuscript draft we could not have done without. Steadfastly professional, Lyn's attention to detail not only helped reduce errors and inconsistencies but also contributed to the clarity of the entries. Jaime Cave provided urgent invaluable assistance preparing the final manuscript, and we thank her very much. Finally, we are grateful for the support of Riawunna, the Centre for Aboriginal Studies at the University of Tasmania, Australia, and for the support and assistance of our academic and administrative colleagues.

Note on Orthography

In 1788, when the first European colony was established in Australia, some 250 different Aboriginal languages were spoken and many more dialects. These languages and dialects belonged to oral cultures. They were not recorded in writing. Many early attempts to write down these languages, which sometimes produced little more than word lists, were by untrained linguists. Their attempts to capture pronunciation through different letter combinations reflected their own ear and native tongue. Some amateur transcribers sought simplicity, modifying the language heard in an attempt to render it more sensible to an English (mostly) speaker. Others were more rigorous. Missionaries in particular, especially those who attained a high level of competence in the language of the Aborigines among whom they worked, did produce valuable written records of Aboriginal languages.

In the late 19th early 20th century, the need for a more standardized orthography was apparent, and from the mid-20th century onward, a great deal of work has been undertaken by Aborigines and linguists. Much of this work has entailed not only the accurate writing (and recording) of languages under threat of extinction but also the production of standard orthographies for the major languages still regularly spoken. Despite these attempts, multiple spellings for many Aboriginal words remain, and spellings once thought standardized are frequently revised. In this dictionary, we have used the most common spelling of most of the Aboriginal words and have provided alternative spellings where these are increasingly being used. This is to provide readers with the best opportunity for locating other relevant literature if they seek further information on a particular topic.

Acronyms and Abbreviations

AAL	Aborigines Advancement League
AAPA	Australian Aboriginal Progressive Association
AC	Companion of the Order of Australia
AIAS	Australian Institute of Aboriginal Studies
AIATSIS	Australian Institute of Aboriginal and Torres Strait Islander Studies
AICCA	Aboriginal and Islander Child Care Agency
ALRA	Aboriginal Land Rights (Northern Territory) Act 1976 (Commonwealth)
ALRC	Australian Law Reform Commission
ALT	Aboriginal Land Trust
AM	Member of the Order of Australia
AMS	Aboriginal Medical Service
ANTaR	Australians for Native Title and Reconciliation
AO	Officer of the Order of Australia
APA	Aborigines Progressive Association
APG	Aboriginal Provisional Government
ARIA	Australian Recording Industry Association
ATSIC	Aboriginal and Torres Strait Islander Commission
BP	Before Present
BRACS	Broadcasting for Remote Aboriginal Communities Scheme
CAAMA	Central Australian Aboriginal Media Association
CAR	Council for Aboriginal Reconciliation
CBE	Commander of the Order of the British Empire
CDEP	Community Development Employment Projects
FCAA	Federal Council for Aboriginal Advancement
FCAATSI	Federal Council for the Advancement of Aborigines and Torres Strait Islanders
HREOC	Human Rights and Equal Opportunity Commission
ICC	Island Co-ordinating Council
MBE	Member of the Order of the British Empire
NADOC	National Aborigines Day Observance Committee

NAIDOC	National Aboriginal and Islanders Day Observance Committee
NATSIAA	National Aboriginal and Torres Strait Islander Art Award
NIC	National Indigenous Council
NNTT	National Native Title Tribunal
Nodom	Northern Development and Mining
Norforce	North West Mobile Force
NTA	Native Title Act
OBE	Officer of the Order of the British Empire
RCIADIC	Royal Commission into Aboriginal Deaths in Custody
SNAICC	Secretariat of National Aboriginal and Islander Child Care
TAIMA	Townsville Aboriginal and Islander Media Association
TEABBA	Top End Aboriginal Bush Broadcasting Association
TI	Thursday Island
TSIMA	Torres Strait Islander Media Association
TSRA	Torres Strait Regional Authority
WAAMA	Western Australian Aboriginal Media Association

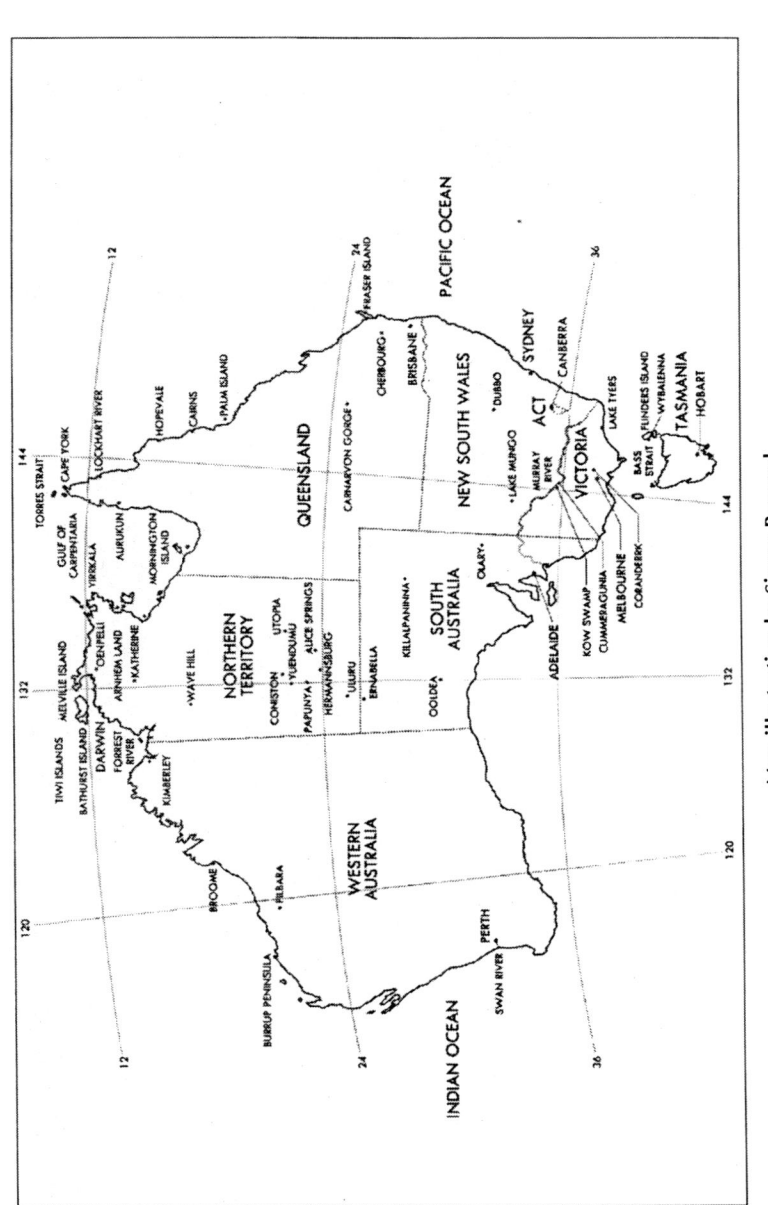

Map illustration by Simon Barnard

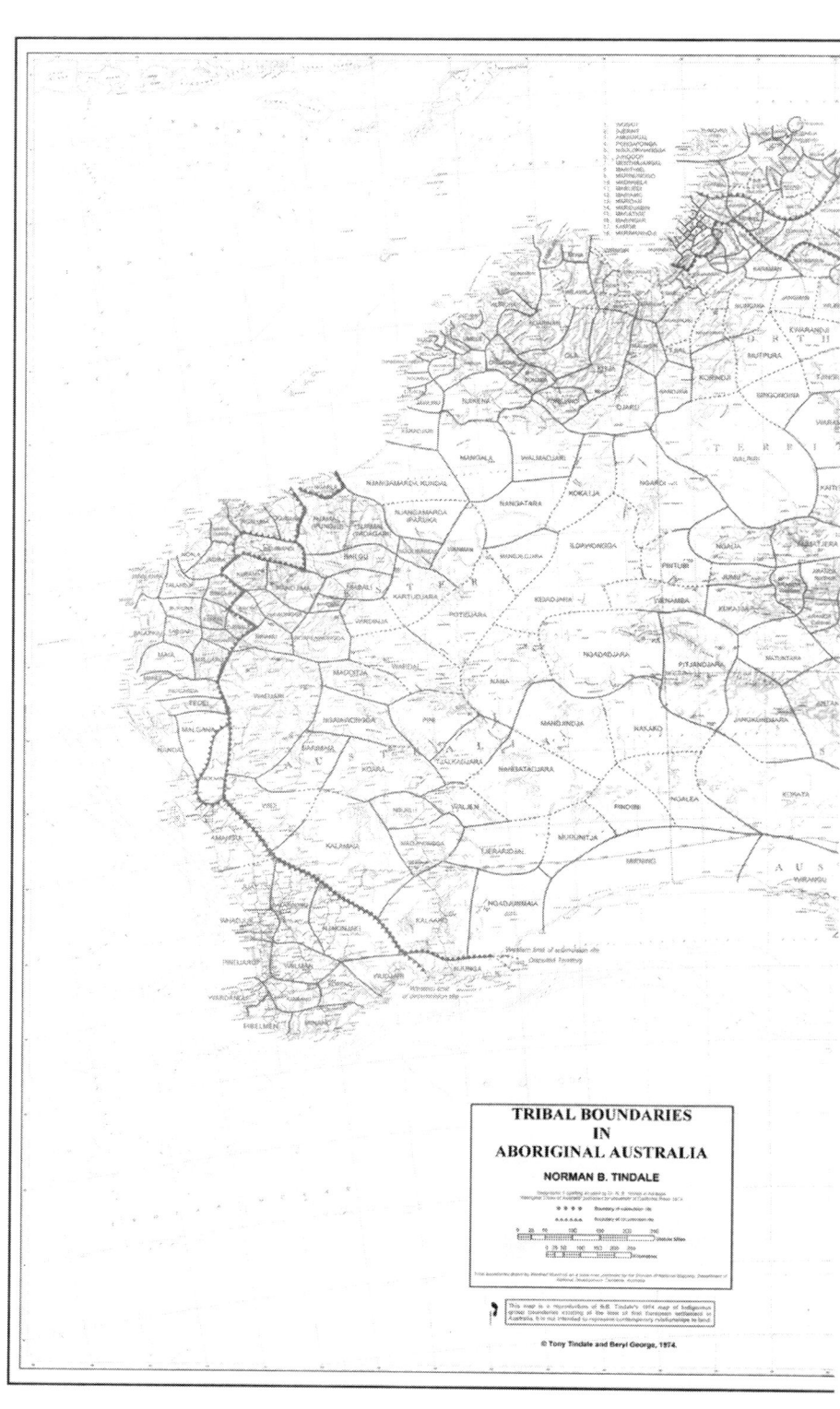

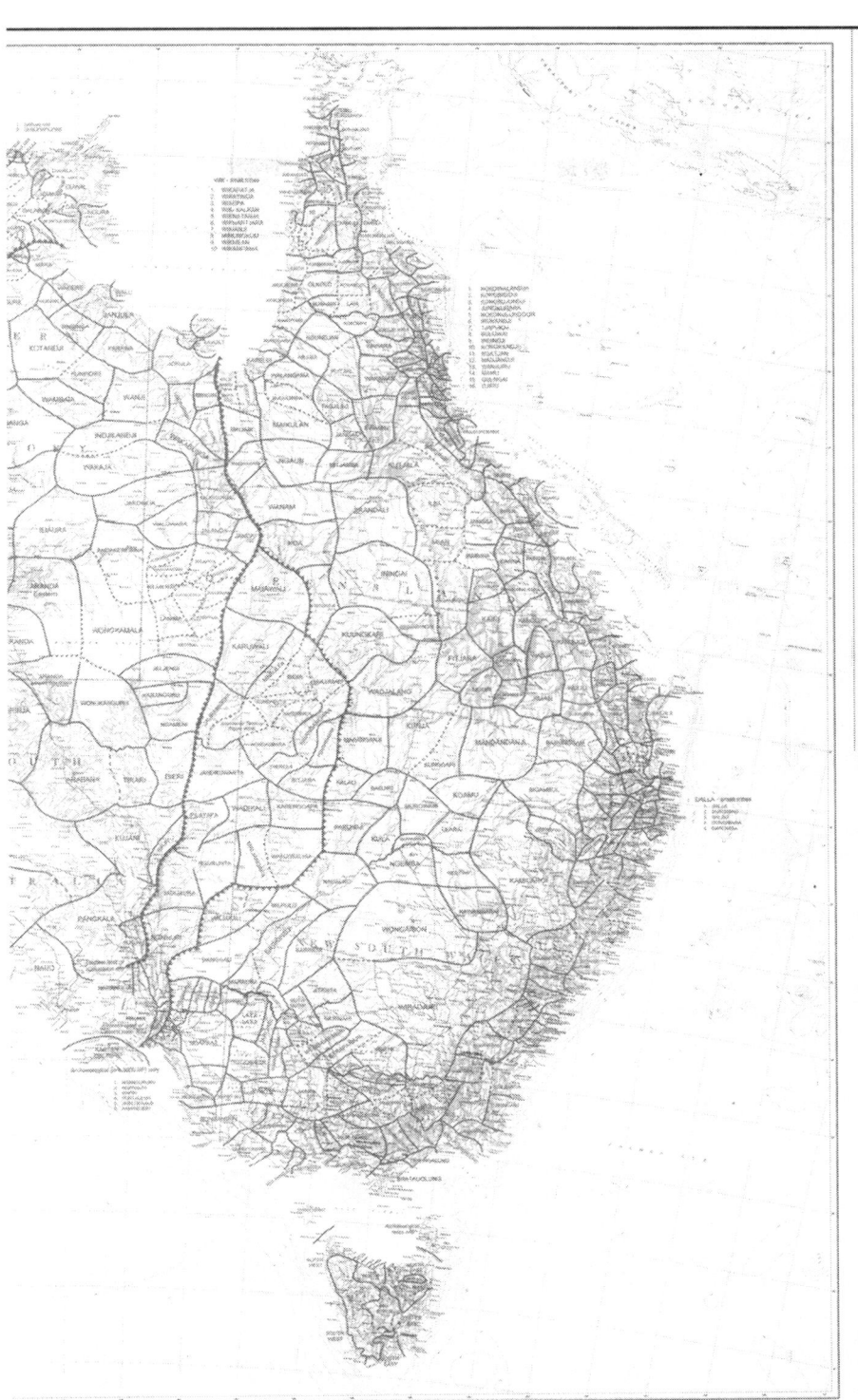

Chronology

c. 60,000 BP The earliest evidence that humans are present on the Australian continent is from this period.

c. 47,000 BP The extinction of the megafauna.

c. 45,000 BP Humans are occupying lakeside campsites at Lake Mungo in New South Wales. First evidence of cremation.

c. 40,000 BP The earliest known Australian engravings in rock are made in the Olary region of South Australia.

c. 35,000 BP There is evidence that humans are occupying parts of Tasmania.

c. 18,000 BP Humans are occupying Kow Swamp in Victoria.

c. 12,000–8000 BP The sea level rises and floods the Bassian land bridge, separating Tasmania from mainland Australia.

c. 4000 BP The dingo is introduced to the Australian continent. The Tiwi Islands are separated from the Australian mainland by rising seas.

c. 2000 BP The Torres Strait Islands are colonized by Melanesian peoples.

c. 1500 BP This period possibly sees the development of the didgeridoo.

1606 March: First known contact between Europeans and Aborigines when the Dutch navigator Willem Jansz sails down the west cost of Cape York in the *Duyfken*. Luis Vaez de Torres is the first European to enter the Torres Strait.

1642 2 December: Dutch mariners under the command of Abel Tasman land on the coast of Tasmania. The Dutch encounter evidence of human occupation but do not record having met with any Tasmanian Aborigines.

1700s Macassan fishermen are trading with Aboriginal people along the Arnhem Land coast.

1770 Captain James Cook charts the eastern coast of Australia.

1788 Retrospective estimates of the Aboriginal population at the time of colonization vary between 200,000 and one million. The estimate continues to vary; however, the figure of 300,000, while probably conservative, enjoys general support. **26 January:** The First Fleet lands in Sydney, commencing British settlement of Australia. **31 December:** Arabanoo is captured by the British with the aim of effecting communication with the Aboriginal people of the Sydney region.

1789 April: A smallpox epidemic strikes the Aboriginal population in the Sydney region. **May:** Arabanoo dies of smallpox. **November:** Bennelong is seized by the British in a new attempt to effect communication with local Aboriginal peoples.

1790 May: Bennelong escapes from captivity. **December:** Pemulwuy fatally spears Governor Arthur Phillip's gamekeeper.

1792 Pemulwuy organizes a series of raids on British farms and settlements west of Sydney. **December:** Bennelong sails to England with Governor Phillip.

1795 September: Bennelong returns to Sydney.

1801 Bongaree accompanies Matthew Flinders on a circumnavigation of the Australian continent. Bongaree has responsibility for establishing cordial relations between the British and Aboriginal groups during the voyage. **November:** Pemulwuy is proclaimed an outlaw, and a reward is offered for his capture.

1802 June: Pemulwuy is shot and killed.

1803 Colonial settlement commences in Tasmania.

1823 Musquito leads a series of raids by the Tame Mob on pastoral properties in Tasmania.

1824 In Tasmania, violent conflict between British settlers and Tasmanian Aborigines intensifies. Eight years of intermittent conflict follow in what is known as the Black War.

1825 Reverend Lancelot Threlkeld establishes a mission in Lake Macquarie on the central coast of New South Wales.

1828 Following the arrival of the ship *Bussorah Merchant*, a second major epidemic of smallpox strikes the Aboriginal population of southeastern Australia.

1829 George Augustus Robinson is appointed "conciliator" in Tasmania.

1830 Robinson commences the first of six expeditions on his Friendly Mission, gathering Tasmanian Aborigines for removal to Flinders Island. **7 October:** The Black Line operation commences in Tasmania. **24 November:** Having failed in its objectives, the Black Line operation ends.

1831 A mission is established in the Wellington Valley by the Church Missionary Society.

1833 11 July: In Western Australia, the Indigenous resistance fighter Yagan is shot and killed. Yagan's head is decapitated, smoke-dried, and sent to England.

1834 August: Robinson's final Friendly Mission concludes.

1835 June: John Batman concludes a treaty with Aboriginal people in what is now southern Victoria. This treaty is the only one of its kind concluded in Australia.

1836 Governor Richard Bourke annuls Batman's treaty. The British claim to sovereignty over Aboriginal peoples in Australia is upheld in Sydney in *Rex v. Jack Congo Murrell*. **September:** The first issue of the *Aboriginal or Flinders Island Chronicle* is published, making it the first periodical produced by Aboriginal people in Australia.

1837 Native Police are first utilized in the Port Phillip District in Victoria.

1838 June: Ten stockmen and hut keepers kill and mutilate 28 Aboriginal people in the Myall Creek Massacre at the Gwydir River in northern New South Wales. **November:** The perpetrators of the Myall Creek Massacre are tried in Sydney and acquitted by the jury. Governor George Gipps orders a retrial for seven of the offenders, who are then found guilty. **December:** Those found guilty of the Myall Creek Massacre are hanged, the first and last time Europeans are executed for killing Aborigines.

1856 Control of Aboriginal matters passes from Great Britain to the then four eastern colonies of Australia: New South Wales, Victoria, South Australia, and Tasmania.

1868 An all-Aboriginal cricket team tours England.

1869 Victoria is the first state to pass "protection legislation" through the Aboriginal Protection Act.

1871 The London Missionary Society arrives in the Torres Strait Islands.

1876 On 8 May, Truganini dies in Tasmania. She was held to be the "last of her race" for many decades.

1878 Truganini's remains are exhumed by the Royal Society of Tasmania.

1883 The Aborigines Protection Board is established in New South Wales.

1886 The Talgai skull is unearthed in southeastern Queensland, the first archaeological evidence uncovered by Europeans suggestive of ancient Aboriginal occupation of the continent.

1894 Jandamarra commences a three-year campaign of organized resistance against European settlers in the Kimberley region of northwestern Australia.

1897 Queensland passes the Aboriginals Protection and Restriction of the Sale of Opium Act, which becomes the model "protection act" for Western Australia, South Australia, and the Northern Territory.

1898–99 The Cambridge Ethnographic Expedition records the cultural life of Torres Strait Islanders in what becomes the oldest surviving ethnographic film in the world.

1904 Daisy Bates commences ethnographic fieldwork in southwestern Western Australia. Truganini's remains are put on display at the Tasmanian Museum.

1911 Estimated Aboriginal population approximately 31,000. The population experienced a rapid decline with the arrival of Europeans in 1788. By the 1930s, however, it had begun to recover.

1912 Bates establishes the first of her isolated camps among Aboriginal people at Eucla on the Great Australian Bight.

1917 May: Military regulations are amended to allow Indigenous Australians to enlist in the armed forces if they can prove one parent to be of European origin.

1924 The Australian Aboriginal Progressive Association (AAPA) is founded.

1926 June: The Forrest River Massacre takes place northwest of Wyndham in Western Australia.

1927 AAPA is dissolved.

1928 In the Northern Territory, 31 Aborigines are recorded killed (with oral testimony putting the number at more than 100 killed) in a series of raids known as the Coniston Massacre, attracting widespread condemnation of the killings.

1930 With the publication of his *Myths and Legends of the Australian Aboriginals*, later reprinted as *Legendary Tales of the Australian Aborigines*, David Unaipon becomes the first Indigenous writer to have his work published in a book, although the work is wrongly attributed to the anthropologist William Ramsay Smith.

1931 The Arnhem Land Reserve is declared.

1933 Estimated Aboriginal population approximately 45,000.

1936 The Australian Aborigines' League (AAL) is formally constituted. The Ernabella Mission is established in the Musgrave Ranges of Central Australia.

1937 June: The Aborigines Progressive Association (APA) is formed.

1938 Daisy Bates's *The Passing of the Aborigines* is published. **26 January:** The Sydney-based Aborigines Progressive Association declares the sesquicentenary of the First Fleet's arrival a Day of Mourning.

1941 8 June: Pearl Gibbs becomes the first Aboriginal person to broadcast a script of his or her own on radio.

1942 At Skull Springs, an estimated 200 Aboriginal people from 23 language groups meet to discuss action for ending their exploitation.

1946 5 May: Aboriginal employees on sheep stations in the Pilbara region of Western Australia engage in the first large-scale industrial action by Aboriginal pastoral workers in what becomes known as the "Black Eureka."

1947 Estimated Aboriginal population approximately 51,000. *Primitive People—The Australian Aborigines* becomes the first ethnographic film professionally produced by Australians. Truganini's remains are removed from public display in the Tasmanian Museum following complaints from the public.

1949 The Commonwealth Electoral Act grants the franchise to Aborigines and Torres Strait Islanders through service in the Australian Armed Forces.

1951 The Native Welfare Conference officially endorses a policy of assimilation.

1952 The Aboriginal mission Ooldea in South Australia is closed prior to the commencement of nuclear tests at nearby Maralinga. For three decades, because of the Maralinga tests, local Aboriginal peoples are denied access to traditional lands.

1956 The Aboriginal-Australian Fellowship is established.

1957 The Aborigines Advancement League (AAL) is formed with the merging of the Australian Aborigines' League and the Save the Aborigines Committee. The National Aborigines Day Observance Committee (NADOC) is formed.

1958 February: The Federal Council for Aboriginal Advancement (FCAA) is established in Adelaide.

1960 The Commonwealth Social Services Act gives Aborigines and Torres Strait Islanders access to Commonwealth pensions and allowances.

1961 The Australian Institute of Aboriginal Studies (AIAS) commences as a research organization.

1962 Aborigines and Torres Strait Islanders are made eligible to vote in federal elections through the passing of the Commonwealth Electoral Act.

1963 14 August: Yolgnu people forward two bark petitions to Federal Parliament protesting against the excision of 390 square kilometers of reserve land for mining purposes. Although the petition was unsuccessful, it did result in the first official acknowledgment that Aboriginal native title had existed.

1964 The Australian Institute of Aboriginal Studies (AIAS) is made a Commonwealth statutory body by the AIAS Act 1964. The Federal Council for Aboriginal Advancement (FCAA) has its name changed to the Federal Council for the Advancement of Aborigines and Torres Strait Islanders (FCAATSI) at the request of Torres Strait Islanders. The protest group Student Action for Aborigines is formed at the University of Sydney. Oodgeroo Noonuccal publishes *We Are Going*, the first volume of poetry published by an Aboriginal writer.

1965 Queensland becomes the last Australian state to grant Aborigines and Torres Strait Islanders the franchise. Charles Nelson Perkins is awarded a bachelor of arts, becoming the first Indigenous Australian to gain a university degree. **February:** The Freedom Ride, organized by Student Action for Aborigines, attracts publicity concerning conditions of poverty and discrimination in northern New South Wales.

1966 Estimated Aboriginal population approximately 85,000. Aborigines of mixed descent are included for the first time in the census data and are counted as Aborigines. **23 August:** Aboriginal stockmen and domestic workers, mostly Gurindji, walk off Wave Hill and Newcastle Waters pastoral properties in a dispute over wages, working conditions, and rights to traditional lands and practices.

1967 27 May: A national referendum is held to formally change two clauses regarding Aborigines in the Australian Constitution, with the referendum carried by the highest "yes" vote ever recorded, at 90.77 percent.

1968 Archaeological excavations at Kow Swamp in Victoria uncover ancient skeletons. The federal government grants a 42-year lease for mining part of the Gove Peninsular in the northeast of the Arnhem Land Reserve, leading to further protest and litigation by the Yolgnu.

1969 The Institute for Aboriginal Development is established in Alice Springs in the Northern Territory.

1971 The first Aboriginal Legal Service and the first Aboriginal Medical Service (AMS) are established in Redfern, Sydney. The Aboriginal Flag is first flown as part of National Aborigines Day. Neville Bonner becomes the first Indigenous federal politician, serving as senator until 1983. The Northern Territory Supreme Court hands down the verdict in the Gove land rights case, holding that the Yolgnu did not enjoy a proprietary interest in their land.

1972 A policy of Indigenous self-determination is introduced by the federal Labor government. A program of bilingual education for Aboriginal Children is established in the Northern Territory. **26 January:** The Aboriginal Tent Embassy is established on the lawns of Parliament House in Canberra. **November:** Douglas Nicholls becomes the first Aborigine to be knighted, at Buckingham Palace.

1973 The Commonwealth Migration Act allows Aborigines and Torres Strait Islanders to obtain passports without a special permit. Justice A. E. Woodward is appointed by the federal Labor government to lead a commission of inquiry into how Aboriginal land rights could be realized in the Northern Territory.

1974 Justice Woodward's second and final land rights report is submitted.

1975 The Commonwealth Racial Discrimination Act is passed. The first portion of Gurindji land is returned to its traditional owners. Prime Minister Gough Whitlam provides a potent symbol of the return by pouring a handful of soil into the hands of Vincent Lingiari, the leader of the Wave Hill strike.

1976 Estimated Aboriginal population is approximately 161,000. The Aboriginal Land Rights (Northern Territory) Act is passed, providing Australia's first statutory land claims process. **April:** Having been returned to the Tasmanian Aboriginal Community, Truganini's remains are cremated.

1977 The Community Development Employment Projects (CDEP) program commences. The National Aboriginal Conference is formed.

1978 The Federal Council for the Advancement of Aborigines and Torres Strait Islanders (FCAATSI) is disbanded due to the withdrawal of government funding. The Kimberley Land Council is established.

1980s A period of intense debate about the nature and impact of European colonization starts in what becomes known as the "history wars."

1982 Eddie Mabo initiates legal proceedings seeking recognition of propriety rights and acknowledgment of traditional ownership that ultimately becomes the Mabo Decision.

1984 The Island Co-ordinating Council (ICC) is created in Queensland. Some of the land associated with the Maralinga Nuclear tests is handed back to the Maralinga Tjarutja under the South Australian Maralinga Tjarutja Land Rights Act 1984.

1985 Uluru National Park is granted to the Anangu as traditional land, and a comanagement 99-year lease is established with the federal government.

1986 The Human Rights and Equal Opportunity Commission (HREOC) is established.

1987 The government-funded Broadcasting for Remote Aboriginal Communities Scheme (BRACS) is launched. **October:** The Royal Commission into Aboriginal Deaths in Custody (RCIADIC) is formally established.

1988 The Aboriginal and Torres Strait Islander Commission (ATSIC) is created through statute by Federal Parliament. NADOC recognizes Torres Strait Islanders and changes its name to NAIDOC. **12 June:** The Barunga Statement is presented to Prime Minister Robert Hawke at Barunga in the Northern Territory.

1989 The Australian Institute of Aboriginal Studies (AIAS) is made the Australian Institute of Aboriginal and Torres Strait Islander Studies (AIATSIS) by the AIATSIS Act 1989. Nitmiluk (Katherine Gorge) National Park in the Northern Territory is returned to Jawoyn ownership.

1990 The Museum of Victoria returns material excavated from Kow Swamp to the local Aboriginal community.

1991 Estimated Aboriginal population approximately 265,000. The Council for Aboriginal Reconciliation (CAR) is established as a statutory authority under the Commonwealth Council for Aboriginal Reconciliation Act. **15 April:** The final report of The Royal Commission into Aboriginal Deaths in Custody (RCIADIC) is tabled. **July:** The Hawke federal Labor government bans mining at Coronation Hill at Kakadu in the Northern Territory.

1992 The Australian Institute of Criminology's National Death in Custody Program is established to monitor deaths in custody. **January:** The Torres Strait Islander Flag is selected by the Island Co-ordinating Council (ICC). **3 June:** The Mabo Decision of the High Court of Australia overturns the legal doctrine of *terra nullius* and recognizes the existence of Native Title. Kakadu National Park in the Northern Territory is listed on the World Heritage List.

1993 Michael Dodson becomes the first Indigenous Aboriginal and Torres Strait Islander social justice commissioner. The Commonwealth Native Title Act (NTA) provides for Indigenous land use agreements and establishes the National Native Title Tribunal (NNTT).

1994 Cathy Freeman creates controversy by carrying the Aboriginal Flag in addition to the Australian flag during a lap of honor after winning the 200-meter sprint at the Commonwealth Games. The Torres Strait Regional Authority (TSRA) is established.

1995 11 May: The enquiry into the impact of the state and federal government policies and practices of forcibly removing Aboriginal children from their families is established, leading to the report *Bringing Them Home*. **June:** The Hindmarsh Island Royal Commission is established by the South Australian government to assess Indigenous claims of sacred associations in an area of proposed development. **14 July:** The Aboriginal and Torres Strait Islander flags are officially proclaimed to be "flags of Australia."

1996 John Howard's new federal Liberal government legislates to allow construction to commence at Hindmarsh Island. **23 December:** The Wik Decision of the High Court finds that pastoral leases do not necessarily confer exclusive possession to the lessee and that such leases do not necessarily extinguish native title.

1997 Yagan's head is returned from England to the Western Australian Aboriginal Community. **26 May:** The report *Bringing Them Home* is tabled in Federal Parliament.

1998 Substantial amendments are made to the Native Title Act (NTA), including the introduction of Indigenous land use agreements. **26 May:** The first National Sorry Day is held.

1999 The Batchelor Institute is established to provide tertiary education to Indigenous Australians.

2000 Cathy Freeman lights the Olympic Cauldron to open the Olympic Games in Sydney. **28 May:** Some 250,000 people participate in the People's Walk for Reconciliation across the Sydney Harbour Bridge.

2001 30 June: Estimated Aboriginal and Torres Strait Islander population of 458,500. This represents 2.4 percent of the total population.

2002   Keith Windschuttle's *The Fabrication of Aboriginal History, Volume One: Van Diemen's Land 1803–1847* is published, exacerbating the history wars by downplaying and denying the violence perpetrated by European colonists. **September:** Prime Minister Howard rejects many of the final recommendations of the report given by the Council for Aboriginal Reconciliation (CAR).

2004   The Aboriginal and Torres Strait Islander Commission (ATSIC) is abolished. Cameron (Mulrunji) Doomagee dies in police custody on Palm Island, Queensland, reigniting concern over Aboriginal deaths in custody. **July:** The Cape York Institute for Policy and Leadership is established. **November:** The National Indigenous Council (NIC), an appointed 14-member advisory body, replaces ATSIC. Its role is to provide expert advice to the federal government with the aim of improving outcomes for Indigenous Australians.

2006   The Tasmanian state government sets aside $AUD5 million in compensation to be paid to Stolen Generations members and their children. **30 June:** Estimated Aboriginal and Torres Strait Islander population of 517,043. **8 August:** The Board of Inquiry into the Protection of Children from Sexual Abuse is established in the Northern Territory.

2007 17 February: Prime Minister John Howard announces the cessation of the Community Development Employment Projects (CDEP) program in cities with unemployment rates of 7 percent or higher. **15 June:** The *Little Children Are Sacred Report* is released. In response, the federal government initiates the Northern Territory Emergency Response through intervention in 73 communities and 45 towns, invoking the constitution to override the powers of the Northern Territory government and passing a legislative package establishing a taskforce and providing exemption from the Racial Discrimination Act. **23 July:** The federal government announces the complete phasing out of the CDEP program in the Northern Territory. **2 August:** The Supreme Court of South Australia awards $AUD525,000 in compensation to Bruce Trevorrow for the injuries and loss he suffered after having been taken from his mother, without her consent, in 1957 by the Aborigines Protection Board.

2008   The Northern Territory abandons the policy of bilingual education for Aboriginal Children as established in 1972. **15 January:** The federal government axes the NIC. **13 February:** Prime Minister Kevin Rudd issues a formal national apology to the Stolen Generations.

2009 8 April: Aboriginal leader Noel Pearson resigns as Director of the Cape York Institute to challenge the Queensland government's "Wild Rivers" legislation, which Pearson claimed would stifle Aboriginal economic development on Cape York Peninsular. **30 November:** Tangentyere Council and 16 Alice Springs Town Camp Housing Associations agree to sublease land to the Commonwealth government in exchange for new housing and infrastructure projects.

2010 12 January: Federal Opposition leader Tony Abbott proposes to introduce a Private Members Bill in Parliament to defeat the Queensland government's Wild Rivers legislation. **30 January:** In a historic deal, the residents of Ilpeye Ilpeye, a major Alice Springs Town Camp, agree to surrender their Native Title to the Commonwealth government. This will allow tenure to be converted to freehold and pave the way for private home ownership. **2 May:** The National Congress of Australia's First Peoples is launched.

Introduction

The Aboriginal Australians first arrived on the continent at least 60,000 years ago. They almost certainly landed on the northwest coast by sea from the nearby islands of the Indonesian archipelago. That first arrival may have been replicated many times over. The following exploration and settlement of a vast and varied continent was a venture of heroic proportions. The new settlers had reached southern Tasmania, the point farthest from the original landfall, at least 35,000 years ago. By the early 17th century, when the first European seafarers arrived in Australian waters, the Aboriginal nations were living in every part of the continent, having colonized the tropical rainforests of the north, the vast arid deserts of the interior, and the cool, damp woodlands of the southeast. In the process, they had learned how to live with the unique flora and fauna, how to shape and manage the landscape with the systematic use of fire, and how to mould their societies to their country with art, religion, and ritual.

The more deeply the Aborigines penetrated into the continent, the farther they traveled from any contact with the outside world. Trade routes and song lines (with their basis in Dreaming stories) crisscrossed the continent, but for great stretches of time, generations lived and died within the boundaries of their own country. It is probable that Aborigines always had intermittent contact with Indonesian people across the Timor Sea, and from at least the 17th century, they also traded regularly with well-organized annual expeditions of Macassans, whose members spent months each wet season camped on hospitable beaches along hundreds of miles of coast from the Kimberley in the west to the Gulf of Carpentaria in the east. Farther east again, at the top of Cape York, local Aborigines had regular and not necessarily friendly contact with the seafaring Melanesian Torres Strait Islanders, who had settled on the spray of small islands in the shallow sea between Australia and New Guinea about 2,000 years ago.

Europeans visited many parts of the Australian coast during the 17th century, but they stayed longer and eventually planted settlements in the southeast (Sydney, 1788; Hobart, 1803–4), among those people with least contact with the outside world. The Tasmanians had been cut off from contact with mainland Australia when the Bassian Plain flooded to form Bass Strait. Hundreds of generations of Tasmanians had known nothing but their own small island and its 5,000 or so inhabitants. However, in the 30 years between 1772 and 1802, the southeast of the island was visited by a parade of French and British expeditions as a prelude to three permanent settlements established in 1803–4.

The most striking feature of the European invasion and settlement was that it took so long to complete. The vastness of the continent was an abiding problem in the era before steamships and trains, but of greater consequence was the arid, inhospitable nature of much of the land, offering little prospect of productive colonization. Aboriginal land was, therefore, wrenched from its traditional owners, serially, over many decades. The result was that many Aborigines never came into contact with Europeans during the first century of settlement. The last groups living beyond the reach of the white man did not "come in" from the bush until the 1960s.

Such slow and fitful settlement over a vast and varied continent meant that the Aboriginal experience differed greatly depending on the time and the nature of the European invasion. The earliest settlements on the sites of the modern port cities—Sydney, Hobart, Adelaide, Perth, and Brisbane—were the least typical. In those places, large parties of Europeans suddenly arrived, instantly outnumbering the resident clans. Their ships disgorged vast quantities of objects and exotic animals. The strangers immediately began building huts, erecting tents, clearing land, and cutting down trees. It must have been an awesome and overwhelming experience. But it was quite unlike what happened to most Aborigines living in the boundless hinterland, where settlement was heralded by small exploring parties and then consummated by parties that were equally small but were accompanied by flocks of sheep or herds of cattle and did not move on but took possession of the best grassland and often the only locally available source of surface water. These encounters on the outer fringes of the pastoral frontier were the most common Aboriginal experience.

There were different patterns of contact in a few places where climate, terrain, and resources determined a distinctive outcome. In some parts of northern Australia, prospectors looking for minerals presaged the arrival in Aboriginal country of large numbers of hopeful miners, who camped in large concentrations near river beds or along promising lines of reef. Around the tropical coast, swamp and mangrove kept the cattlemen away, but nearby waters held promise of pearls, trochus shell, and trepang. European and Japanese seamen came ashore seeking women, water, and young men to assist in their labor-intensive industries. Also in the north, there were some places hitherto hostile to settlement where missionaries of numerous faiths, seeking souls rather than resources, preceded other Europeans.

The experience of settlement, therefore, differed depending on where and when it occurred. But for all the variety, there were common and, ultimately, all-powerful themes. Central to the whole history of European–Aboriginal relations was the decision of the British government to disregard both Aboriginal sovereignty and land ownership. No recognized treaties were ever signed with indigenous Australians, and the whole continent was treated as a *terra nullius*—a land without owners. From the moment of the major claims of sovereignty in 1788 in eastern Australia, 1824 in the center, and 1829 in the west, the British Crown became both the sovereign and the beneficial owner of all the land on the continent. These were momentous and fateful decisions. There was no need to deal with the Aborigines diplomatically, to learn their languages and conduct negotiations with them about matters of common concern. Nor was there any recognition given to Indigenous law. The British carried their law with them, and it became the only law that could be formally recognized. The settlers naturally concluded that the land they sought was either vacant and open to occupation or could be accepted as an unencumbered grant from the Crown. It made the expropriation of land a simple, and in most cases a guiltless, procedure. Aboriginal resistance could be seen as criminal behavior, their attacks on the ubiquitous livestock wanton destruction.

The question of land rights became a major issue of Australian politics in the 1970s. Legislation recognized indigenous ownership in the federally controlled Northern Territory in 1976. The High Court of Australia finally recognized native title and overturned the doctrine of *terra nullius* in the Mabo Decision in 1992. The linked questions of Aboriginal traditional law and of sovereignty remain both contentious and unresolved.

The other question that has been at the forefront of national debate in recent years is the nature of settlement and the violence that accompanied it. The resulting controversy has been a major component of what have been called the "history wars." There has been dispute over the question of whether the occupation of Australia could be regarded as an invasion or as a more-or-less peaceful occupation. The extent of frontier violence has been at the center of this debate, with widely differing interpretations of the likely death toll from the small-scale violence that accompanied Australian settlement from the first few weeks at Sydney Cove in 1788 until the last documented mass killing of Aborigines in 1928.

Attending the debate about violence, invasion, and expropriation are the unavoidable questions of apology and reparation. State governments and assorted churches offered apologies to the Aborigines during the 1990s—a course of action resisted by the conservative federal government of John Howard between 1996 and 2007. The apology was finally given by the incoming Labor government of Kevin Rudd in 2008. Much of the agitation during the 1990s was associated with the long-standing practice of all Australian governments of removing Aboriginal children from their families and placing them in state and religious institutions. A report into the practice by the Human Rights and Equal Opportunity Commission attracted intense interest and genuine anguish and regret. But the focal point of controversy was the determination of the commissioners to refer to child removal as being genocidal in intent. Beyond that specific application of the text of the Genocide Convention is the broader and even more contentious question of whether the whole colonial venture can be considered as genocidal in its overall impact on the indigenous population. Even if that question is left aside, there is no doubt about the devastating consequences of the European invasion. Many Aboriginal nations disappeared within a generation of contact. The overall population declined relentlessly every year for well over a century under the impact of disease, violence, deprivation, and a catastrophic decline in the birth rate. When the population began to recover, the most rapidly increasing communities were those with large numbers of mixed descent children. By then, the Aborigines were commonly living in fringe camps on the outskirts of rural towns or on cattle stations. Many of the young men and women worked casually in the towns or among the cattle, often receiving in return food, tobacco, and clothing instead of money. The communities were half in and half out of the colonial economy, maintaining culture where they could, remaining in their own country whenever possible, and hunting and gathering to supplement food acquired from the Europeans. They rarely shared in the life of town or station, except for providing casual labor and casual sex. But the de facto segregation was often welcome and provided protection from both the casual aggression and often well-meaning interference from white people.

Another theme that runs through most of white Australia's history is the abiding view that the Aborigines were a primitive, inferior people. This underlying assumption drew intellectual strength from many sources. In the early years of settlement, the common belief among the educated officials, explorers, and missionaries was that the Aborigines were the victims of their isolated and unpromising environment and that they could, with careful attention, be raised up to a higher plane of development by becoming farmers and industrious day laborers. Many experiments premised on these assumptions failed, and the indigenous communities living in proximity to the Europeans continued to decline.

The Australian colonies were receptive to the scientific racism that began to filter into the Antipodes from Europe and North America during the 1820s and 1830s, and earlier optimism about a civilizing mission ebbed away. In the second half of the 19th century, social Darwinism found eager local recruits who embraced ideas that appeared to confirm common experience while easing troubled consciences. The Aborigines were clearly victims and exemplars of the iron laws of evolution. They were primitive people, trapped in the Stone Age and destined to die out in the struggle for existence. There was little that anyone could do to ease the dictate of nature itself. Indeed, the fate of the Aborigines appeared to be among the strongest evidence available globally to confirm the ideas of evolution. It was for this reason that the death of the Tasmanian woman Truganini in 1876 assumed such ecumenical importance. She was thought to be the last of her race. In the space of one lifetime, under the observant eyes of a resident European population, a unique race had disappeared. It was both proof and prognosis, heralding the impending fate of other indigenous societies all over the world.

This putative death sentence gave great impetus to ethnography and anthropology in both the colonies and in the metropolitan countries. Time pressed. Indigenous elders had knowledge that was both perishable and irreplaceable. It was also uniquely valuable because it contained information about human origins, about the ancient roots of religion, art, and social organization. European savants wove colonial ethnography into their theories about human nature and society. Anthropologists were attracted to Australia from the early years of the 20th century, drawn by the prospect of studying tribal people still with little contact with the European colonists and in a relatively safe and salubrious environment. By the 1930s, Australia had begun to develop its own schools of anthropology, which dispatched scholars into the still remote and little visited parts of the continent.

The legal status of the Aborigines during the 19th century was that they were British subjects with the same rights and privileges as the colonists. This meant little in practice and even less after 1856, when the five eastern Australian colonies were granted responsible government and effective control over their own internal affairs. There were always men and women who spoke out about the treatment of the Aborigines, about the gap between promise and reality. They wrote angry letters to local papers and occasionally to the British press. They sent petitions to the Colonial Office and the Aborigines Protection Society in London, with little measurable effect. Death and dispossession traveled in the wake of the pioneer settlers all over the continent. In the late 19th and early 20th centuries, all the major colonies adopted protectionist policies, giving government officials extraordinary powers to control indigenous lives, to confine people to closed reserves and missions, to manage what money they earned, to determine who they would marry, and, often enough, to take their children away from them. When the colonies federated in 1901, Aborigines were subsequently excluded from the franchise through a narrow definition of Section 41 of the Australian Constitution. The universal assumption of the time was that they were a dying race with no long-term future. Nature could be left to finish its work of extinction.

What was unexpected was the demographic recovery by the 1920s of communities in the closely settled parts of the country, calling forth anguished calls for something to be done to counter the "half-caste menace." By this time, new generations of activists were about. Aboriginal ones looked to developments in Afro-American politics and particularly the charismatic appeal of Marcus Garvey. White humanitarians looked with hope and eventual frustration to the League of Nations and the International Labour Organization. The powerful Anti-Slavery Society took renewed interest in Australia and applied pressure to the Australian government.

But the great changes in the political and legal status of indigenous Australians did not come until the 1950s and 1960s. The winds of change blew through the Antipodes as surely as they did through Africa. Local activists were greatly assisted by developments outside Australia. The Universal Declaration of Human Rights of 1948 stripped away the constant Australian claim that Aborigines were Stone Age people who could not participate in the political life of a modern nation state. Rapid decolonization and the proliferation of new non-European nations increased pressure on racist policies and overt discrimination in all the white settler societies. Australia became an easy target for countries of the Soviet bloc in Cold War skirmishing at the United Nations. One by one, the discriminatory policies developed since the early 20th century were dismantled. Formal political equality was put in place even while great disparities in all the social indicators remained and have continued to shame and vex national life to the present day.

The emphasis in political debate and social commentary on the problems besetting many Aboriginal communities should not distract attention from the achievements of contemporary indigenous society. The demographic recovery is pronounced. The Aboriginal population is growing faster than mainstream Australia, and it is much more youthful. In 2008, the total fertility rate for all women in Australia was 1.97 babies per woman, while the fertility rate for Aboriginal women was 2.52. From the 1970s, Aboriginal politics has been led and inspired by a generation of indigenous leaders, a number of whom have developed national profiles. Aborigines and Torres Strait Islanders have played a significant role in global fourth world politics, both at the United Nations and in other international fora. They have ensured that Australia continues to be the focus of critical international attention. Underpinning much of the formal political activity is the work of a large number of indigenous-managed community organizations providing services relating to health, housing, law, and culture. These are to be found all over the continent.

Even more remarkable has been the cultural renaissance of the past generation. Novelists and poets have won admiring audiences and national literary prizes. Filmmakers have won praise both at home and abroad. The national indigenous dance company Bangarra performs all over the world, presenting dances created by Aboriginal and Islander choreographers. But the most extraordinary development has been the global success of traditional Aboriginal painting, transferred from bark, body, and the ground itself to canvas, frequently with quite spectacular results. The often very old leaders of this movement have become international, if frequently reluctant, celebrities, with their work displayed in the major galleries of the world.

The significant cultural achievements notwithstanding, the Aboriginal and Torres Strait Islander communities still face a wide range of problems. Almost every social indicator points to a story of poverty and deprivation. Taken as a whole, the indigenous population is the poorest in the nation, with higher unemployment and lower wages for those in work. Educational standards are far below the national average, with fewer students completing their secondary schooling or going on to university. Levels of health and well-being are still far below the national average at every stage of life. Child mortality is three times higher than the national average, and for adults, the average age of death is between 15 and 20 years below that for the rest of the nation. Aboriginal communities suffer from higher average rates of death by accident or violence. Alcoholism, petrol sniffing, and addiction to drugs beset many communities, although there are numerous remote settlements that have chosen to be alcohol free. Levels of domestic violence are very high, the overall crime rate far outreaches that in the general population, and Aborigines and Islanders are imprisoned at 10 times the rate of the wider community.

This dispiriting array of social indicators is well known and often widely publicized in the national media. Both state and federal governments introduce programs that they hope will improve the situation, and slow but measurable progress is often reported. The federal government has recently launched a large and varied range of ameliorative measures collected under the "aspirational" slogan of "Closing the Gap" between the life chances of white and indigenous Australians. A more radical series of measures have been implemented in communities in the Northern Territory, collectively known as the "Intervention." Alcohol has been banned, and individual welfare payments have been controlled to ensure the money is spent on food and other essentials.

National statistics can have the effect of suggesting a homogeneity of condition that distorts rather than reflects the reality of indigenous life in Australia. In fact, few communities in the world would match the diversity of condition or lifestyle found across the continent. There are, for instance, hundreds of small, remote outstations scattered across the north and the center where traditional owners live in a way that still echoes their presettlement way of life. Traditional law is still observed, and languages are maintained.

But at the other end of the spectrum are the urban communities, which within themselves contain great diversity. There are pockets of extreme poverty, but equally there are many Aborigines and Islanders who live in suburban affluence and work at high levels in both the public and the private sector where indigenous background can be an advantage rather than an obstacle. Some of the members of the new indigenous middle class have emerged from the remote tribal communities, although they would more commonly come from mixed-descent families that have lived in the wider society for generations and have, in some cases, only recently identified as Aborigines or Islanders.

Despite the array of social indicators, which portray an unmistakable picture of distress and deprivation, they do not capture the whole picture of indigenous Australia and the sense of identity and purpose. The most popular slogan at the time of Australia's bicentenary in 1988 was "We Have Survived," and that still seems to be the foundation on which the community seeks to build a new relationship with the modern world.

Henry Reynolds

A

ABORIGINAL AND ISLANDER CHILD CARE AGENCY (AICCA). Until the mid-1970s, the welfare of Indigenous Australian children rested almost solely in the hands of non-Indigenous authorities. To address this issue, Indigenous people held a conference on the adoption policy in 1976, and a subcommittee that was subsequently formed precipitated a wider movement calling for the creation of Indigenous child care and adoption agencies. With the assistance of government funding, the first such body was established in Sydney, and within a decade, AICCA had proliferated throughout Australia. Since 1981, they have been linked by the Secretariat of National Aboriginal and Islander Child Care (SNAICC), although individual agencies remain semiautonomous and operate in conjunction with mainstream government services that have responsibility for running their respective state and territory child welfare systems.

The main functions of the AICCA are to organize the placement of Aboriginal and **Torres Strait** Islander children who require substitute care and to provide support services to monitor their placement. Support services are usually arranged with the relevant state or territory department. The majority of state and territory governments provide funding for AICCA to train and employ suitably qualified Indigenous staff, and in some areas of Australia, the agencies have been able to exert considerable influence in relation to the welfare of Indigenous children. Indeed, a number of agencies have played a significant role in the development of policies and legislation.

ABORIGINAL AND ISLANDER SPORTS HALL OF FAME. *See* SPORT.

ABORIGINAL AND TORRES STRAIT ISLANDER COMMISSION (ATSIC). First proposed by the federal government in 1987, ATSIC was intended to be representative of Indigenous people and to perform executive and administrative functions.

Following extensive consultation, the government introduced the ATSIC bill into parliament in 1988. Throughout the legislation's passage through federal parliament, the Coalition (Liberal and National parties) opposition, led by future Prime Minister John Howard, criticized the principles behind ATSIC, arguing it would divide Australia by giving separate representation to a minority group. Parliament finally passed the bill, with substantial amendments, in early November 1989. The amendments included provisions to strengthen ATSIC's public accountability. **Lowitja O'Donoghue** was appointed as ATSIC's first chairperson. Future chairpersons were Gatjil Djerrkura (1996–2000), Geoff Clark (2000–04), and Lance Quarterman (acting, 2004).

ATSIC was responsible for advising the government on Indigenous issues, advocating the recognition of Indigenous rights, and delivering and monitoring some of the government's Indigenous services and programs. Its 35 regional councils were grouped into 16 zones, and each zone elected one representative to the ATSIC board. Elections for the regional councils were held every three years.

In 2003, an independent committee appointed by Prime Minister John Howard conducted a formal review of ATSIC. The review found that although it was in need of major structural reform, ATSIC should not be abolished. Despite this, on 15 April 2004, following further controversy, Prime Minister Howard and Minister for Indigenous Affairs Senator Amanda Vanstone announced the government's intention to abolish ATSIC. A few weeks prior to this, the Australian Labor Party had announced that it would abolish ATSIC if it won the forthcoming election. With both sides of politics having withdrawn their support, on 27 May 2004, the government introduced legislation to abolish ATSIC. The bill was passed by parliament, and ATSIC was formally abolished at midnight on 24 March 2005.

Many regarded the dismantling of ATSIC as the loss of the only democratic forum for Indigenous representation in Australia. In its stead, in 2004, the government established the National Indigenous Council (NIC) as its main advisory body on Indigenous policy, program, and service delivery. Fourteen members from various backgrounds were appointed to the NIC. While the government maintained that the NIC was not a replacement for ATSIC or a representative body for Indigenous people, it was the key source of advice provided to the government on Indigenous issues. In early 2008, the Kevin Rudd-led federal Labor government abolished the NIC. On 2 May 2010, the **National Congress of Australia's First Peoples** was launched in its stead.

ABORIGINAL AND TORRES STRAIT ISLANDER SOCIAL JUSTICE COMMISSIONER. This position was established in 1992 by the federal government in response to the findings of the **Royal Commission into Aboriginal Deaths in Custody** and the National Inquiry into Racist Violence. The incumbent is one of five commissioners forming part of the

Human Rights and Equal Opportunity Commission and is responsible for consulting widely with Indigenous people, reviewing laws, policies, and practices that impact upon Indigenous people, and preparing an annual report on social justice and **native title** tabled in federal parliament. Past commissioners are **Michael Dodson** (1993–98), Zita Antonias (acting, 1998), Dr. William Jonas (1999–2004), and Tom Calma (2005–9). Former **Aboriginal and Torres Strait Islander Commission** Chief Executive Mick Gooda assumed the position in 2010.

ABORIGINAL–AUSTRALIAN FELLOWSHIP. *See* BANDLER, FAITH; GIBBS, PEARL.

ABORIGINAL FLAG. The Aboriginal flag was first flown in 1971, as part of National Aborigines Day (now **National Aboriginal and Islander Day Observance Committee**). In 1972, the flag was flown at the **Aboriginal Tent Embassy** as a symbol of Aboriginal people's struggle for **land rights**. It has become an important symbol of unity and **identity** for all Aboriginal people. On 14 July 1995, the Aboriginal flag, together with the **Torres Strait Islander flag**, was officially proclaimed to be a "flag of Australia," under the Commonwealth Flags Act 1953. It is now common for state governments and local councils to fly the Aboriginal flag.

Harold Thomas, a Luritja elder from central Australia, designed the flag in 1971. The flag comprises a red lower half below a black top half, with a central yellow disc. The red represents the red earth and spiritual affinity to it, the black the Aboriginal people, and the yellow disc the life-nurturing sun. Some hold that the red also represents the blood lost during the period of colonial conquest. In 1997, Thomas was recognized by the Federal Court of Australia as holding copyright for the design under the Commonwealth Copyright Act 1968.

ABORIGINAL LAND RIGHTS (NORTHERN TERRITORY) ACT 1976 (COMMONWEALTH) (ALRA). A legislative act of Federal Parliament providing for the granting of specific lands to Aborigines in the Northern Territory, the ALRA contained a 20-year sunset clause for making claims, and this period ended in 1997.

Following a **referendum** in 1967, the Commonwealth obtained the powers to make laws applicable to Aborigines in the Northern Territory, the Australian Capital Territory, and all Australian states. The ALRA is widely believed to be the first **land rights** legislation to be passed and the first attempt to recognize Aboriginal systems of land tenure. However, in 1966, South Australia passed significant preceding legislation: the Aboriginal Lands Trust Act

(South Australia). This act placed all reserve lands under the authority of the trust, which effectively returned some land to Aborigines and gave Aborigines some control over the land held by the trust.

Under the ALRA, unalienated Crown land (government-owned land not designated for any specific purpose) or land where interests not held by the Crown were held by, or on behalf of, Aboriginal people was available to be claimed. The act established a land-claims process whereby Aboriginal people could seek grants of land upon establishing traditional ownership of that land through traditional use or occupation. An Aboriginal land commissioner was responsible for assessing the validity of claims and making recommendations as to whether a grant should be made by the government. Successful claims resulted in a grant of land being made to an Aboriginal land trust (ALT), which held that land on behalf of the traditional owners. The act also established land councils in the Northern Territory to act as the representative bodies for Aboriginal people in respect to the claiming and management of land under the act, including financial management. An ALT can only deal with land granted as instructed by the relevant land council, and the ALRA restricts how land can be dealt with. For example, it cannot be disposed of or sold. The ALRA also controls access to Aboriginal land through a permit system and access to **sacred sites**.

Aboriginal groups obtaining land granted under the act receive freehold, communal, and inalienable title to their land. Freehold title means full and complete ownership; communal title means that instead of individuals owning the land, Aboriginal groups collectively own their land, and title is vested in ALT; inalienable title means that the land cannot be sold, mortgaged, or otherwise made available for purchase, although it can be leased, subject to specific conditions.

Under the ALRA, there are procedures for granting mining interests and other leases over land held by an ALT. The ALRA also establishes a regime for royalty payments to be paid for mining activities on Aboriginal land. It requires that the Aboriginal Benefit Account (formerly the Aboriginal Benefit Reserve) distribute funds from federal revenue in amounts equal to those paid to the federal or Northern Territory government by the mining companies for those activities undertaken on Aboriginal land.

The Commonwealth Aboriginal Land Rights (Northern Territory) Amendment (Township Leasing) Act 2007 was enacted on 28 June 2007. Due to the restrictions on how Aboriginal land could be dealt with, the Coalition government introduced an amendment to permit other nonmining leases to be granted over townships on Aboriginal land. The government argued that the amendment would promote economic development in Aboriginal communities by encouraging individual home ownership and business leases over Aboriginal land.

Despite indications in the early 1980s that Federal Parliament would introduce national land rights legislation, to date it has not done so. However, all states have subsequently passed some form of land rights legislation or, as in the case of Tasmania, have handed selected lands back to Aboriginal ownership through ad hoc legislation. The Native Title Act has to some extent superseded land rights legislation, but the latter remains an important avenue for Aborigines to secure land where **native title** might have been extinguished and for managing land already returned under the act. *See also* ABORIGINAL LAND RIGHTS COMMISSION; GOVE LAND RIGHTS CASE; LAND CLAIMS; LAND OWNERSHIP; LINGIARI, VINCENT; WAVE HILL; WOODWARD INQUIRY.

ABORIGINAL LAND RIGHTS COMMISSION. Land rights were a central concern driving Aboriginal activism in the late 1960s and early 1970s. In 1973, the federal Labor government established a commission of inquiry into Aboriginal land rights and appointed Justice A. E. Woodward its commissioner. The inquiry was to report on ways that traditional rights to land could be legislatively recognized and established. Justice Woodward produced two reports: an interim report in 1973 and a final report in 1974. These two reports formed the basis upon which the Coalition government led by Prime Minister Malcolm Fraser introduced the Commonwealth **Aboriginal Land Rights (Northern Territory) Act 1976**. *See also* GOVE LAND RIGHTS CASE; LAND CLAIMS; LAND OWNERSHIP; LINGIARI, VINCENT; WAVE HILL; WOODWARD INQUIRY.

ABORIGINAL LAND TRUST. *See* ABORIGINAL LAND RIGHTS (NORTHERN TERRITORY) ACT 1976 (COMMONWEALTH) (ALRA).

ABORIGINAL LEGAL SERVICES. Although influenced by the activities of African-Americans in the civil rights movement in the United States, the genesis of the Aboriginal legal services is to be found in local conditions and the experiences of Aborigines. In the late 1960s and early 1970s, rising levels of concern over a number of issues, including increased police harassment following the rapid growth of the Aboriginal population in inner-urban Sydney, **Koori** activists established a free shop-front Aboriginal legal service in the Sydney suburb of Redfern in 1971. Legal advice and assistance were first provided by non-Indigenous lawyers on a volunteer basis (there were no Koori lawyers in 1971). The opening of the Redfern service was quickly followed in 1973 by the opening of a service in regional New South Wales and another in the Melbourne suburb of Fitzroy. Aboriginal legal services now operate in all Australian states, the Australian Capital Territory, and the Northern Territory. As well as providing legal advice and assistance to Aborigines, they play an important advocacy role, promoting social justice for all Indigenous Australians.

ABORIGINAL MEDIA. The *Aboriginal or Flinders Island Chronicle*, issued between September 1836 and December 1837, was the first periodical produced by Aboriginal people. Notwithstanding that it was controlled by George Augustus Robinson, superintendent of the **Wybalenna** Aboriginal settlement on Flinders Island in Bass Strait, at least three of the exiled **Tasmanian Aborigines** on the island directly contributed to the publication. Little is known of any other Aboriginal print media until 1938, when Aboriginal activist **John (Jack) Patten** edited the *Australian Abo Call*, which ran for only six months. The *Westralian Aborigine* was published in Perth during the 1950s, but it was not until the height of the Aboriginal protest movement in the 1970s that Aboriginal print media finally found a permanent niche.

One of the best known and most influential publications was the *Identity*, published from 1971 to 1975 and continuing until 1982 as the *Aboriginal and Islander Identity*. Between 1976 and 1978, the *Koori-Bina*, published by the Redfern-based Black Women's Action Committee in inner-Sydney, took a vigorous stand against social injustices, while another militant newsletter, the *Koorier 2*, circulated widely throughout New South Wales and Victoria during the 1970s and early 1980s. The *Land Rights News* newsletter, first published in Darwin in July 1976, is today the longest-running Aboriginal publication, while the *Koori Mail*, published at Lismore in northern New South Wales since 1991, is distributed nationally and is now the best known Aboriginal periodical.

There are a number of other media outlets where Australian Indigenous people have made their mark. Sydney-based Radio Redfern, now known as Koori Radio, began operating under a broadcasting license first granted in 1983 to community access station Radio Skid Row. By 2000, there were more than 100 licensed Indigenous radio stations operating across Australia.

The Central Australian Aboriginal Media Association (CAAMA), based in Alice Springs, began as an FM radio station in 1980 before expanding into AM and shortwave broadcasting. In 1984, a video unit was added to CAAMA's communication network, and two years after the launch of Australia's first communication satellite in 1985, CAAMA's bid for the central Australian downlink license proved successful. The private commercial television station, known as Imparja, began broadcasting in January 1988 and continues to cater for both Aboriginal and non-Aboriginal viewers.

CAAMA's lead has been followed elsewhere in regional Australia. The Western Australian Aboriginal Media Association (WAAMA), the Townsville Aboriginal and Islander Media Association (TAIMA), the Top End Aboriginal Bush Broadcasting Association (TEABBA), and the Torres Strait Islander Media Association (TSIMA) are among those that have made significant contributions to Indigenous Australia. Much of this has been made possible by the government-funded Broadcasting for Remote Aboriginal Communities Scheme (BRACS). First launched in 1987, BRACS provided 83 Aboriginal and Torres Strait Islander communities with equipment and facilities necessary to receive radio and television services by 1992. Under the scheme, Indigenous communities are also able to produce and broadcast their own radio and television programs. Sydney-based Indigenous television programs "Living Black" and "Message Stick" are screened nationally. A 24-hour television broadcasting service via satellite throughout Australia commenced in November 2007. National Indigenous TV is a subscription and cable-based network designed to promote Indigenous languages and culture.

ABORIGINAL MEDICAL SERVICE (AMS). A new era in Aboriginal **health** policy began in July 1971 when the first AMS started operating in the inner-Sydney suburb of Redfern. The service owed its genesis to the concerns of several Aboriginal people regarding the state of health within their local community. Despite government opposition and limited funding, the service was supported by a number of non-Aboriginal medical practitioners who were similarly alarmed at the poor state of Aboriginal health in Redfern.

The following year, a second AMS opened in the Melbourne suburb of Fitzroy, while a third opened in Perth in 1974. By 1990, there were 68 AMS organizations across Australia, and this rate of growth has continued to the present day. Part of their success has been due to government funding, but all services remain independent and are controlled by their individual communities through an annually elected board of directors.

The main function of AMS has been to provide a full range of accessible and affordable primary health care in a culturally appropriate manner. They strive to work alongside, rather than in conflict with, mainstream health services, and some of the larger AMS organizations have expanded their activities to include dental clinics, nutritional programs, and training for health workers.

ABORIGINAL PROTECTION BOARDS. By 1911, the Northern Territory and every state except Tasmania had "protectionist legislation" in place that gave either a chief **protector** or an Aborigines protection board extensive power to control Indigenous peoples' lives. Such power included regulating where Indigenous people could live, when they could travel, what employment they could take up, whom they could marry, and other daily social interactions. In some states and in the Northern Territory, the chief protector was the legal guardian of Aboriginal children.

Victoria was the first state to enact such "protection legislation," passing its Aboriginal Protection Act in 1869. In New South Wales, the Aborigines Protection Board was established in 1883, but it was not vested with legal authority until 1909, with the passing of the New South Wales Aborigines Protection Act 1909. In Western Australia, a board operated between 1887 and 1898 and was then replaced by an Aborigines department under the chief protector of Aborigines. Queensland passed the Aboriginals Protection and Restriction of the Sale of Opium Act in 1897. Although ostensibly an act providing "for the better Protection and Care of the Aboriginal and Half-caste Inhabitants of the Colony, and to make more effectual Provision for Restricting the Sale and Distribution of Opium," it became the instrument for the exercise of the most oppressive and punitive control over all aspects of Aborigines' lives. Although replaced in 1939 by the Aborigines Preservation and Protection Act and the Torres Strait Islanders Act, there was no improvement in the administration of Aboriginal lives. A chief protector was also appointed under legislation in South Australia and the Northern Territory.

The policy motivating this legislation was initially one of **segregation** (*see* GOVERNMENT RESERVES) but later shifted to that of **assimilation**. The segregationist policy was driven by a belief that Indigenous people should be allocated reserve land and moved off their traditional lands to these reserves. This approach shifted in the late 19th century when increasing numbers of Indigenous people were of "**mixed descent**," and it was thought that because such people had some European ancestry, they could be successfully assimilated into white society. This prompted the "protectionist legislation" to be amended to reflect the governments' new assimilationist aspirations. Increased powers were given to the boards, chief protectors, and, later, government departments so that Aboriginal children, and particularly "half-caste" children, could be removed from their families without the consent of their parents. Those individuals forcibly removed from their families under this policy became known as the **Stolen Generations**. The ongoing impacts of this policy were investigated in the report *Bringing Them Home*.

ABORIGINAL STUDIES PRESS. *See* AUSTRALIAN INSTITUTE OF ABORIGINAL AND TORRES STRAIT ISLANDER STUDIES.

ABORIGINAL TENT EMBASSY. In response to the federal government's refusal to recognize Aboriginal **land rights**, an Aboriginal protest was held on Australia Day (26 January) 1972 on the lawns of Parliament House (now Old Parliament House) in Canberra, the nation's capital. Its establishment on

Australia Day is of symbolic importance. Since the early 19th century, 26 January has been celebrated by Australia's colonial and settler population. The day commemorates the arrival in 1788 at Sydney Cove of the First Fleet under the command of Captain Arthur Phillip, who was also the first governor of New South Wales.

Aboriginal people believed that the failure to recognize their land rights made them "aliens" in their own country and argued that they therefore required an embassy in Canberra to represent their interests. In addition to lobbying for land rights, the Tent Embassy argued for compensation for the lands taken from Aboriginal people as a result of European settlement. The Tent Embassy continues to work for recognition of Aboriginal sovereignty, **land rights** (including rights to minerals and natural resources on Aboriginal land), protection of **sacred sites**, and compensation for the lands taken.

Although the federal government has never recognized it as an official embassy, the Aboriginal Tent Embassy continues to occupy a prominent position in the Australian political landscape. It is currently being assessed by the Australian Heritage Council for possible addition to the National Heritage List as a living record of Australian history.

ABORIGINAL TREATY COMMITTEE. *See* COOMBS, HERBERT "NUGGET"; *MAKARRATA*.

ABORIGINES ADVANCEMENT LEAGUE (AAL). Claiming to be the oldest Aboriginal organization in Australia, the AAL was formed in 1957 when the **Australian Aborigines' League**, founded by **William Cooper**, merged with the Save the Aborigines Committee. The merger was triggered by the report of retired Stipendiary Magistrate Charles McLean, who had been commissioned by Victorian Premier Henry Bolte to investigate his state's Aboriginal affairs policy. McLean advocated greater emphasis on **assimilation** and recommended that large sections of the Lake Tyers Aboriginal Reserve should be sold. The AAL, which included non-Aboriginal members, led the campaign against these anticipated changes.

On a broader front, the AAL also campaigned for a **referendum** to effect constitutional change that would allow the federal government to take control of Aboriginal affairs. When famed Aboriginal artist **Albert Namatjira** was charged with supplying an Aboriginal ward in the Northern Territory with **alcohol**, the AAL established a fund to provide him with legal counsel.

By 1967, the league was fully controlled by Aboriginal people, with William Onus elected as the inaugural Aboriginal president. Based in the

Melbourne suburb of Northcote, the AAL today provides a range of services for Victorian Aboriginal people in need of assistance.

ABORIGINES PROGRESSIVE ASSOCIATION. *See* FERGUSON, WILLIAM; PATTEN, JOHN (JACK).

ABORIGINES PROTECTION BOARD. *See* ABORIGINAL PROTECTION BOARDS.

ALCOHOL. Contrary to popular belief, Aboriginal people across Australia produced and consumed an array of mood-altering substances prior to the arrival of Europeans. In northern Australia, an alcoholic beverage was made from *Pandanus* seeds, while cones from grass trees served the same purpose in southwestern Australia. In Tasmania, an alcoholic cider was made from Gunn's eucalypt, and across a wide swath of the southeastern mainland, mood-altering substances were manufactured from roots, bushes, barks, and fruits. In the more arid central regions, native tobaccos such as *pitcheri*, which were chewed not smoked, produced strong psychoactive effects, particularly when mixed with alkaline ash. Without exception, however, the manufacture and consumption of mood-altering substances throughout the continent was subject to rigid social controls, a situation that altered markedly in northern Australia from the early 18th century when **Macassan** fishermen introduced tobacco and alcohol as trade goods.

Yet this paled into insignificance as massive amounts of alcohol became available to Aboriginal people in southeastern Australia after British colonization in 1788. From the earliest years, Aboriginal men were paid for their casual labor, and **women** for their sexual services, with alcohol. This system of exchange was to continue throughout the 19th century and beyond, notwithstanding government regulations that attempted to prohibit Aboriginal access to alcohol from 1838. By the late 19th century, many pastoralists in the rural districts had also begun supplying their Aboriginal workers with opium obtained from Chinese manufacturers to create a dependent labor pool. Opium addiction among Aborigines was used in Queensland as a major plank in its segregationist policy from 1897, legislation that served as the blueprint for similar policies throughout Australia. While Commonwealth immigration restrictions from 1901 drastically reduced the availability of opium, the continuing demand for Aboriginal labor ensured that **segregation**, despite all its harsh controls, did not entirely eliminate Aboriginal access to alcohol.

Moreover, as Aboriginal people slowly began to gain citizenship during the 20th century, they were also granted the right to purchase and consume alcohol. In a perverse way, alcohol thus became inextricably linked with equality and status, and, partly owing to discriminatory practices in the retail sector as well as through preference, Aboriginal people frequently consumed alcohol in public spaces where they came to the attention of policing authorities. That situation has remained much the same to the present day, contributing to the high rates of Aboriginal incarceration for public order offenses.

Despite the media focus on Aboriginal drinkers and associated violence, per capita there are more teetotalers among the Aboriginal than the non-Aboriginal population. The major difference lies in the fact that Aboriginal drinkers, particularly those in the under-24 age bracket, tend to consume hazardous amounts of alcohol. Numerous explanations have been given for this unequal pattern: the breakdown of traditional social mechanisms, sharing of resources, unemployment and boredom, dislocation, and resistance to imposed controls. There can be little doubt that excessive alcohol consumption among the young is linked to depressed socioeconomic circumstances as it is a social phenomenon that transcends the urban and rural divide.

A number of strategies have been introduced in a bid to curb the excessive consumption of alcohol, many of which are community based. Some, such as the substitution of kava in eastern Arnhem Land in the early 1980s, have proved disastrous. Others have shown more positive outcomes. Group therapy and counseling have achieved some measures of success, as have preventative campaigns using Aboriginal **art** on posters and audiovisual materials presented through local media. Despite considerable government support, much has depended on the strength or otherwise of local community commitment.

ALICE SPRINGS TOWN CAMPS. Following the establishment of a telegraph station at the central Australian town of Alice Springs in 1872 and a subsequent influx of European graziers, the local Arrernte people were gradually dispossessed of their ancestral lands. In 1915, an institution for part-Aboriginal children known as the Bungalow was built near the telegraph station, resulting in a number of Arrernte people settling in fringe camps around the town's perimeter. When the Bungalow was relocated 170 kilometers west to Jay Creek in 1928, Alice Springs was proclaimed a prohibited area for Aboriginal people.

Seven years later, a **mission** at Charles Creek encouraged the Arrernte people to again settle in camps around the town's perimeter, and despite widespread forced removals to Aboriginal reserves at Jay Creek, Hermannsburg, and Artlunga between 1940 and 1945, a small number of Aboriginal people continued to reside in the camps. When the Bungalow was moved back to Alice Springs in 1945, the population of the camps increased substantially, and attempts to drive the Arrernte people away proved futile. The Bungalow was closed down in 1960, and its 360 residents were resettled at Amoonguna, 15 kilometers south of Alice Springs, resulting in the proliferation of more camps along the road between the two locations. A dramatic increase in the population of existing town camps, along with the creation of others, was a direct result of the 1965–1968 Equal Wages Case, which left large numbers of Aboriginal pastoral workers homeless and unemployed and was a contributory factor to the landmark Gurindji strike on **Wave Hill**.

In 1970, the Alice Springs Town Management Board officially recognized 16 town camps, 5 of which were granted town leases and provided with basic services. The remainder were left to their own devices until 1974, when a volunteer group calling itself Tunkatjira began assisting the residents. When Tunkatjira formally became a nonprofit organization three years later, it began to receive funding from the Northern Territory administration, which also granted freehold to a number of camps nominally under Tunkatjira's control after the territory achieved self-government in 1978.

A number of the larger camps subsequently formed their own **housing** associations to campaign for services and improved housing, with Tunkatjira acting on their behalf. In 1979, the organization was incorporated as a municipal council, the spelling of the name was changed to Tangentyere, and after reaching agreement with the Department of Aboriginal Affairs, the council opened an office in Alice Springs.

Funding has been a perennial problem for the Tangentyere Council, which attempts to cater for 21 town camps—six more than it officially controls—with a combined permanent population of around 2,000 people. Following the **Northern Territory Emergency Response** in 2007, the federal government began negotiating with Tangentyere Council for a five-year lease of the town camps in exchange for a massive injection of funding to improve the living conditions of the residents. After protracted opposition and a legal challenge in 2009, the government succeeded in gaining a 40-year lease of the camps.

ANANGU. *See* ULURU.

ANCESTRAL BEINGS. It is believed by many Aboriginal people that during the **Dreaming** ancestor spirits came to Earth in human and other forms. Through their varied activities and travels, they gave shape to the land, created the mountains, hills, plains, and watercourses, and formed the plants and animals. Wherever they traveled or rested, their legacy is inscribed in the landscape. Numerous sites associated with ancestral beings have particular significance. These include sites where particular activities took place, or perhaps where an ancestral being rested from its labors, or where it first arrived or finally departed or merged into the landscape or a particular feature. Many such places are considered **sacred sites**.

The ancestor spirits also created relationships between groups and individuals (both human and animal) and determined the laws that govern social and political life. Following their activities, most did not then leave the Earth but changed form into animals, plants, landscape features, or objects, and in doing so, they remain powerful and present. Their ongoing presence and power reflects the continual cycle of the Dreaming.

ANUNGA RULES. These Northern Territory guidelines for the interrogation of Aboriginal suspects who do not speak standard English were laid down by the Supreme Court of the Northern Territory in *R. v. Anunga* [1976] 11 ALR 412. They consist of nine rules that are advisory rather than legally binding. Their purpose is to afford some protection to Aborigines who are the subject of a police interview. They draw attention to cross-cultural differences, particularly with respect to communication, and strive to avoid the problem of gratuitous concurrence, whereby a person under interrogation agrees with propositions or questions put to them.

APOLOGY TO THE STOLEN GENERATIONS. *See BRINGING THEM HOME*; NATIONAL SORRY DAY; RECONCILIATION; STOLEN GENERATIONS.

ARABANOO (?–1789). First Aboriginal Australian to have extended contact with British settlers. Arabanoo was captured by a party led by lieutenants Ball and Johnston at Manly Cove in Port Jackson (Sydney Harbour) on 31 December 1788. The aim of his abduction was to effect communication with the Aboriginal people of the Sydney region and to learn something of their society. Variously described as between 24 and 30 years of age and with a robust physique, Arabanoo was initially chained to a convict guard and housed in a building adjacent to the residence of Arthur Phillip, the first governor of New South Wales. He dined with Phillip and soon became a general favorite with the colony's educated elite. A man of great dignity and good humor, Arabanoo quickly adapted to his altered circumstances, and when his fetters were finally removed, he chose to remain with the colonists. At no time, however, did he become an intermediary between the two groups.

When a **smallpox** epidemic struck the Aboriginal population around Sydney in April 1789, the British brought two adults and two children suffering from the disease into the settlement, where Arabanoo assisted with their care. The two adults quickly succumbed to the virus; the children survived. Arabanoo also contracted smallpox, dying on 18 May 1789.

ARMY SERVICE. *See* MILITARY SERVICE.

ARNHEM LAND. Extending across the northeastern section of the Northern Territory from Groote Eylandt in the east to Cobourg Peninsula in the west and the Rose River in the South, Arnhem Land comprises approximately 97,000 square kilometers of vast floodplains, rugged escarpments, and rainforest. It is home to 16 major Aboriginal groups, of which the best known are the Yolngu people, famed for their **bark paintings** and as the originators of the **didgeridoo**. Arnhem Land has a number of significant archaeological sites, and the earliest evidence of ground axes anywhere in the world has been found here. **Macassan** fishermen traded with Aboriginal people along the Arnhem Land coast from the early 1700s, a lengthy contact, which is well documented in rock **art** found in some of the 1,500 significant galleries scattered throughout the region.

Arnhem Land was named by British navigator Matthew Flinders in 1802 to commemorate the Dutch vessel *Arnhem*, which sailed these northern waters in 1623. Apart from establishing a number of Christian **missions** along the coast from the late 19th century, Europeans had very little impact on Arnhem Land and its Aboriginal population until comparatively recently. It was gazetted an Aboriginal reserve in 1931 and is today an Aboriginal land trust territory (*see* ABORIGINAL LAND RIGHTS [NORTHERN TERRITORY] ACT 1976) with restricted access to all areas except the main service center of Nhulunbuy. In recent decades, mining has become extremely important, royalties providing a major source of funds that are increasingly supplemented by income from **tourism**. *See also* BARK PETITIONS; GOVE LAND RIGHTS CASE.

ART. Australian Indigenous art, in all its diversity, is now one of the most recognizable art forms in the world. Nevertheless, its rise to international prominence has been recent and fast. Early observers of Australian art (in the late 18th and early 19th centuries) dismissed it as having little artistic merit. Convinced of its rudimentary nature, few non-Indigenous people made any attempt to understand the various motifs and symbols, and Aborigines were seldom asked their meaning or significance. In the late 19th and early 20th centuries, museums and art galleries began collecting artworks, mostly as examples of primitive cultural artifacts. This was in keeping with contemporary evolutionary theories. Some institutions amassed large collections. Since the 1960s and 1970s, Indigenous art has successfully negotiated the temperamental fine art market and is now exhibited in the world's major galleries. A great deal of art is also created for the tourist market. Although the majority of art produced today is for sale—the annual estimated value is in excess of

$AUD130 million—much still conforms to traditional designs and motifs determined by the **Dreaming**. Partly for this reason, distinctive regional diversity is maintained. Northeastern and western **Arnhem Land** is renowned for **bark paintings**, the desert regions for **dot paintings**, the **Kimberley** for representations of **Bradshaw art** and **Wandjina**, and the **Tiwi Islands** for **pukumani poles**.

Adherence to discrete forms does not mean replication of static tradition. Within the constraints of tradition, considerable innovation is still possible and apparent, and leading artists, such as the late **Emily Kngwarreye**, manage to be respectful of tradition as well as innovative.

In general, traditional art and much contemporary art is subject to stringent restrictions as to who has the appropriate authority and standing to paint particular motifs, symbols, and figures. Authority can depend on gender, initiatory status, **conception** site, place of birth, classificatory position in the **kinship** system, and the **ancestral beings** one is affiliated with, among much else. Many groups depend on the cooperation of two contrasting kinship divisions in order for appropriate authority to be realized for the production of artwork. Loosely described as a system of owners and managers, one division has the authority to paint but only in the presence or with approval of the other division, who ensures that the painting (or performance or story) is executed appropriately and correctly.

In respect of rock art, the most detailed and extensive painted galleries are found in the more northern regions of Australia. The major rock engraving sites are in the southern two-thirds of the continent, including central Australia. There are notable exceptions to this.

Many Aboriginal artists, particularly (but not exclusively) urban-based artists, do not conform to traditional strictures but instead engage in the full range of artistic practices and media now available. Much of this work, but by no means all, contains a political edge, whether a statement over loss of land, cultural degradation, loss of **language**, community dysfunction and domestic violence, or white racism, among much else. This is not to dismiss or patronize this work with the label "protest art," for the leading artists are producing work that transcends such a label. *See also* BARAK, WILLIAM; BODY DECORATION; DENDROGLYPHS; ENGRAVING; MARIKA, WANDJUK; MCRAE, TOMMY; MORGAN, SALLY; NAMATJIRA, ALBERT; ONUS, LIN; PAPUNYA TULA; THANCOUPIE; THOMAS, ROVER; TJAPALTJARRI, CLIFFORD POSSUM; *TOAS*; WESTERN DESERT ART; X-RAY ART.

ARTHUR, WALTER GEORGE (c. 1820–61). Aboriginal leader and political activist. Separated as a boy from his **tribe** and country in northeast

Tasmania, the circumstances of which are unknown, Arthur learned little of his people's **language** and culture. Much of his early life was spent among colonists in Launceston, where he survived through petty crime. He came to the attention of G. A. Robinson, with whom he went to **Wybalenna** on Flinders Island, where he spent most of 1832, before being sent to an orphan school on the outskirts of Hobart. It was here he learned to read and write. In 1835, he returned to Flinders Island, where he put his literacy skills to use teaching other Aborigines to read and write and writing articles for the *Aboriginal or Flinders Island Weekly Chronicle*, a small newspaper established by Robinson to promote Christianity and literacy among those detained at Wybalenna.

Arthur enjoyed good rapport with Robinson. When Robinson left Wybalenna in 1839 to take up the position of chief protector of Aborigines in the Port Phillip District, Arthur and Mary Anne, his wife, went with him. Returning to Wybalenna in 1842, Arthur conflicted with the new superintendent, Dr. Henry Jeanneret. Arthur's nascent political activism was given impetus by this conflict. Arthur wanted Jeanneret replaced. However, his criticisms were broadened with claims that promises made by the colonial government of Van Diemen's Land to the Aborigines when they agreed to go to Flinders Island had been broken. These protests were formalized in a petition dated 17 February 1846 to Queen Victoria. Eight men were signatories to the petition, with Arthur signing "Walter G. Arthur, Chief of the Ben Lomond **Tribe**." Following the petition, Arthur and Mary Anne continued to write letters from Wybalenna to the governor seeking better conditions for all there.

Arthur and his wife were with the surviving Aborigines who were removed from Wybalenna to Oyster Cove in 1847. He farmed in the district until 1859, when he joined the whaling bark *Sussex* as a crewmember. Throughout this period, he continued to agitate for better conditions for his people. Arthur drowned on 11 May 1861, having fallen overboard from a rowing boat en route to Oyster Cove. *See also* FRIENDLY MISSION; TASMANIAN ABORIGINES.

ASSIMILATION POLICY. Beginning with Governor Lachlan Macquarie's Native Institution on the outskirts of Sydney in 1814, there were a number of restricted and sporadic attempts during the first half of the 19th century to educate and indoctrinate Aboriginal people into European ways. Much of the emphasis fell on children. Resistance by the Aborigines, as well as a widespread refusal to accept Aboriginal people as equals, defeated all preliminary efforts at assimilation. Government policies steadily moved toward **segregation**, and it was not until the 1930s that a noticeable increase in the part-Aboriginal population resulted in official policies turning once again toward assimilation. Owing to the disruption caused by World War II, a universal assimilation policy was not officially adopted until the Native Welfare Conference of 1951. Although seemingly a far more positive response toward the Aboriginal population, the assimilation policy has nevertheless been the subject of harsh criticism. While some argue that it was motivated by concern for Aboriginal welfare, others critique the underlying principle that expected all Aborigines, including those of **mixed descent**, to eventually enjoy the same rights and adhere to the same customs and beliefs as settler Australians. This is widely held to be a rejection of Aboriginal cultures, values, and beliefs and, hence, assimilatory in that Aborigines were expected, in time, to become indistinguishable from settler Australians. By the early 1970s, the policy of assimilation lost temporary impetus in favor of integration and later **self-determination**.

The policy of assimilation justified the government's extensive intervention into Aboriginal people's lives and has had long-lasting, destructive consequences, including the removal from their families of children who have come to be known as the **Stolen Generations**. *See also BRINGING THEM HOME*; SEGREGATION.

AUSTRALIAN ABO CALL. *See also* ABORIGINAL MEDIA; DAY OF MOURNING; PATTEN, JOHN (JACK).

AUSTRALIAN ABORIGINAL PROGRESSIVE ASSOCIATION (AAPA). Recognized as Australia's first formally constituted Indigenous protest organization, the AAPA was founded in Sydney in 1924 by the Aboriginal activist and wharf laborer Frederick Maynard. The aims of the organization were threefold: to improve the material conditions of Aboriginal people and have them granted the franchise, thus ending political oppression. The AAPA also vigorously campaigned for Aboriginal people to be granted farming land with security of tenure. It is relevant that the AAPA arose during a period when Aboriginal reserves throughout New South Wales were being drastically reduced in size, with Aboriginal people often being forcibly evicted from land that they had successfully farmed for decades.

The AAPA received support from a number of European sympathizers, one of the most prominent being Elizabeth McKenzie-Hatton, who operated a hostel in Sydney for abused Aboriginal girls. Maynard's organization used innovative strategies to champion their causes, including street rallies, public meetings, conferences, and petitions. Throughout the three years of its existence, the AAPA was actively opposed by the government-run Aborigines Protection Board (*see* ABORIGINAL PROTECTION BOARDS), which unsuccessfully attempted to publicly discredit Maynard on a number of occasions. The board also failed in its bid to prevent the AAPA from being registered as a limited company, but the organization was finally dissolved in 1927 following serious internal dissent and police harassment. Maynard continued to agitate for Aboriginal rights until he was seriously injured in an industrial accident in the early 1930s, complications from which directly contributed to his **death** in 1946.

AUSTRALIAN ABORIGINES' LEAGUE. Based in Melbourne, the league developed from a number of loose-knit Aboriginal protest groups and became a formally constituted body in 1936. Headed by **William Cooper**, who was officially the league's secretary, the organization also received considerable support from Arthur Burdeau, a white trade unionist, and the Communist Party of Australia. Membership was nevertheless restricted solely to people of Aboriginal descent, and the main aim of the league was to campaign for equal rights and citizenship under the motto, "A fair deal for the dark race."

An important aspect of the league's activities was to protest against the loss of Aboriginal reserve land in Victoria and southern New South Wales that had been successfully farmed by the occupants during the late 19th and early 20th centuries. Above all, the league was an **assimilation**ist rather than a separatist organization and formulated its policies to accord with prevailing white ideologies. To this end, the league deliberately avoided radical campaign strategies, opting instead for moderate tactics, including open-air meetings, concerts, and letters to newspaper editors, politicians, and government departments. Although the outbreak of World War II in 1939 and Cooper's **death** two years later resulted in the league losing much of its drive, the organization continued until 1957, when it merged with the Save the Aborigines Committee to form the **Aborigines Advancement League**.

AUSTRALIAN INSTITUTE OF ABORIGINAL AND TORRES STRAIT ISLANDER STUDIES (AIATSIS). The AIATSIS is involved in research related to Aboriginal and Torres Strait Islander studies, which it publishes through its publishing house, Aboriginal Studies Press. The research organization began in 1961 and, in 1964, became a Commonwealth statutory authority known as the Australian Institute of Aboriginal Studies (AIAS), governed at the time by a 22-member non-Indigenous council. The Commonwealth AIATSIS Act 1989, which replaced the Commonwealth AIAS Act 1964, not only recognized **Torres Strait** Islanders but also established a Research Advisory Council. A majority of council members is now Indigenous, and the current chairperson is **Michael Dodson**.

AUSTRALIANS FOR NATIVE TITLE AND RECONCILIATION (ANTaR). ANTaR is a national network of predominantly non-Indigenous organizations and individuals initially formed to counter hostility toward, and suspicion of, **native title** and promote **reconciliation** between Indigenous and non-Indigenous Australians. It has expanded its charter to advocate for Aboriginal rights on a range of issues. It is not aligned with any political party, and it guards and cherishes its independence. Most recently, it commenced publishing a new national quarterly magazine called *Seachange*. ANTaR sees its role as advocacy and community **education**.

AYERS ROCK. *See* ULURU.

B

BANDLER, FAITH (1918–). Activist and writer. Born Ida Lessing Mussing at Tumbulgum, northern New South Wales, Faith Bandler was the daughter of a former Melanesian indentured laborer from Vanuatu and a **woman** of mixed Indian and Scottish descent. Bandler left school in 1933 and moved to Sydney, where she first worked as a dressmaker's assistant, before entering domestic service. In 1942, Bandler and her sister Kath joined the Australian Women's Land Army and worked on fruit farms, where they were paid at the same low rate as Indigenous workers. After Bandler's discharge in 1945, she mounted an unsuccessful campaign to gain equal wages for Indigenous workers.

In 1952, she married Hans Bandler, an Austrian Jew who had been persecuted under the Nazi regime, and four years later, she became a full-time activist, after assisting **Pearl Gibbs** to form the Aboriginal-Australian Fellowship in Sydney. Following the establishment of the **Federal Council for Aboriginal Advancement** in 1958, Bandler became general secretary and remained with the organization until 1973. She played a leading role in the campaign for constitutional change that led to the successful 1967 **referendum**.

Bandler began writing both fiction and nonfiction works during the 1970s, including a novel based on her father's experiences as an indentured laborer. In 1974, she also began campaigning for the rights of South Sea Islanders, a distinct social group who experienced a similar level of discrimination to Aborigines and Torres Strait Islanders.

Bandler has been honored with numerous awards in recognition of her work with Indigenous Australians. In 1984, she was appointed a Member of the Order of Australia (AM), and in 2009, she became a Companion of the Order of Australia (AC). Three years after receiving an honorary doctorate from Macquarie University in 1994, Bandler was awarded the Human Rights Medal and named by the National Trust as one of Australia's Living National Treasures.

BANGARA DANCE THEATRE. Formed in 1989 as a company for Indigenous performance artists and graduates from what is now the National

Aboriginal and Islander Skills Development Association, it quickly established itself as one of Australia's preeminent **dance** companies. It tours its productions nationally and internationally and performed at the closing ceremony of the Atlanta Olympic Games in 1996 and performed *Awakenings* at the Sydney Olympic Games in 2000. While drawing extensively from Australia's Indigenous cultures and traditions, it fuses this with contemporary Western performance. It has performed with the Australian Ballet, both in Australia (*Rites* 1997) and New York (*Rites* 1999). Those productions most critically acclaimed include *Praying Mantis Dreaming* (1992), *Ochres* (1995), *Fish* (1997), *Skin* (2000), *Corroboree* (2001), and *Fire* (2009). Stephen Page is the theatre's long-serving artistic director. He was appointed to this position in 1991 from his role as a dancer with the Sydney Dance Company. *See also* CORROBOREE; MUSIC.

BARAK, WILLIAM (1824–1903). Indigenous artist. Together with **Tommy McRae**, William Barak was one of the better-known Aboriginal artists of the 19th century. He was an elder of the Woiworung people of southern Victoria and, from 1863, lived at Coranderrk (the Woiworung name for *Prostanthera lasianthos*, a white-flowered native shrub), a government reserve for Aborigines near Healesville, northeast of Melbourne. Aborigines living on the reserve were determined to manage their own affairs, and Barak was at the forefront of agitation to secure better conditions for his people, including the right for Indigenous **self-management** on **government reserves**. To these ends, he provided evidence to an 1881 parliamentary board of inquiry.

Craft production was the primary source of income for Coranderrk residents, but Barak was the only regular painter. Two subjects dominate his artwork. Firstly, many paintings and drawings depict ceremonial and communal life, particularly ceremonial **dance**s. Secondly, he painted figures wearing possum-skin cloaks. These cloaks were not peculiar to the region, being made and worn across southern Australia, but the Victorian examples were the largest, being composed of some 50 to 80 skins. Barak did not include Europeans in any of his work. His subject matter remained exclusively Aboriginal. *See also* ART.

BARK PAINTING. There are records of painted barks from what are now the states of New South Wales, Tasmania, Victoria, and the Northern Territory and from isolated areas in Queensland. However, there are no early records of precontact bark paintings from Western Australia, central Australia, or most of Queensland. Although, in some areas, the inside of bark shelters were painted and/or scratched with charcoal, indicating, perhaps, an everyday aesthetic, painted barks using a range of media were also produced for the esotery of ceremonial, ritual, and mortuary practices.

The best-known examples of bark painting are from **Arnhem Land** in the Northern Territory. There are distinct regional styles within this broad expanse, which can be loosely grouped into northeastern, central, and western geographical areas. It is in the western region that the renowned **x-ray** style of **art** is produced. Most of the bark used is cut from the stringybark tree (*Eucalyptus tetradonta*).

Many of the motifs and designs used in bark painting are said to have originated in the **Dreaming**, and **ancestral beings** are said to have issued instructions as to their use. Bark paintings are still used to affirm cultural and clan **identity** and to demonstrate traditional affiliation with particular territories in land and sea rights claims, as well as native title claims. They are also used in **initiation** ceremonies, other rites of passage, mourning practices, and a range of ritual activities. Bark paintings are one of the conduits between Aborigines and the ever-present Dreaming and form an explicit link with relevant ancestral beings. Although continuing to have profound foundations and functions, bark paintings also form an integral part of the **economy** of many small Aboriginal communities, with many barks being produced for the market.

Contemporary bark painters draw inspiration from a range of sources, yet many remain influenced by the various styles of rock and/or body art peculiar to their region. Hence, it is still possible to discern regional styles in today's barks, including those produced solely for the purposes of sale. Both considerable innovation and adherence to traditional designs and motifs are evident, not only between different bark paintings within and across regions but also often in a single painting. Because of their conformance to traditional templates, the innovativeness of many bark paintings is often overlooked or goes unrecognized.

The bark paintings of northeastern Arnhem Land are distinctive from those produced in the central and western geographical areas. Whereas in western Arnhem Land figures are painted on a monochrome background, in northeastern Arnhem Land, extensive crosshatching generally fills the space not occupied by figures or other motifs and symbols, the interior of which is largely monochrome. The crosshatching is constrained within two specific differing patterns: a diamond-shaped pattern that indicates the artist is from the Yirritja moiety and a rectilinear pattern indicating the Dhuwa moiety. Unlike art from the **Western Desert**, paintings from northeastern Arnhem Land generally focus on specific sites associated with the Dreaming and are less concerned with the links between sites across vast areas.

BARK PETITIONS. In 1963, the Commonwealth government excised 390 square kilometers of land near Yirrkala in the Northern Territory's **Arnhem Land** for bauxite mining. In response, senior members of the local Gumatj clan of the Yolngu people forwarded two bark petitions, written in English and the Gumatj **language**, to Canberra. The petitions pointed out that the Yolngu had a close relationship to the land in question and the importance it held for them as a people was simply being ignored. Although the petitions in themselves were unsuccessful, they did result in the government agreeing that the Yolngu should be compensated either monetarily or through the exchange of alternative land. This was the first time that the existence of **native title** was officially acknowledged by the Commonwealth government, and the petitions were later accorded a prominent place in the new Parliament House, which opened in 1988.

BARUNGA STATEMENT. Written on bark, the Barunga Statement was a document that outlined the national objectives of the Aboriginal and **Torres Strait** Islander people. It was presented to Prime Minister Robert Hawke when he attended the cultural and sporting festival held at Barunga, 65 kilometers east of Katherine in the Northern Territory, on 12 June 1988. High on the agenda was a call for Indigenous **self-determination** and **self-management**, a national system of **land rights** and compensation for the loss of ancestral lands, respect for and promotion of Aboriginal **identity** and Indigenous culture, an end to discrimination, and the granting of full civil, economic, social, and cultural rights in accordance with international covenants. The prime minister responded by stating his desire to conclude a treaty with Australia's Indigenous people. Aboriginal interest in a treaty still remains unfulfilled, an issue which continues to wax and wane in Australian politics and Indigenous activism.

BATCHELOR INSTITUTE OF TERTIARY EDUCATION. Established as an independent provider of tertiary **education** in 1999, the institute offers a range of vocational courses and training programs for Indigenous Australians. It is situated approximately 96 kilometers south of Darwin, the capital of the Northern Territory, in the small town of Batchelor.

BATES, DAISY MAY (1863–1951). Non-Indigenous journalist and ethnographer. A controversial ethnographer who won fame during her lifetime for welfare work among the Aboriginal people of the Nullarbor Plain, Daisy Bates was born in Tipperary, Ireland, in 1863. Her mother died while she was still an infant, and although her father, James O'Dwyer, was described as a "gentleman," she experienced a very unstable childhood. From around the age of eight, she was raised by the family of Sir Francis Outram in London.

Suspected of having contracted tuberculosis, Bates immigrated to northern Queensland in 1884. She remained there only briefly before moving to southern New South Wales and working as a governess. In 1885, she married Jack Bates, a local cattleman, at Nowra. In 1894, Daisy Bates abandoned her husband and the son who was the only child from their union to return to England, where she spent five years learning journalism.

Returning to Australia in 1899, Bates investigated allegations of atrocities committed against Aboriginal people near Broome in Western Australia. This was the beginning of her interest in Aboriginal people, which would dominate the remainder of her life. After a short-lived reunion with her husband, Bates began her first serious ethnographic fieldwork in 1904, when she was commissioned by the Western Australian government to research Aboriginal people in the state's southwest. In 1910, she was a member of A. R. Radcliffe-Brown's anthropological expedition in northwestern Australia, where she directed most of her energy to welfare work among the Aborigines. Two years later, Bates established the first of her isolated camps among Aboriginal people at Eucla on the Great Australian Bight. In 1915, she relocated to Yatala and, in 1918, to Ooldea, where she remained for 16 years.

Bates published a number of important academic papers on Aboriginal society and culture as well as some 270 newspaper articles, income from the latter supplementing the meager stipends she received from government sources. Her most significant work was *The Passing of the Aborigines* (1938), in which she insisted that **segregation** was necessary to save the Aboriginal people from extinction. Although this and many of her other views have long since been discredited, her widely read book did result in a number of state governments taking action to address some of the problems relating to Aboriginal **health** and child care. Bates died at Adelaide in April 1951.

BATMAN'S TREATY. In June 1835 John Batman, a northern Tasmanian landholder and frontiersman, concluded the only formal treaty with Australian Aboriginal people. A member of the Port Phillip Association, which was anxious to acquire land in what is now southern Victoria, Batman and a small party comprising Europeans and seven Aboriginal men from Sydney journeyed to Port Phillip Bay, where Batman claimed an agreement was reached with local Aboriginal leaders for 600,000 acres of land. Two deeds were produced, one covering the site of modern Melbourne, the other an area of land on the western side of Port Phillip Bay around what is now Geelong.

In exchange for these parcels of land, Batman's party provided the Aboriginal people with a large quantity of European goods, with further consignments to be made annually as rent or tribute. Although Batman adhered to the agreement, the following year his treaty was annulled by Governor Richard Bourke in Sydney, who insisted that the Crown had the exclusive right of preemption. Bourke's decision was later upheld by the Colonial Office in London, and £7,000 was offered to the Port Phillip Association as compensation.

Whether Batman's treaty was merely a duplicitous act or carried out with honest intentions has been debated since, but for all the questions that surround this episode, it was the only time in Australian history when Europeans offered a formal treaty to the Aboriginal people for possession of their land. There were a number of attempts to negotiate treaties during the 20th century. In late 1972, the Larrakia people of Darwin petitioned the federal government, calling for Queen Elizabeth II to negotiate a treaty with the Aboriginal people of Australia. It was ignored. In the late 1970s, **Herbert Coombs** and a number of other prominent non-Aboriginal people formed the Aboriginal Treaty Committee, which, despite strong support in some quarters, failed to achieve its purpose. Finally, in 1988, Prime Minister Robert Hawke promised to negotiate a treaty with the Aboriginal people in his response to the **Barunga Statement**. It was not accomplished. *See also* LAND OWNERSHIP.

BENNELONG (1764?–1813). The **death** of **Arabanoo** from **smallpox** in May 1789 temporarily destroyed Governor Arthur Phillip's hopes of opening up a direct line of communication with the Aboriginal people around Sydney Harbour. A second attempt was made in November 1789, when Bennelong was forcibly seized and brought to the British settlement. He adapted quickly to his captivity, enjoying the food prepared by his captors, gaining a grasp of the English **language**, and forming an affection for Governor Phillip, in whose residence he lodged. Bennelong also acquired a liking for liquor that would remain with him for the rest of his life.

Bennelong escaped from the settlement in May 1790, reappearing at a gathering of Aborigines at Manly Cove the following September, when Governor Phillip was wounded by a spear. Bennelong, who had taken no part in this action, thereafter began to frequent the British settlement with a number of close associates. In 1791, Phillip erected a brick hut for Bennelong on what is now known as Bennelong Point.

Bennelong sailed to England with Governor Phillip in December 1792 and was presented to King George III. After being feted by English society, Bennelong returned to Sydney in September 1795, where he experienced great difficulty readjusting to his old way of life. Frequently intoxicated, he became a virtual fringe dweller until his death at Kissing Point in 1813.

BILINGUAL EDUCATION. An initiative of the Whitlam federal government in the early 1970s, attempts to promote bilingual **education** had precursors in South Australia in the 1840s and north Queensland in the 1880s, where it was introduced by Lutheran missionaries. It is designed to teach formal subjects through both English and local Aboriginal **language**. By 1998, there were 21 bilingual programs operating in the Northern Territory when the territory government announced its plan to replace bilingual education and focus on teaching English to Aboriginal children as a second language. Following opposition from a number of Aboriginal communities, bilingual education continued as a variant of two-way education. Over the next decade, the number of bilingual schools in the Northern Territory was steadily reduced to nine, and in early 2009, the Northern Territory government announced that these remaining schools would be expected to deliver the first four hours of classes in English by 2010. Affected Aboriginal communities and a number of academics have again opposed the government's policy on the grounds that bilingual education is an important means of preserving Aboriginal languages while allowing Aboriginal students to engage with formal, Western-style education.

BLACK ARMBAND HISTORY. *See* HISTORY WARS.

BLACK EUREKA. The first large-scale industrial action by Aboriginal pastoral workers occurred on 5 May 1946, when employees on 20 sheep stations in the Pilbara region of Western Australia struck for better wages and conditions. Aboriginal workers on the remaining five sheep stations followed suit shortly after. Black Eureka had its genesis in 1942, when an estimated 200 Aboriginal people representing 23 **language** groups gathered at Skull Springs on the Davis River to discuss action necessary to end their continuing exploitation. In the interests of national security, the strike was delayed until the end of World War II. Although the graziers finally capitulated in 1948, the majority of the Aboriginal strikers did not return to paid employment, opting instead to earn money from tin prospecting and the sale of marsupial skins.

With assistance from Don McLeod, a European contractor and miner sympathetic to the Aboriginal cause, they formed Northern Development and Mining (Nodom) in 1951, the first Aboriginal-owned company in Western Australia. Solely reliant on the mining of wolfram, the company went into liquidation three years later, but in 1954, a new company, called Pindan, was established with more diverse economic interests. Internal dissent during the mid-1960s led to McLeod and a breakaway group setting up a separate company called Nomad, with both businesses and their respective communities continuing to the present day.

BLACK JACK. *See* MUSQUITO.

BLACK LINE. The **Black War** intensified in Tasmania during the mid to late 1820s and escalated further in the 1830 winter when a number of settlers were killed. Seemingly incapable of ending the violence, Lieutenant Governor George Arthur in August 1830 authorized a military strategy to push all Aborigines of the Tasmanian mainland into the Tasman and Forestier peninsulas in the southeast. This strategy required that the colonists, soldiers, and convicts form a human chain and walk the Tasmanian country. Over six weeks, between 7 October and 24 November 1830, more than 2,200 men formed part of this line. The strategy was ultimately a costly failure. It was thought that the Aborigines' skill and knowledge of the terrain enabled them to escape the Black Line. Following this failed campaign, George Augustus Robinson began the **Friendly Mission**, which brought an end to the violence. As a result of the mission, the **Tasmanian Aborigines** agreed they would leave their land and move to **Wybalenna** on Flinders Island, and, in exchange, the Crown would provide food, clothing, and shelter. They were promised that they would be permitted to return to their lands. However, this promise was never fulfilled, and many Tasmanian Aborigines died in exile.

BLACK WAR. This indicates the period between 1824 and 1832 in what was then named Van Diemen's Land (from 1856, officially renamed Tasmania) when there was intense violence between the British settlers and **Tasmanian Aborigines**. While war was never officially declared, it is thought that this violent conflict intensified when British settlers spread into new regions of Van Diemen's Land, populating vital Aboriginal hunting grounds. The Black War reached its peak in 1830 and came to an end following the **Friendly Mission**. The number of European deaths by the end of 1831 was 175. The number of Aboriginal deaths, although uncertain, is thought, according to the evidence available, to have been considerable. Disagreement about the actual number of deaths caused by the conflict and whether it was, in fact, a "war," contributed to the so-called **history wars** of the 1990s. *See also* BLACK LINE.

BLAIR, HAROLD (1924–76). Indigenous tenor and activist. Born on the Cherbourg Aboriginal settlement northwest of Brisbane in Queensland, Harold Blair grew up at Purga Aboriginal Mission near Ipswich, which was run by the Salvation Army. After receiving a limited **education**, he worked briefly as a farm laborer and entertained visitors to Purga with his singing. During World War II, he worked in the cane fields near Childers and performed in a number of local concerts.

Blair's first major break came in March 1945, when he performed on the popular radio program *Australia's Amateur Hour* and achieved a record number of votes. After a series of setbacks, Blair finally enrolled in Melbourne's

Conservatorium of Music, where he was awarded a diploma of music in 1949. The same year, he married a fellow European student, Dorothy Eden, and was shortly afterwards encouraged to study singing in the United States by the visiting African American baritone Todd Duncan.

Unable to afford the passage for his wife, Blair arrived in New York without her and soon found work as an assistant choirmaster, but his limited finances meant that he also had to take on menial work to pay for his lessons. The highlight of Blair's relatively brief sojourn in America came in March 1951, when he performed at a benefit concert in the New York Town Hall.

On his return to Melbourne, Blair was offered a three-year contract by the Australian Broadcasting Commission, but damaged vocal chords forced him to break the contract after the first extensive tour, and he was prohibited from singing professionally until the contract expired. In 1956, he taught singing part time at the Albert Street Conservatorium in Melbourne, and it was around this time that he became actively involved in Aboriginal affairs. From 1957 to 1959, he served as one of two Aboriginal representatives on the Victorian Aborigines Welfare Board, following which he joined the **Aborigines Advancement League** and, later again, the **Federal Council for the Advancement of Aborigines and Torres Strait Islanders**. Blair also initiated the Aboriginal Children's Holiday Project, whereby thousands of Aboriginal children living on **missions** in Queensland (and later New South Wales) were brought to Melbourne for holidays. It was later alleged that these excursions were used by welfare authorities to remove and separate Aboriginal children from their families.

In 1959, Blair and his wife attended a number of Moral Rearmament conferences in Europe, where he was invited to sing in various countries. Blair proved so popular in Finland that he was persuaded to produce three television programs. In 1962, the couple returned to Australia, where Blair worked in diverse occupations, interspersed by theatrical performances. In 1967, he was appointed a **music** teacher in the Victorian Education Department, winning acclaim for his work with choirs from Ringwood and Sunshine technical schools. Blair continued to sing publicly until just before his death, one of his last major performances being in the Aboriginal opera *Dalgerie* at the Sydney Opera House in 1973. He died of a heart condition in May 1976, four months after being appointed a Member of the Order of Australia (AM). In 1998, the Queensland electoral division of Blair was named in his honor.

BODY DECORATION. This takes many forms and varies widely throughout Aboriginal and Torres Strait Islander cultures, but it may include ritual scarification (cicatrices), tooth avulsion (as part of **initiation** rites), septum piercing, hair plucking, face and body painting, and headdresses. Body decoration is often a feature of ceremonial performance and has important spiritual significance. *See also* BORA.

BONGAREE (?–1830). Indigenous mediator. From the central coast of New South Wales—possibly the Broken Bay area—Bongaree (also known as Bungaree) settled with the remainder of his people in the Sydney district during the 1790s. In 1799, he accompanied Matthew Flinders in the *Norfolk* to explore Moreton Bay, and in 1801–02, he again accompanied Flinders, this time in the *Investigator*, on a circumnavigation of the Australian continent. His role was to establish cordial relations with Aboriginal groups, and he was commended for his exemplary conduct and bravery by both Flinders and Phillip Parker King, the latter of whom Bongaree accompanied during a survey of the Western Australian coast in 1817.

Wearing uniforms presented by various governors and senior military officers, Bongaree became a well-known personality in Sydney. He reputedly spoke English very well, and often mimicked the mannerisms of governors and other leading dignitaries. Although lacking traditional authority, Bongaree became the acknowledged leader of the Aboriginal people living in Sydney.

In 1815, Governor Lachlan Macquarie set aside land at Georges Head for Bongaree and his people to farm, though even the provision of buildings and convict labor did not result in any success. Viceregal patronage was continued by Governor Thomas Brisbane, who supplied Bongaree with a fishing boat and net. In this instance, the catch was often bartered for **alcohol** to which Bongaree had long been addicted. After a lengthy illness, Bongaree died in November 1830 and was buried at Rose Bay.

BONNER, NEVILLE (1922–99). Indigenous politician. An elder of the Jagera people, Neville Bonner was the first Indigenous federal politician, serving as an Australian senator from 1971 to 1983. Bonner was born on Ukerebagh Island in northern New South Wales. Following an array of laboring jobs, in 1946, he moved with his wife and children to Palm Island Aboriginal Reserve in northern Queensland. Developing interests in promoting Aboriginal rights, in 1960, he moved his family to the Ipswich region in Queensland. In 1965, he became a member of the board of directors of the One People of Australia League, which promoted Aboriginal rights, welfare, **housing**, and **education**. He served as its president from 1970 to 1976. Following the changes that occurred as a result of the 1967 **referendum**, Bonner decided to enter politics. He joined the Liberal Party and became a senator in 1971. Bonner was named Australian of the Year in 1979.

An independent thinker and possessed of great integrity, Senator Bonner crossed the Senate floor 23 times to vote against the Liberal Party. In 1982, after having been demoted by his party to an unwinnable third place on the ticket for reelection, he unsuccessfully sought reelection as an independent.

After leaving federal politics, Bonner maintained his interest in public service. He served on the board of directors of the Australian Broadcasting Corporation from 1983 to 1991, as a member of the Griffith University Council from 1992 to 1996, as senior official visitor for all Queensland prisons from 1990 to 1997, and from 1997, chairperson of the Indigenous Advisory Council. Shortly before his death in 1999, Bonner was involved in the 1998 Constitutional Convention. He opposed Australia becoming a republic and supported the existing model of constitutionalism in Australia. In 1984, he was named an Officer of the Order of Australia (AO).

BOOMERANG. The boomerang (a carved hardwood club) is probably the best known of all Aboriginal clubs. Together with the **didgeridoo** (*yidaki*), it is popularly seen as emblematic of Aboriginality and thought of as an Australia-wide cultural artifact. Best known of all is the so-called returning boomerang, a boomerang that when thrown by a skilled practitioner carves an elliptical trajectory in its return to the thrower. Contrary to popular belief, the boomerang is not unique to Australia. Among other locations, they were found in the tombs of pharaohs, including that of Tutankhamen. Non-returning boomerangs, or throwing clubs, have been sourced from many countries. In several cultures, their abandonment as a hunting tool followed the invention of the bow and arrow, which was not developed in Australia.

Boomerangs have a long and continuous history of use in Australia, being produced over many thousands of years. The oldest discovered so far was found in a peat swamp (Wyrie Swamp in southeastern South Australia), where it had lain preserved for between 9,000 and 10,200 years. The returning boomerang was/is only one form of this specialized club. For example, the hunting boomerang of central Australia was a non-returning throwing club. Among other functions, it was used for hunting, fighting, and digging and as a percussive musical instrument. Similarly, the returning boomerang had various functions: in the treed coastal regions of Western and southeastern Australia, it was used for hunting wildfowl and in various games, again, among other uses. Irrespective of their purpose, nearly all boomerangs were augmented with painted and/or incised designs on their upper surface. As with most Aboriginal designs, these designs on boomerangs were not simply decorative but were also invocations of **Dreaming** ancestors, **identity** markers, such as clan or moiety membership, and/or indications of affiliation with local territory. Hence, beyond their more utilitarian uses, boomerangs usually had social and religious significance too.

Boomerangs were used across much of Australia, resulting in subtle regional differences between form and type of boomerang, and the uses to which they were put. They were not, however, produced in Tasmania. There is some speculation that **Tasmanian Aborigines** may once have made boomerangs, but the practice ceased some time after the land bridge between Tasmania and the mainland flooded between 12,000 and 8,000 years BP. The dense forests of Tasmania would certainly have limited some of the functions of a throwing club. Although boomerangs were traded into far northern Australia and the Western Desert, they were mostly not thrown in these regions but used as ritual objects.

BORA. The *bora* is an **initiation** ceremony in which Aboriginal youths reaching puberty are instructed in the duties and obligations of adulthood. Although the word originates from southeastern Australia, variants of the *bora* were practiced across the continent. Depending on the region, the ceremony also included ritual scarification (cicatrices), circumcision, subincision (which is practiced among all Western Desert Aborigines), or tooth avulsion. While it was generally held in summer, the *bora* could be conducted at any time of the year and was an important means of strengthening the authority of the older men while instilling in the young knowledge of the law and traditions of the group. The *bora* ceremony commenced in a large stone circle or circular mound of earth, known as the *bora* ring, and concluded in a smaller ring connected by a sacred pathway. **Women** and children were forbidden to attend. *See also* BODY DECORATION.

BOXING. *See* ROSE, LIONEL; SPORT.

BRADSHAW ART. Bradshaw **art** (now also known as *gwion gwion*, *jungardoo*, and *kiera-kirow*) forms part of a graphic schema in the northern **Kimberley region** of Western Australia that differs significantly from artwork found in the rest of the continent. There is, however, some stylistic overlap with specific artwork from the **Kakadu** region in the Northern Territory—that of the Dynamic tradition—but contiguity or disjunction between these two styles remains speculative. The Bradshaw figures are finely executed, small (approximately 25 centimeters, although there are life-size exceptions), red human figures of solid uniform color. They are elegant, are usually male, and almost always sport elaborate, tightly bound headdresses. They are often wearing sash belts and carry paraphernalia such as weapons. Hanging tassels frequently appear, suspended from limbs, hair, waist belts, and the neck. Their adornments and equipage do not inhibit movement, with the figures usually depicted as active (dancing, running, hunting, and so on). Despite this activity, the figures retain their elegance. Dating remains provisional, but they are at least 6,000 years old and perhaps as much as 16,000 years old, or even older.

The Bradshaws have attracted some controversy. Grahame Walsh, an amateur rock art specialist who has systematically documented a great many galleries of Bradshaw art, contends that the execution of these figures is so delicate and different from other contemporary Aboriginal art that they must have been produced by another people. Aboriginal elders have also confirmed that they have no knowledge of the artwork. They have attributed it to others or to a small bird that beat its beak upon the rock surface until it bled and then made the images by daubing its blood on the rock with its beak and feathers. However, the local traditional owners of the region have now incorporated the Bradshaws into their artistic lexicon and argue that they form an element of their ancestral and continuing heritage. *See also* WANDJINA.

BRAMBUCK CULTURAL CENTRE. *See* TOURISM.

BREAST PLATES. *See* KING PLATES.

BREELONG BLACKS. A part-Aboriginal bush worker, James (Jimmy) Governor, was born near the New South Wales town of Dunedoo in 1875. In 1898, he married a European girl named Ethel Page, at Gulgong, and two years later, the couple were working on the property of John and Sarah Mawbey at Breelong in northwestern New South Wales. They were joined there by Jimmy's brother, Joe, and Jacky Underwood, a lame Aboriginal man from Queensland. Owing to her marriage to a part-Aboriginal man, Ethel Governor was ostracized by the small European community, and in July 1900, she was openly insulted by Ellen Kerz, the local school teacher who boarded with the Mawbey family. Jimmy Governor decided on revenge, and with his brother and Underwood, he killed the five **women** and children in the homestead while John Mawbey and the other men were elsewhere on the property. The town of Breelong, close to where the brutal murders were committed, became indelibly linked to the killers, possibly as a means of dehumanizing the Governor brothers and their actions.

Underwood was captured soon after, tried, and executed in Dubbo Jail. Jimmy and Joe Governor were on the run for three months, eluding some 2,000 police and civilian volunteers as they continued to exact revenge against settler society, self-consciously molding themselves as bushrangers. After four more deaths and three woundings, Jimmy Governor was himself wounded and captured near Taree on 27 October 1900. Joe was ambushed and shot dead near Singleton in the Hunter River Valley four days later. Jimmy Governor was tried, found guilty of murder, and hanged at Darlinghurst Jail in Sydney on 18 January 1901. *See also* FILM.

BRIDGE WALK. *See* NATIONAL SORRY DAY.

BRINGING THEM HOME. Formally titled *Bringing Them Home: Report of the National Inquiry into the Separation of Aboriginal and Torres Strait Islander Children from Their Families*, the report was tabled in Federal Parliament on 26 May 1997. The *Bringing Them Home* report was the result of an inquiry established on 11 May 1995 examining the impact of the state and federal government policies and practices of forcibly removing Aboriginal children from their families. The individuals who were forcibly taken have become known as the **Stolen Generations**. The inquiry also examined whether existing laws, practices, and policies were adequate to address the ongoing effects of these policies and whether compensation should be paid.

The *Bringing Them Home* report concluded that the forcible removal of children from their families violated basic human rights and has had a deep and long-lasting impact upon individuals, families, and entire Aboriginal communities. The *Bringing Them Home* report made 54 recommendations. The recommendations included: that governments and churches involved in administering the policy formally apologize for these past wrongs; that governments, through **education**, training, and instituting **self-determination** for Indigenous people, ensure that such injustices are never repeated; that counseling services be provided to those affected; and that compensation be paid to members of the Stolen Generations.

These recommendations became the subject of intense public debate. The government, under Prime Minister John Howard, rejected the appropriateness of paying compensation and refused to make a formal apology, arguing that current generations could not be held accountable for past wrongs. The then minister for Indigenous affairs went so far as to question the very existence of the Stolen Generations. The government maintained that "symbolic" gestures, such as an apology, would not advance **reconciliation** and argued instead that what was needed was "practical reconciliation." Despite the government's refusal, the wider public supported an apology, and a community-based **National Sorry Day** Committee was formed. The first National Sorry Day was held on 26 May 1998.

The Australian Labor Party won office in 2007, and on 13 February 2008, Prime Minister Kevin Rudd issued a formal national apology to the Stolen Generations. By then, many churches and state governments had already issued their own apologies. The Tasmanian government has moved further, legislating in 2006 to set aside $AUD5 million in compensation to be paid to Stolen Generations members and their children. In Federal Parliament in 2007, Andrew Bartlett, an Australian Democrats senator from Queensland, tabled the Stolen Generation Compensation Bill, which, if enacted, would create a national compensation framework modeled on the Tasmanian scheme. However, a Senate Standing Committee on Legal and Constitutional Affairs' inquiry into the bill recommended that it not proceed.

On 2 August 2007, in a landmark decision, the Supreme Court of South Australia awarded $AUD525,000 in compensation to Bruce Trevorrow for the injuries and loss he suffered after having been taken from his mother, without her consent, in 1957 by the **Aborigines Protection Board**. Following his removal, he had been fostered by a white family. Unless appealed and overturned, this decision creates a precedent for other Stolen Generations members to initiate similar court claims for compensation. *See also* ASSIMILATION POLICY.

BUCKLEY, WILLIAM. *See* MCRAE, TOMMY.

BULLROARER. Usually a flat elongated piece of wood with twine affixed to one end, the bullroarer is swung in a circular motion and produces a buzzing sound that varies in intensity depending on the speed. It was frequently used to signal the commencement of **initiation** ceremonies and thus warn **women** and children to keep away. Despite its common association with Aboriginal culture, the bullroarer was used by Indigenous societies in North and South America, Polynesia, and Africa, and it was also known from ancient Egypt and Greece. In Australia, it was widely distributed and was only absent from Tasmania and the extreme southwestern and northwestern regions of the continent. Bullroarers made from slate have also been recorded from the central districts of Western Australia.

BUNGALOW. *See* ALICE SPRINGS TOWN CAMPS.

BUNGAREE. *See* BONGAREE.

BURIAL. There was considerable diversity in Aboriginal mortuary practices across Australia. Burial was common, especially in the last few thousand years, though much older graves exist, such as those at **Lake Mungo**. Most burial sites located to date reveal an individual burial. However, along the Murray River in southeastern Australia, there are cemeteries that have been used continuously over many thousands of years. Sometimes remains would be adorned and/or artifacts would be interred with the body. Cremation or partial cremation and burial were practiced in some regions. Other mortuary practices included the wrapping of bodies in bark, skin, or woven-grass matting prior to shallow burial or prior to placing the body in rock fissures or a tree hollow. In other regions, remains would be first sun- or smoke-dried (depending on the region) and then dismembered (again, depending on region). Various elaborate rituals associated with mortuary practices were conducted throughout Australia. *See also* DEATH; PUKUMANI POLES.

BURNUM BURNUM (1936–97). Indigenous activist. Born Harry Penrith in 1936 at Wallaga Lake, near Bermagui in southern New South Wales, Burnum Burnum was orphaned as a child. He spent many years in a children's home at Bomaderry run by the United Aborigines **Mission** before being sent to Kinchela Boy's Home at Kempsey, operated by the New South Wales Welfare Board. He achieved local fame as a sportsman while attending Kempsey High School, after which he spent 13 years working for the Department of Agriculture. In the late 1960s, Burnum Burnum, who adopted the name of his great-grandfather, moved to Tasmania and entered university to study law. It was during his three years as a student that Burnum Burnum led the campaign to have **Truganini**'s remains returned to the Aboriginal community for burial. In 1972, he was also heavily involved in planning the **Aboriginal Tent Embassy**, which was erected opposite Parliament House in Canberra. Remaining active in Aboriginal affairs, Burnum Burnum's most public protest coincided with the Australian bicentenary celebrations on 26 January 1988, when he raised the **Aboriginal flag** on the cliffs of Dover and offered the British a chance to begin their relationship with the Australian Aborigines all over again. After appearing in three Australian **film**s during the 1980s, Burnum Burnum settled in the Sydney suburb of Woronora and gave regular talks to school children on Aboriginal mythology before his death from heart disease on 18 August 1997.

BUSH CRAFT. This refers to Indigenous people's ability to use their traditional knowledge of land and skills to live on country and to develop new skills and knowledge through their relationship with their natural environment. These skills/knowledge can include tracking, hunting, **fire-stick farming**, making/using tools, and constructing various objects and artifacts, including **watercraft** and seacraft. Indigenous Australians developed a comprehensive and intimate knowledge of their environment, enabling them to exploit its resources and survive in what were often harsh conditions. Rather than being passive occupiers of their country, they used their detailed knowledge to actively manage it.

BUSH FOODS. Aboriginal people across Australia exploited an extraordinarily diverse range of plant and animal foods prior to European colonization. All of it was dependent on expert **bush craft** and ecological knowledge, although the availability of particular foods varied according to both season and location. Thus, different species usually comprised the bulk of the diet at specific times of the year. In rich coastal areas, fish and mollusks featured prominently in the diet, whereas in more arid regions, reptiles were crucial to survival.

Apart from fortuitous bounty, such as a stranded whale, or seasonal harvests that included bunya nuts in southeastern Queensland and Bogong moths migrating to the Australian and Victorian Alps every summer, the plant and small animal foods necessary for daily sustenance were generally provided by **women** in Aboriginal society. Men tended to hunt the larger game, but this did not provide a regular or reliable food source.

When meat was available—in the form of mammals, birds, reptiles, fish, mollusks, and insects—Aboriginal people consumed prodigious quantities. Techniques employed in the hunt depended on the species. Large kangaroos, for example, were stalked (often over a number of days) and speared or were driven into nets, into waterholes, or along narrow pathways set with crippling sharpened stakes.

Virtually all species of Australian mammals were hunted, and they provided lean meat throughout the year. Unlike domesticated animals, native mammals were an important source of polyunsaturated fatty acids, while their organs provided high levels of cholesterol, minerals, and nutrients such as vitamin C. This high intake was supplemented by protein-rich insect foods, one of the most favored being the wood-boring caterpillars of the cossid moth, commonly known as witchetty grubs.

A balanced diet was also dependent on plant foods, some of which required considerable preparation. Although the cycad is highly toxic and contains carcinogenic properties, it featured regularly in the diet of Aboriginal people living in eastern, northern, and southwestern Australia. After being sliced into thin strips, the kernels of the cycad were leached in running water before being ground and baked into a form of bread. Aged kernels exposed to the elements for lengthy periods could also be processed. The advantage of the cycad lay in its high nutritional content and the fact that the various species produce more food per hectare than many modern cultivated plants.

Depending on the region, Aboriginal people also harvested a wide range of tubers, grass seeds (which were also ground and baked into a form of bread), nuts, berries, and fruits. These provided essential vitamins, with many being extremely rich sources of protein, minerals, and dietary fiber.

Although bush foods are still harvested by rural and remote Aboriginal people, they largely subsidize their predominantly European diet. Conversely, Aboriginal bush foods are gaining increasing acceptance among Europeans, appearing regularly on the menus of gourmet restaurants. At the same time,

European scientists are working closely with Aboriginal people in a number of regions in Australia to identify and study the chemical components of their traditional bush foods for possible future use.

BUSH MEDICINE. In traditional Aboriginal society, illness resulted from one of three causes: malevolent spirits, sorcery, or natural sickness and injury. To combat the latter, Aboriginal people in all parts of Australia drew on an extensive pharmacopoeia that included animal, vegetable, and mineral substances. The consumption of white clay was used as a treatment for coughs, stomach upsets, and diarrhea, much as kaolin and aluminum-hydroxide mixtures are used in contemporary European society to remove bacteria. Skin ailments were commonly treated with wood ash, while animal fats from monitor lizards, snakes, emus, muttonbirds, and dugongs were used as a liniment for the relief of rheumatism and muscular pain. Crushed green ants were combined with other medicines to treat chest complaints, spider web was used to stop bleeding, and in more arid regions, finch droppings were mixed with eucalyptus gum to heal sores.

Plants representing more than 100 genera comprised the bulk of Aboriginal medicines, extracts being obtained by infusion, decoction, crushing, or maceration. Many Australian medicinal plants contain a mix of alkaloids, tannins, steroids, sugars, essential oils, and complex carbohydrates, in addition to elements such as iron, selenium, and silica. They are also known to have antiseptic, analgesic, antipyretic, and carminative properties. Aboriginal people used a number of plants as stimulants or for their hallucinogenic effects, the latter being subject to strict social controls. Aromatherapy was practiced, and herbal tonics are still made today from roots, barks, infused leaves, and flowers.

Bloodletting was a widespread treatment for headache and other ailments, but major surgery was limited to occasional amputation and cauterization by fire. Aboriginal people were well versed in orthopedic procedures, with fractured limbs being immobilized by splints made from either bark or human bone.

Scientists are attempting to unravel the many mysteries of Aboriginal bush medicine in the face of rapidly declining traditional knowledge. Despite the inroads of European medicine and treatments, it is relevant that many traditional treatments remain in use, while a number of Aboriginal remedies manufactured from monitor lizards (goanna oil), emus, dugongs, eucalyptus, and ti tree became an important part of the pharmacopoeia of early European settlers. *See also* HEALTH.

C

CAMPBELL, JOHNNY (1846–80). Indigenous outlaw. Born at Imbil, in the Mary Valley near Gympie in Queensland, the Aboriginal Johnny Campbell spent most of his working life on Manumbar Station, and it was there that he attacked the wife of a European shepherd in 1872. Sentenced to 10 years' imprisonment, Campbell was released in June 1879 and almost immediately embarked on a series of armed robberies, holding up homesteads, isolated huts, and bush camps across a wide area of southeastern Queensland. Captured by Aborigines near Noosa Heads in March 1880, Campbell was sentenced to 14 years' imprisonment, but 3 months later, he was again brought before the court after it was alleged that he had sexually assaulted a European girl near Esk the previous February. In the racially tense atmosphere of colonial Queensland, the rape of a European female by an Aborigine was regarded as a particularly heinous offense. Campbell was found guilty and hanged at Brisbane Jail on 16 August 1880.

CAPE YORK. Named by Lieutenant James Cook on 21 August 1770, Cape York is Australia's northernmost extension and approximately 137,000 square kilometers in area. The peninsula is home to around 18,000 people, the majority of whom are Indigenous. Lying within the monsoon belt, the region is subject to roughly defined wet and dry seasons and, with its extensive geographical size, has a wide range of distinctive ecosystems that have resulted in the development of specialized cultures among its 33 major Aboriginal groups.

On its northeastern coast, the Wuthathi, or "white sand" people of Shelburne Bay, are semi-maritime, while further south the Lama Lama and other related groups of the Princess Charlotte Bay area have adapted to the wetlands, open grass plains, and rocky offshore islands. Their **economy** and cultural practices remain heavily marine-based, unlike the Kuku-Yalanji, who inhabit the dense rainforests of the southeast, or the riverine and floodplain cultures of western Cape York. The region is also noted for the unique Quinkan rock-art galleries found in the Laura district.

Cape York has also been a significant cultural contact point between Papua New Guinea via the islands of **Torres Strait**. Communities of Torres Strait

Islanders exist at Bamaga and Seisia, while Aurukun, Kowanyama, Mapoon, Umagico, Hopevale, and Lockhart River are among the major Aboriginal communities found throughout the region.

CAPE YORK INSTITUTE FOR POLICY AND LEADERSHIP. Jointly established in July 2004 by the federal and Queensland governments, Griffith University, and the Indigenous people of **Cape York** Peninsula, the Institute is charged with the task of conducting policy research on social and economic issues directly affecting the Indigenous people of the region. Although primarily funded from government sources, it remains an entirely independent organization. **Noel Pearson** was the inaugural director of the institute, and he has remained in that position except for a brief period during 2009, when he resigned to campaign against the Queensland government's Wild Rivers Act, which threatens to stifle economic opportunities for many of the region's Indigenous people. *See also* ECONOMY.

CARMODY, KEVIN (KEV) (1946–). Indigenous singer-songwriter. Kevin Carmody was born in Cairns in northern Queensland in 1946. His father was of Irish descent, while his mother was Aboriginal. In 1950, the Carmody family moved to a cattle property near Dalby in southern Queensland, where both parents worked as drovers. In 1956, Kevin Carmody and his younger brother, Laurie, became part of the **Stolen Generations** when they were forcibly removed to Toowoomba and placed in a Christian school. Leaving at the age of 15, he spent almost two decades working in a variety of rural occupations before enrolling at the Darling Downs Institute of Advanced **Education** in 1979. While completing a bachelor of arts degree with honors, Carmody began taking a serious interest in **music**, and while he went on to gain a diploma of education at the University of Queensland and begin a doctorate in history, music became his passion. Performing a blend of country and folk styles, Carmody released his first album, *Pillars of Society*, in December 1988. A second album, *Eulogy (For a Black Person)*, followed in November 1990. *Bloodlines*, which included a track about the Gurindji walk-off on **Wave Hill** Station in 1967 called "From Little Things Big Things Grow," appeared in July 1993. It won him the Country Music Association of Australian Heritage Award, the first of a number of outstanding achievements in the music industry. Other albums, including two compilations, have been released, and on 27 August 2009, Carmody was inducted into the Australian Recording Industry Association Hall of Fame.

CARVED TREES. *See* DENDROGLYPHS.

CENTRAL AUSTRALIAN ABORIGINAL MEDIA ASSOCIATION. *See* ABORIGINAL MEDIA.

CHRISTIANITY. *See* DODSON, PATRICK (PAT); MISSIONS; RELIGION.

CHURINGA. Also spelt *tjuringa*, this was originally an Arrernte (central Australia) term for profoundly sacred objects. Usually made of carved wood, though sometimes of stone, most were also engraved and/or painted. Although varying in size, the majority were portable: wooden *churinga* were commonly tapered, no longer than 60 centimeters and at the widest point no more than eight centimeters. Although symbols of the **Dreaming**, they were more than merely representative, for they were themselves Dreaming, hence their profundity and the reverence in which they were held. There was an array of different *churinga* used for different purposes, not all of which were concerned with the sacred. Some were carried by hunters in order to sharpen their skills. Game killed with this assistance could be the subject of a number of restrictions, such as who could share the food. As Dreaming, *churinga* were frequently used in ceremonies and rituals. When not in use, they were invariably covered, and the most sacred *churinga* were housed in safe repositories, often small caves. Today, use of the term has spread beyond the Arrernte to describe a range of sacred objects.

CITIZENSHIP. While all Aborigines and **Torres Strait** Islanders (and non-Indigenous Australians) born after 26 January 1949 technically became Australian citizens when the Commonwealth Nationality and Citizenship Act 1948 came into effect, equality before the law and voting rights were very different matters. Aboriginal men were not excluded when the adult franchise was granted in the Australian colonies between 1856 and 1900, but the right to vote in elections was steadily eroded through their lack of property qualifications or, later, by virtue of their being welfare recipients under state protection acts. Through a narrow definition of Section 41 of the Australian Constitution, they were also denied the right to vote in federal elections in 1902. At the same time, Aborigines and Torres Strait Islanders were excluded from the census, and although there were individual exceptions during the first half of the 20th century, it was not until the years immediately following World War II that Aborigines and Torres Strait Islanders began to gain full citizenship rights.

The Commonwealth Social Services Consolidation Act of 1947 allowed some Aboriginal people to be exempted from state protection laws and to receive old age, invalid, and widows' pensions along with the maternity allowance. Two years later, the Commonwealth Electoral Act granted the franchise to Aborigines and Torres Strait Islanders who were either serving in or had served in the Australian armed forces. In 1960, the Commonwealth Social Services Act gave all Aborigines and Torres Strait Islanders access to Commonwealth pensions and allowances, and with the passing of the 1962 Commonwealth Electoral Act, they also became eligible to vote in federal elections. In the same year, Western Australia similarly granted the franchise to all Aboriginal people residing in that state, and in 1965, Queensland became the last Australian state to grant Aborigines and Torres Strait Islanders the franchise, although it remained heavily qualified. There was no official encouragement for Aborigines and Torres Strait Islanders to enter their names on the electoral rolls, and voting did not become compulsory for Indigenous people in Western Australia until 1984.

A major turning point for Aborigines and Torres Strait Islanders had come in 1967, when a **referendum** provided the federal government with the power to legislate on their behalf and to include them in the census. In 1973, the Commonwealth Migration Act made it possible for all Aborigines and Torres Strait Islanders to obtain a passport without a special permit, and the 1975 Commonwealth Racial Discrimination Act made it illegal to discriminate against any person in Australia on the grounds of race, color, **religion**, descent, or their national and ethnic origins.

CLAPSTICKS. These are a pair of stick-shaped instruments struck against each other. They are widely used by Aboriginal people across the various regions of Australia. **Boomerang** clapsticks are also widely used as musical instruments. Striking together the tips of a pair of boomerangs facing in opposite directions not only marks rhythm but also produces a pleasing visual aesthetic as the central elliptical space between them opens and closes. *See also* MUSIC.

COLBUNG, KEN. *See* DJIRDJARKAN, NUNDJAN.

COMMUNITY DEVELOPMENT EMPLOYMENT PROJECTS (CDEP). Operating since 1977, the CDEP is currently the government's largest Indigenous program. It assists unemployed Indigenous people in rural and remote areas by developing training and skills that enable them to be employed in the mainstream labor market. The program requires participants to work in community-based activities in exchange for income support benefits.

On 17 February 2007, the then federal government, under Prime Minister John Howard, announced that the CDEP would cease in cities and towns where the unemployment rate was 7 percent or higher. Then, on 23 July 2007, the government announced that the CDEP program would be phased out entirely in the Northern Territory as a result of the government's **Northern Territory Emergency Response**. The government argued that the program perpetuates welfare dependency within Aboriginal communities by creating a disincentive for Aboriginal people to find mainstream employment.

CONCEPTION. Whether Aborigines recognized the male role in conception or were ignorant of physical paternity and instead believed in spirit conception is a debate of long standing that seems unlikely to be resolved. The full range of recorded beliefs on this point, and anthropological interpretations of the data, is voluminous.

Across Australia, a number of different explanations were provided for conception and the development of the fetus. Even within particular groups, different explanations were proffered, and men's explanations could vary from **women**'s. Although they might not have understood the role of semen, for example, some groups believed the fetus developed through a combination of semen and menses. A growing, but by no means universal, consensus is that even those Aborigines who did recognize that sexual intercourse was a necessary precursor to conception did not consider it sufficient: spirit conception remained essential for pregnancy. Some speculate that one reason Aboriginal men emphasized the centrality of spirit conception was precisely because they were uncertain of their role in physical paternity. By emphasizing an essential spiritual basis to procreation, they were able to ensure through cultural means that the issue of conception remained in a religious domain over which men held primary responsibility.

CONISTON MASSACRE. Occurring in 1928 near Coniston Station to the east of Yuendumu, approximately 350 kilometers northwest of Alice Springs in the Northern Territory, this was the last recorded **massacre** of Aboriginal people. Frederick Brooks, a **dingo** trapper and prospector, was murdered by Aborigines for allegedly interfering with the wife of an Aborigine. Later, a party under police guidance admitted to the murder of 17 Aborigines in reprisal for Brooks' murder. In a subsequent raid, another 14 Aborigines were killed. Aboriginal oral testimony holds that 100 or more were killed in a series of raids, and there is evidence to support a far higher figure of Aboriginal deaths than the 31 recorded. Although no parties were punished for their roles in these deaths, the massacre received national and international press and attracted widespread condemnation. For this reason, the Coniston massacre is regarded as a turning point in Aboriginal-settler relations. *See also* FORREST RIVER MASSACRE; MYALL CREEK MASSACRE.

COOLAMON. This multifunctional utensil is a shallow or steep-sided wooden dish, usually manufactured from tree burls and often completed with fine fluting marks. Temporary *coolamons* can also be made from eucalypt bark. Widely distributed throughout Australia, they were used for carrying water, grass seeds, and other foods, as well as infants and personal effects. In some areas of Australia, *coolamons* were also used as a digging implement.

COOMBS, HERBERT "NUGGET" (1906–97). Non-Indigenous economist and public servant. Herbert Coombs exerted considerable influence on Aboriginal affairs from the late 1960s to the early 1980s. Born at Kalamunda in Western Australia on 26 February 1906, Coombs began his public career as a country school teacher before pursuing economics at the University of Western Australia and the London School of Economics. Shortly after returning to Australia in 1934, Coombs became an economist at the Commonwealth Bank, before moving to the Department of Treasury in Canberra. From 1949 to 1960, he served as governor of the Commonwealth Bank and, from 1960 to 1968, was governor of the Reserve Bank. Retiring in 1968, Coombs became chancellor of the Australian National University and continued his interest in the Australian arts. The period from 1968 also marked his first serious foray into Aboriginal affairs after he became chairperson of the Australian Council for Aboriginal Affairs, established in the wake of the 1967 **referendum**.

Although few of the council's recommendations were accepted by Liberal prime ministers John Gorton and William McMahon, an important era began in 1972 when Coombs became consultant to Labor Prime Minister Gough Whitlam. Coombs was a powerful advocate of **self-determination**, a policy designed to allow Indigenous Australians to gain semi-autonomy by administering their own communities. A necessary corollary was to return ancestral land to Aboriginal groups, which, following the **Aboriginal Land Rights Commission** of 1973–74, culminated in the **Aboriginal Land Rights (Northern Territory) Act** of 1976, which gave legal recognition to Aboriginal **land rights** in the Northern Territory.

Coombs resigned from all official positions in 1976 but retained his interest in Aboriginal affairs. In 1979, he launched the Aboriginal Treaty Committee with the intention of concluding a formal treaty with Indigenous Australians. While the idea received considerable public support, it failed to gain a firm commitment from either the Fraser Coalition government (1976–83) or its Labor successor. Coombs died in Sydney on 29 October 1997. *See also* WOODWARD INQUIRY.

COOPER, WILLIAM (1861?–1941). Indigenous activist. William Cooper was born in northern Victoria near the junction of the Goulburn and Murray rivers. Raised by his parents on the Maloga **Mission** and nearby Cummeragunja Aboriginal Reserve outside Moama in southern New South Wales, Cooper spent much of his working life as a shearer and general handyman on grazing properties. He joined the Australian Workers' Union and, after attending adult literacy classes, became a prominent spokesman for disadvantaged Aboriginal communities throughout northern Victoria and western New South Wales.

After moving to Melbourne from Cummeragunja in 1933 to become eligible for the old-age pension, Cooper joined with other exiles from the reserve to form the **Australian Aborigines' League**, which actively campaigned for Aboriginal enfranchisement, parliamentary representation, and **land rights**. He traveled widely to collect signatures from Aboriginal people as part of a petition to King George VI aimed at seeking royal intervention to have responsibility for Aboriginal affairs taken away from individual states.

Cooper joined with members of the Sydney-based **Aborigines Progressive Association** to declare a **Day of Mourning** on 26 January 1938, the sesquicentenary of the arrival of the First Fleet in 1788, protesting the seizure of Aboriginal land and callous treatment over 150 years. Two months later, Prime Minister Joseph Lyons and his Cabinet refused to forward Cooper's petition to the king, a move that greatly disappointed the aging activist. Despite failing **health**, Cooper continued to campaign against the alienation of Aboriginal reserve land in Victoria, and in 1940, he played a prominent role in the establishment of a National Aborigines Day (*see* NATIONAL ABORIGINAL AND ISLANDER DAY OBSERVANCE COMMITTEE). He died the following year. *See also* LAND OWNERSHIP.

CORONATION HILL. Known as Guratba by the Jawoyn people—the traditional owners of the area—this site, which is now in **Kakadu National Park** in the South Alligator River valley in the Northern Territory, came to prominence when the interests of the Jawoyn and the environmental movement conflicted with mining interests. Coronation Hill contains significant deposits of gold, platinum, and palladium. It was these ores, not the possibly equally significant uranium deposits, that a consortium of mining companies sought. The necessary excavations would have caused considerable damage to the local terrain.

To the Jawoyn, Coronation Hill is the final resting place of Bula, an important creator **ancestral being**. Mortally wounded by a hornet sting, Bula made his way with his two wives from the sea to Coronation Hill. Frequently needing to rest, Bula would enter the ground to emerge again whenever disturbed and continue his journey. Wherever Bula rested, he would leave behind powerful life essences. So as to ensure Bula would not be further disturbed, the Jawoyn protected his resting sites with sheets of bark and, in more recent times, tin. A number of prohibitions and restrictions pertained (and still pertain) to sites associated with Bula. The Jawoyn were fearful that the proposed mining operations would disturb Bula's final resting place, and the consequences would be cataclysmic, not only for the Jawoyn, but for all humankind. Conservationists, who mostly supported the Jawoyn, were concerned about environmental damage to ecologically sensitive areas and argued that the area excised from Kakadu National Park to permit mining be reincorporated into the park.

The debate was polarized and bitter. Nevertheless, on 17 June 1991, in what was regarded as a victory for the Jawoyn (and the environmental movement), the Hawke-led federal Labor government refused permission for mining to proceed.

CORROBOREE. In this public performance of song and **dance**, participants reenact mythical stories and scenes of the **Dreaming**. As such, the corroboree differs from many other Aboriginal ceremonies, which may be either gender-specific or exclude outsiders. Corroborees involve the entire group and, frequently, neighboring groups who are invited to both attend and perform. The term itself is a corruption of an Aboriginal word from the Sydney region of New South Wales, and in more recent times, it has been applied indiscriminately to a number of other genres of song and dance as well as to sporting events and rallies.

Aboriginal corroborees became popular entertainments in colonial Australia, and by 1845, they were a regular feature in the European social life of Melbourne and Adelaide. Aboriginal entrepreneurs made them as spectacular as possible to maximize profits, and each performance was usually preceded by spear and **boomerang** throwing demonstrations and contests. Cultural artifacts were sold as a profitable sideline. Later, in the 19th century, corroborees were important adjuncts to European celebrations and events, including **cricket** and football matches.

Aboriginal people also formed traveling troupes, often following the same pattern of seasonal movement that had underlain their pre-European lifestyle. In summer, corroborees were regularly performed at seaside resorts, some of which were located on old Aboriginal camping grounds. By the mid-1890s, traveling troupes were operating in Queensland and northern New South Wales. In the latter, in 1896, one group of Aborigines became the star act of the Tenterfield Show when it performed a corroboree under electric light.

While Aboriginal troupes regularly entered into arrangements with European agents, they still retained a strong measure of control over specific performances. Importantly, corroborees provided a vehicle that reinforced the value and status of Aboriginal cultural practices and beliefs. Corroborees were later carried into the 21st century by the Tjapukai Aboriginal Dance Theatre in Cairns, Queensland. A number of other Aboriginal and Islander dance companies draw on a panoply of Aboriginal cultural traditions in their productions. *See also* BANGARA DANCE THEATRE; MUSIC.

COUNCIL FOR ABORIGINAL RECONCILIATION (CAR). Established in 1991 as a Commonwealth statutory authority under the Commonwealth Council for Aboriginal Reconciliation Act 1991, the CAR was given a 10-year mandate, ending on 31 December 2000, to promote the process of **reconciliation** between Aboriginal and Torres Strait Islander people and the wider Australian public. The first chairperson was **Patrick Dodson**. The government appointed 25 council members representing diverse community groups within Australia.

The CAR produced a *Document Towards Reconciliation* and *Roadmap to Reconciliation* that were launched at **Corroboree** 2000 at the Sydney Opera House. The CAR then submitted its final report, calling upon the government to establish a formal framework for advancing the process of reconciliation and, for this purpose, to create the foundation Reconciliation Australia. This foundation was to continue CAR's work by addressing what was seen to be the "unfinished business" of reconciliation and, more controversially, to progress work toward negotiation of a treaty with Indigenous people. In 2001, the CAR was replaced by the private organization Reconciliation Australia.

The federal government took more than two years to respond formally to these recommendations. In September 2002, Prime Minister John Howard rejected many of CAR's final recommendations, including setting out a formal process that would lead toward reconciliation. The prime minister also rejected the recommendation of a treaty as inappropriate and divisive. The government reaffirmed its approach to reconciliation as a form of "practical reconciliation." Nevertheless, outside of formal treaties, there was broad support for the more sanguine, less confronting aspects behind the concept of reconciliation. Sensing that the CAR's initiative might be lost and that supportive sentiment might wane, an inquiry by the Senate Legal and Constitutional References Committee was established. It presented its report to Federal Parliament in October 2003. The report made various recommendations, including that the government adopt all of the recommendations set out in the final CAR report, that the government acknowledge that reconciliation encompasses more than "practical reconciliation," and that the government had a duty to demonstrate national leadership on the issue of reconciliation. *See also* AUSTRALIANS FOR NATIVE TITLE AND RECONCILIATION (ANTaR).

CRICKET. The first Australian cricket team to tour England was composed entirely of Aboriginal players from Victoria. Impressed by the athletic prowess of local Aboriginal people, European settlers around Edenhope in western Victoria had begun to include them in district cricket teams by the mid-1860s. In late 1866, an all-Aboriginal team was formed at Edenhope, with the highly respected Melbourne cricketer Thomas Wills being hired as coach. In December, the team traveled to the Victorian capital, where they played the Melbourne Cricket Club before an estimated 10,000 spectators. Although the Aboriginal team lost the match, two of its members were selected for the Victorian team to play against Tasmania. Interest in the Aboriginal cricketers led to a return match against Melbourne and a tour of regional Victoria. In February 1867, the team played in Sydney, before embarking on another round of matches in the New South Wales towns of Newcastle, Maitland, and Wollongong.

In 1868, the Aboriginal cricket team was taken to England, where it played at many of the leading grounds. Of its 47 matches, the team won 14 and drew 19, on each occasion entertaining the English crowds during intervals with athletic displays and demonstrations of **boomerang** throwing. On their return to Australia, the players again toured regional Victoria before the team was disbanded after a final match against the Melbourne Cricket Club in March 1869. Remarkably few Aboriginal players have appeared in representative teams since the 1860s, aside from **Edward Gilbert**. *See also* CORROBOREE; SPORT.

CUSTOMARY LAW. In view of the diversity of Indigenous people and their specific histories and cultures, there can be no single definition of what constitutes Indigenous customary law. What Indigenous people share is an **oral history** and tradition in which their religious beliefs and practices, laws, way of life, and understanding of the past are encoded. Customary law is, therefore, not written or codified as are many Western laws but passed on orally through generations. Further, for many Indigenous people, customary laws are sacred, and some laws can only be known and enforced by those with the appropriate authority and knowledge.

The Australian Law Reform Commission (ALRC) published a report in 1986 entitled *The Recognition of Aboriginal Customary Laws*, which considered whether existing legal institutions should recognize Aboriginal customary law. It found that no single overarching approach should be taken in recognizing customary law, but its recognition should respond to the unique context within which Aboriginal customary law is practiced. More recently, the law reform commissions of the Northern Territory (November 2003) and Western Australia (September 2006) reported on the issue of customary law and its intersection with Australia's criminal justice system. The reports did not substantially progress the 1986 ALRC findings.

Concepts of customary law interplay strongly with notions of **self-determination**, in which Indigenous peoples maintain their right to decide matters that impact upon their lives, including the right to live under the provisions and sanctions of their customary laws.

D

DALGERIE. *See* BLAIR, HAROLD.

DANCE. Dance was a regular feature of Aboriginal social and religious life. Through dance, Aborigines were able to invoke the **Dreaming** and not so much tell the myths describing the exploits of the **ancestral beings** but reveal their continuing presence. This could be done through reenacting segments of particular myths or through the dancers themselves manifesting as an ancestral being. Dance of this sort was profoundly symbolic and was integral to sacred ceremonial performance and song. Some of these performances were secret, with participants and audience strictly limited according to age, initiatory status, **kinship** position, and social category (*see* SOCIAL ORGANIZATION). Much dance activity however, was performed publicly and spontaneously. These dances could still contain mythical referents, but the focus (and joy) was in the dance itself, singing, and any other musical accompaniment. Many early observers of Aboriginal peoples reported that singing and dancing were a usual evening activity. These ad hoc performances were public and prosaic, providing an avenue for commentary on day-to-day life. Such performances did not foreclose mythological allusions. Dance, like **music** and visual **art**, remains integral to contemporary expression and continues to be widely practiced. *See also* CORROBOREE; MUSIC.

DAY OF MOURNING. Held on 26 January 1938 to coincide with the celebrations marking the sesquicentenary of British colonization in 1788, the Day of Mourning was the idea of **William Cooper** of the Melbourne-based **Australian Aborigines' League**. **William Ferguson** and **John (Jack) Patten** of the Sydney-based **Aborigines Progressive Association** organized the alternative Aboriginal protest, which brought together 100 Aboriginal activists from New South Wales and Victoria. This was Australia's first national Aboriginal conference, with much of the discussion focusing on **citizenship** and equal rights. The proceedings were later published in a new Aboriginal monthly journal, the *Australian Abo Call*. The conference concluded after producing a 10-point manifesto that, inter alia, called for Commonwealth control of Aboriginal affairs and an advisory board of six members, three of whom were to be of Aboriginal origin.

A few days after the conference, a deputation of 20 delegates, including Jack Patten, presented the manifesto to Prime Minister Joseph Lyons and Federal Minister for the Interior John McEwen, neither of whom acted upon the document's recommendations. Although it achieved little in the short term, the Day of Mourning received extensive media coverage and is widely recognized as having been a powerful symbolic moment in the struggle for Aboriginal equality.

DEATH. A wide range of mortuary and ritual practices are conducted across Australia. In most instances, these practices were religious and were concerned with the spiritual essence of the dead person, such as ensuring the spirit returned to the country to which it belonged and ensuring the spirit did not linger and interfere with the living. In many instances, the cause of death had to be found, with sorcery or some other spiritual interference considered the likely explanation. This could lead to retaliation against the perpetrator or some other resolution.

Many of these beliefs and practices continue. In some regions, for example, mourners still gash their heads and bodies with stones or other implements. Depending on the region and/or circumstances of death, a family or even an entire camp might move to a new site following a death. The ritual cleansing of property and house following a death, often through the medium of smoke, continues to be practiced in some regions. The prohibition on using the name of a recently deceased person or showing his or her image remains widespread. Most media in Australia carry a standard warning that a program could offend some members of the Indigenous community if it contains the names or images of Aborigines who may be deceased. *See also* BURIAL; PUKUMANI POLES; RELIGION.

DECLARATION ON THE RIGHTS OF INDIGENOUS PEOPLES. *See* DODSON, MICHAEL (MICK).

DEMOGRAPHICS. The June 2006 census estimated the total Aboriginal and Torres Strait Islander population to be 517,043, with a median age of 21. New South Wales was the state with the highest Australian Indigenous population (152,685, representing 28.7 percent of the total Indigenous population), followed by Queensland (144,885, representing 28.3 percent of the total Indigenous population). The estimated total Australian resident non-Indigenous population was 20,180,837, with a median age of 37. While New South Wales and Queensland have the highest Indigenous population, they also have large non-Indigenous populations—6,663,402 and 3,946,023, respectively. This means that in New South Wales, Indigenous Australians comprise just 2.2 percent of the total population of that state and in Queensland, 3.6 percent. The Northern Territory, on the other hand, with an estimated total non-Indigenous population of 146,622 (median age 34.6), has an Indigenous population of 64,005 (median age 22.3), representing 31.6 percent of the total population of that territory and 12.9 percent of the Australian Indigenous population. Despite the popular misconception, the majority of Indigenous Australians do not live in the Northern Territory or in the remote regions of central, western, and northern Australia.

From the early 1960s until the mid-1990s, the Indigenous fertility rate (measured by births to Indigenous mothers) followed (but did not parallel) the falling birth rate for all **women** in Australia. This trend saw the total fertility rate for Indigenous women fall from 5.8 babies per woman in the early 1960s to 1.97 babies per woman in 1996, with the 1970s being the period of greatest decline. Whereas the total fertility rate for all women in Australia shows a consistent decline and no evident upward trend (from 3.2 babies per woman in the early 1960s to 1.97 in 2008), from 1996, the fertility rate for Aboriginal women has increased. In 2008, it was 2.52 babies per Indigenous mother.

Due to a number of factors, the data upon which the statistics measuring the fertility rate of Aboriginal women (and Aboriginal births) are based is likely to underestimate the actual rate.

DENDROGLYPHS. These are trees with large areas of bark removed and carved lines etched into the underlying wood. The practice was not widespread, with dendroglyphs only found in the eastern and central regions of New South Wales and southeastern Queensland. Etchings took many shapes, mostly following the geometric patterns carved into weapons, skin cloaks, and assorted paraphernalia. Diamond-shaped and herringbone patterns are typical. More rarely, human figures or animals would be carved. Dendroglyphs are primarily associated with ceremonial grounds, **burial**, and **sacred sites**. *See also* ART.

DIDGERIDOO. The didgeridoo is an aerophone. It produces sound when a player blows into one end of the hollow instrument while vibrating the lips. This apparently simple instrument is, however, rather more complex. Playing it requires mastering "circular breathing." This allows for the continuous production of sound. It is achieved by the player inhaling through the nose while simultaneously expelling and then replenishing air held in the cheeks. This technique allows for considerable augmentation of the underlying rhythmic drone, the drone being varied through changes in rhythm. Overtones (once a feature of specific areas only) are produced through vocalizations and control of the diaphragm.

As with the **boomerang**, the didgeridoo is popularly regarded as emblematic of Aboriginality. Although popularly thought to be a traditional instrument of all Aborigines, it was traditionally confined to northern Australia, above the latitude of approximately 17 degrees south. And unlike the boomerang, which has been in use for many thousands of years, the didgeridoo is a comparatively recent artifact that may not be more than 1,500 years old. It is made from a tree branch or small trunk hollowed out by either termites or fire. The tube is then cleaned of any residual obstructions and dirt, and a mouthpiece of wax or resin is added to one end. This covers the end fibers of the wooden tube but does not significantly (if at all) narrow the opening.

While the didgeridoo is still used in secret-sacred contexts, particularly in the north of Australia where it originated and where it is used to accompany singers in ceremonial performances, it is now made and used by Aborigines throughout Australia for a range of purposes, just as it is made and used by people throughout the world for different purposes. For example, the Yolngu of northeastern Arnhem Land, who call the didgeridoo the *yidaki*, still use it for secret-sacred performances but have also brought it into mainstream popular musical entertainment through the rock band **Yothu Yindi**. *See also* MUSIC.

DIGGING STICK. A heavy dependence on plant and small animal foods ensured that the multifunctional digging stick was one of the most important implements in Aboriginal material culture. Depending on the region, wooden digging sticks varied in length from 30 centimeters to just under two meters, with fire-hardened tips either pointed or fashioned into a chisel- or spade-like blade. Diggings sticks were used to harvest underground tubers and roots, excavate the burrows of small animals, break open termite mounds, and peel bark from trees to make shelters. They provided **women** with extra reach to harvest fruits, berries, and nuts from trees and large shrubs, and in coastal areas, they were used to prize mollusks from rocks. Digging sticks could also be wielded as a weapon, and after the arrival of Europeans, they were frequently manufactured from discarded iron.

DINGO. Australia's largest native mammalian carnivore is a type of dog (*Canis lupus dingo*), now thought to be related to a subspecies of wolf. Its origins and length of time in Australia are yet to be precisely determined. However, most scientists believe the dingo originated in Asia and some 3,500 to 4,000 years BP was introduced to Australia, either by Aborigines or, more likely, by Asian seafarers. The dingo rapidly spread throughout most of the

Australian mainland and a number of its offshore islands. Tasmania was an exception and remained dingo-free. The dingo is implicated in the extinction of the thylacine (*Thylacinus cynocephalus*, also known as the Tasmanian tiger) on the Australian mainland, but to what extent is still the subject of debate. While Aborigines did not ever entirely domesticate the dingo, a number of groups utilized the dingo for hunting and as camp dogs, and it was incorporated into the **Dreaming** and the pantheon of **ancestral beings**. The pups were also eaten.

DISPOSSESSION. This term is used to describe the alienating of Aborigines and Torres Strait Islanders from their lands and the failure of consecutive generations to acknowledge that Indigenous Australians were the traditional owners and possessors of Australia. *See also* LAND RIGHTS; MABO DECISION; MABO, EDDIE ("KOIKI"); NATIVE TITLE; *TERRA NULLIUS*.

DJIRDJARKAN, NUNDJAN (1931–2010). Indigenous leader and activist. An elder of the Noongar people, Nundjan Djirdjarkan (Ken Colbung) was born in Moore River settlement. In 1950, at 19 years of age, he joined the Australian Army and served in Korea and Japan. Discharged from the army in 1965, Djirdjarkan moved to Sydney to work as a welfare officer for the Foundation for Aboriginal Affairs and, in 1970, returned to Perth and was involved in the Aboriginal Advancement Council. He was an advocate for Aboriginal **land rights** and for the preservation of cultural **identity** and spirituality.

Djirdjarkan was awarded the Member of the Order of the British Empire (MBE) in 1979 and, in 1988, became a Member of the Order of Australia (AM) in recognition of his service to the Indigenous community. One of his most recognized accomplishments was his successful lobbying of the Australian and British governments for the return of the remains of **Yagan**, a Noongar warrior who had been killed in 1833 and whose decapitated head had been taken to England.

DODSON, MICHAEL (MICK) (1950–). Indigenous political leader and Aboriginal rights activist. Born in Katherine in the Northern Territory, Mick Dodson is a member of the Yawuru people from the Broome area, Western Australia. He is an activist for Indigenous **land rights** and prominent figure in Indigenous politics. Dodson is director of the Australia National University's National Centre for Indigenous Studies and chairperson of the **Australian Institute of Aboriginal and Torres Strait Islander Studies**. He was Australia's first Indigenous **Aboriginal and Torres Strait Islander social justice commissioner** and held this position from 1993 to 1998. Prior to this, he worked with the Victorian Aboriginal Legal Service and became a barrister at the Victorian Bar. Dodson was senior legal advisor for the Northern **Land Council** from 1984 and was appointed director of the council in 1980. From 1988 to 1990, he acted as counsel assisting the **Royal Commission into Aboriginal Deaths in Custody**.

Dodson has been involved in developing the Draft Declaration on the Rights of Indigenous Peoples in the United Nations Working Group on Indigenous Populations. In 2003, he became a Member of the Order of Australia (AM) for service to the Indigenous community, particularly in recognition of his work in raising awareness of social justice, as a contributor to advancing **reconciliation**, and as an advocate for **native title**. Michael Dodson's brother is **Patrick Dodson**.

DODSON, PATRICK (PAT) (1947–). Indigenous political leader and Aboriginal rights activist. A member of the Yawuru people from the Broome area, Western Australia, Patrick Dodson has a very high public profile and is readily recognizable by his Akubra hat and long, flowing white beard. He is the former chairperson of the **Council for Aboriginal Reconciliation** and was a commissioner in the **Royal Commission into Aboriginal Deaths in Custody** and a former director of the Central **Land Council** and **Kimberley Land Council**. Currently, he is chairperson of the Kimberley Development Commission and the **Lingiari** Foundation. He was the first ordained Aboriginal Catholic priest, but he left the Catholic Church in the early 1980s as a result of his belief that Christianity and Aboriginal ceremonies were not irreconcilable practices as was preached by the Church. He continues to be actively involved in promoting Indigenous rights and culture and is a frequent, harsh critic of government policy on Indigenous affairs. Patrick Dodson's brother is **Michael Dodson**.

DOG TAGS. During the era of the **Aboriginal Protection Boards**, Aboriginal people were permitted exemptions from the strictures governing their lives if they demonstrated that they had assimilated into non-Aboriginal society. Such people were provided with a certificate of exemption granting freedom from the Aboriginal Protection Board's far-reaching control, but to obtain an exemption, Aboriginal people were required to renounce their Aboriginality and forego contact with Aborigines who were not similarly exempted. Those Aboriginal men who served in the Australian Army often sought these exemptions to avoid further racism and discrimination. Without this exemption, they were not treated equally with non-Aboriginal servicemen. Aboriginal people referred to these exemptions as "dog tags" or "dog licenses." *See also* ASSIMILATION POLICY.

DREAMING, THE • 65

DOOMADGEE, MULRUNJI (CAMERON). *See* ROYAL COMMISSION INTO ABORIGINAL DEATHS IN CUSTODY.

DORA DORA BLACKS. In February 1890, two Aboriginal men from Fraser Island in Queensland—Boolyal and Thunimmberi (known respectively to Europeans as Jacky and Willie)—were recruited as trackers by the Victorian Police Force. Jacky had previously served as a police tracker in Victoria during the hunt for Ned Kelly and his gang of outlaws in 1878–80. On this occasion, the recruits believed their term of enlistment was to be for 12 months, and when they were not repatriated back to Queensland as expected, they absconded to make their own way home. In March 1891, they killed a European **woman** named Smith at Benalla in Victoria before crossing the border into New South Wales, where they mortally wounded a Polish settler at Dora Dora, near Albury, after being refused provisions. Despite a massive police manhunt, both escaped to Queensland, where they disappeared until December 1893, when Willie was finally arrested at Bundaberg. Jacky was captured the following February near Mackay in northern Queensland, with both men being extradited to New South Wales to stand trial for murder. After widespread calls for clemency, Willie was sentenced to 15 years' imprisonment and Jacky to life. Willie was released from Grafton Jail in April 1909, while Jacky served nearly 20 years in Maitland Jail before his release in January 1914.

DOT PAINTINGS. Now iconographic of acrylic **Western Desert art**, so-called dot paintings are a recent aesthetic. The name refers to the practice of infilling the expanse of a canvas not already painted with imagery with dots, often in alternating color bands. While dotting using natural media was a feature of some traditional aesthetic practices, the early acrylics from the desert region had few or no dots. Dotting is partially a response to market forces, partially the enjoyment of the brilliant visual effect that well-executed dotting produces, and partially a traditional practice emergent in new media.

DREAMING, THE. This term refers to a complex system of beliefs, knowledge, and law. It arises from Baldwin Spencer and F. J. Gillen's 1896 translation of the Arrernte word *altyerrenge*. Each Aboriginal **language** group has its own word for this corpus of beliefs, and in no instance is the word "dreaming" a literal translation of the universal experience to dream. Rather, the Dreaming describes the period, stories, and mythology telling of the creation era when the **ancestral beings** came to or arose from the earth and/or seas and commenced their activities. Prior to this period, there was no humankind, and the extant medium was, depending on Aboriginal group, a flat, featureless terrain or watery body. With the coming of the ancestral beings, the landscape began to take form and shape: every action they performed left its mark.

The Dreaming, however, is not a straightforward record of past events. Through **conception**, ritual, and day-to-day life, the Dreaming is continually reanimated in the present and projected into the future. In attempting to encapsulate the manner in which the Dreaming simultaneously evokes past, present, and future, the anthropologist W. E. H. Stanner coined the neologism "everywhen." Significantly, the evocation is dynamic, in that while the Dreaming influences Aboriginal life, the relationship is one of participatory engagement and mutual influence, not passive succumbing to its dictates.

Formerly an oral culture, Aboriginal people use **initiation** ceremonies, rituals, song, **dance**, painting, and storytelling to impart this knowledge and law to future generations and, in doing so, have input into the Dreaming's content and form. Individuals acquire this knowledge at different stages of their life, and access to esotery is dependent upon age, gender, initiatory status, and position in the **kinship** structure. The Dreaming is a living and lived experience. It continues to be a powerful force structuring Aboriginal peoples' lives today.

E

ECONOMY. The land, sea, estuaries, and rivers provided the means of production for traditional Aboriginal societies, with hunting and gathering the primary means of exploitation (*see* BUSH FOODS). There was a marked division of labor between men and women. Women provided the majority of foodstuffs through their gathering activities, which included small game (reptiles, small marsupials) and a very wide range of edible plants collected (including tubers, seeds, fruits, nuts, and succulents). Women mostly gathered collectively and often in the accompaniment of young children of both sexes, though in few societies some women on occasion gathered alone. Men hunted the less reliably obtained larger game. This was frequently a collective effort involving considerable teamwork. Sometimes, it was a singular (and more opportunistic) pursuit. Food was distributed among family and beyond in accordance with **kinship** obligations. The tools of production predominately were constructed from organic materials, such as wood, bone, grasses, reeds, and kelp (the latter three being woven into an assortment of implements, such as baskets, nets, and water carriers). Stone was used to make ax heads, grinding stones, cutting tools, spearheads, and fire-making flints and in the construction of fish traps and weirs. Aborigines were quick to utilize the availability of new materials that European colonization introduced. For example, both glass and iron were fashioned into spearheads. Trade between near and distant groups occurred, particularly of ceremonial material, such as ochre and pearl shell, and also of tool- and flint-making stone. It was not a significant method of procuring foodstuffs.

Across Australia, fire was used as a land management tool (*see* FIRE-STICK FARMING), and although cultivation, as such, was not practiced, some societies did replant pieces of yam tubers so as to ensure a continuing supply. One popular misconception is that Aborigines had no means of preserving foodstuffs. A number of groups utilized smoke as a preservative for particular foods, including eels and fish. Aborigines in the desert regions would occasionally dry strips of kangaroo meat on hot stones. A number of groups stored quantities of grass seed for later grinding. With the exception of the **dingo** (which arrived in Australia 3,500 to 4,000 years BP and which did not reach Tasmania), no animals were pressed into service as an instrument of production or for companionship.

Another popular misconception (although one now quickly abating under the influence of a more romantic vision of traditional life) is that Aborigines eked out a precarious existence that offered little comfort or security against the ravages of hunger and thirst. This is countered by suggestions that the richness of Aboriginal spiritual life points to sufficient leisure time to indulge in elaborate and arcane metaphysical pursuits (*see* DREAMING, THE; RELIGION). However, much ceremonial and ritual activity was devoted to ensuring that the socioeconomic conditions that provided the means for Aboriginal societies to prosper were satisfied. The spiritual life of Aborigines was, therefore, not a luxury permitted by an abundant time-rich life but an integral element of their economy. Nevertheless, across Australia, the traditional economy provided for what we would now describe as a reasonably balanced life (between work, leisure, and rest), and the wide variety of foodstuffs obtained and consumed provided a healthy diet.

The dispossession of land from Aborigines following European colonization in 1788, their alienation from resources, and imposition of the subsequent settler economy ultimately destroyed the capacity of Aborigines to practice their traditional means of production. As a direct consequence of this, today key socioeconomic indicators reveal Aborigines to be the most disadvantaged group in Australia. Unemployment is high, and few who are employed are in high status or professional positions. Very few run their own businesses or are self-employed. Because far fewer Aborigines have formal **education** qualifications than those in the total population, most who are employed are in laboring and unskilled jobs. For those with qualifications, the largest single employer is the public sector, with many Aborigines working in the areas responsible for service delivery to Aboriginal communities. Until its recent demise, the **Community Development Employment Projects** (CDEP) skills-based training program was the primary means of employment in many Aboriginal communities. The 2006 census reported the Aboriginal unemployment rate being approximately 16 percent for both men and women, a little over twice that of the total population. This figure is conservative, for Aborigines "employed" under the CDEP training program are not included.

Welfare is for many their only source of income, producing a high level of dependency and what has been called the "sit-down economy." A number of programs are aimed at addressing this concern, including an initiative by a prominent mining magnate who, in concert with the federal government, Indigenous groups, and a number of other major companies, is striving to create 50,000 jobs for Indigenous Australians. Called the Australian Employment Covenant, it was launched in October 2008. **Noel Pearson**, the

Aboriginal leader from Cape York, has proposed a series of reforms to end welfare dependency, including the garnishing of income and compulsory school attendance, which some communities in that region have adopted. A number of national parks have been returned to Aboriginal ownership, including **Kakadu** and **Uluru-Kata Tjuta**. These provide limited employment opportunities for traditional owners as park rangers, tourist guides, and the like and some income from gate and licensing fees. Mining royalties provide income for a number of groups where mining occurs on Aboriginal-owned land. **Tourism** provides a limited income for some communities, but despite its potential, this industry remains mostly underdeveloped. A number of large pastoral leases are owned by Aborigines (purchased on the open market or gained under **land rights** or **native title** legislation) in central, northern, and northwest Australia. Some of these are run profitably and provide limited employment opportunities. There are many **art** centers and dealers distributing Aboriginal art to the fine art and tourist market. Despite contributing some $AUD130 million annually to the Australian economy, little filters back to the artists or their communities. Education, skills-based training, greater emphasis on individual responsibility instead of communal and/or individual rights, curtailing welfare, and encouraging people to move to where there are better employment (and educational) opportunities provide the underlying impetus for current policy aimed at redressing enduring socioeconomic disadvantage.

EDUCATION. Only comparatively recently have Aborigines and Torres Strait Islanders been afforded the same educational opportunities as all other Australians. While little attempt was made at first to cater for Indigenous culture in formal education settings, a raft of programs and initiatives, including Indigenous, community-controlled schools staffed by Indigenous teachers, now aims to do so. Many argue that formal, Western education represents a double bind for Aborigines. While desirous of an education and the opportunities it presents and recognizing the necessity of having Indigenous people with the range of formal qualifications necessary for today's society, there is concern that Western educational settings, syllabi, and methodologies undermine Indigenous cultures and values. However, despite the deployment of considerable resources in an effort to improve the educational outcomes for Indigenous students and the efforts to incorporate culturally sensitive teaching practices and syllabi, Indigenous Australians are still not achieving educational parity with their non-Indigenous peers. In particular, they are underrepresented proportionately at university and other higher education institutions, and school attendance in many regional and remote settings remains a concern. A number of private boarding schools have responded to the challenge of Indigenous education by offering scholarships and other support mechanisms to Indigenous students who would not otherwise have had the opportunity to attend boarding school.

As has been the experience in other settler nations, the **language** of instruction is contested. Partly in an attempt to improve performance at school in junior age groups and in response to concerns about language and culture loss, in 1972, a program of **bilingual education** was introduced in the Northern Territory. Under this program, children commenced their schooling using their native tongue. Following acquisition of reading and writing proficiency in their first language, English successively became the language of instruction. In late 2008, following concerns over educational standards in Indigenous schools, the Northern Territory government enforced the abandonment of bilingual education by insisting that the first four hours of instruction in schools be in English. Mastery of English is seen as essential to equipping students to succeed in contemporary society and lessening dependence on welfare. *See also* BATCHELOR INSTITUTE OF TERTIARY EDUCATION; INSTITUTE FOR ABORIGINAL DEVELOPMENT.

ENGRAVING. Also known as carvings or petroglyphs, engravings on rock are found throughout Australia. Broadly speaking, however, and with notable exceptions, Australia's major rock painting galleries are found in an arc across the northern regions of Australia, from the **Kimberley**, across **Arnhem land** to the **Cape York** Peninsula, and south to Carnarvon Gorge. The major rock engraving sites, by contrast, are mostly in the southern two-thirds of the continent. The Burrup Peninsula in the northwestern corner of this sector in Western Australia is a significant engraving site, and there are a number of sites in central Australia, such as N'Dhala Gorge to the east of Alice Springs. Engraving sites north of this sector are sparse and generally not as elaborate as those found in the south.

In the Olary region of South Australia, there is an extensive engraving site (there are many thousands of engravings) of particular significance. The oldest engravings have been dated to 40,000 years BP, and the most recent to 1,500 years BP. This suggests a continuity of cultural traditions and engraving technology over countless generations.

Three main methods of engraving rock surfaces were employed. One method (pecking) was to pit and mark the rock by direct percussion with a hand-held stone hammer. Another method (also known as pecking) used a stone hammer and chisel. Interestingly and contrary to previous opinion, recent trials have demonstrated that the direct percussion method produced more precise delineation than the stone hammer and chisel method. The third principal engraving technique employed was abrasion, whereby grooves were created by repeatedly pushing an implement over the surface to be marked. Motifs and figurative engravings often combined both pecking and abrading techniques.

From the late 19th century, both emu eggs and the fruit of the boab tree have been carved by Aborigines. This practice continues. *See also* ART.

F

FAMILY. *See* SOCIAL ORGANIZATION.

FEDERAL COUNCIL FOR ABORIGINAL ADVANCEMENT (FCAA). *See* FEDERAL COUNCIL FOR THE ADVANCEMENT OF ABORIGINES AND TORRES STRAIT ISLANDERS (FCAATSI).

FEDERAL COUNCIL FOR THE ADVANCEMENT OF ABORIGINES AND TORRES STRAIT ISLANDERS (FCAATSI). Originally the Federal Council for Aboriginal Advancement, this organization played a major role in Aboriginal and **Torres Strait** Islander affairs between 1960 and 1972. At the request of Torres Strait Islanders, the name was changed to the Federal Council for the Advancement of Aborigines and Torres Strait Islanders in 1964. The organization's greatest triumph came in 1967, with the successful referendum giving the federal government the power to legislate on behalf of all Australian Indigenous people. FCAATSI was also heavily involved in campaigns for **citizenship** and voting rights to be extended to all Indigenous Australians, improvements in living conditions and **education**, equal wages for pastoral workers, and Indigenous **land ownership**.

An umbrella organization that drew together diverse bodies, such as trade unions and church groups, FCAATSI was formed in Adelaide during February 1958. Only three of the 30 founding members were Aboriginal people, and as the latter's numbers expanded during the following decade, tensions developed over control of the organization. A major schism occurred at the general meeting held at Easter 1970, when a number of Indigenous members formed the National Tribal Council. The Council survived for only three years, and by 1973, FCAATSI itself was under full Indigenous control. This development coincided with the establishment of the Commonwealth Department of Aboriginal Affairs and the National Aboriginal Consultative Committee, both of which seriously undermined FCAATSI's influence. The organization was finally wound up in 1978 when the federal government refused further funding.

FERGUSON, WILLIAM (1882–1950). Indigenous activist. Outspoken critic of the **Aborigines Protection Board**, William Ferguson was born at Darlington Point in New South Wales in 1882 and became one of the most important figures in the struggle for Aboriginal rights during the 1930s and 1940s. A professional shearer, Ferguson spent his entire working life in the rural areas of New South Wales and was actively involved in the trade union movement. From the early 1920s, his interest turned to the discriminatory policies of the Aborigines Protection Board, which he vigorously opposed. Along with **Jack Patten**, Ferguson played a pivotal role in the formation of the **Aborigines Progressive Association** in June 1937, an organization that was at the forefront of the fight for Aboriginal civil rights. When the Aborigines Protection Board was replaced by the Aborigines Welfare Board in 1940, Ferguson and his associates campaigned for Aboriginal representation, a move that was rewarded in 1943, when Ferguson and Walter Page were elected as the first Aboriginal representatives. Although obstructed on numerous occasions, Ferguson remained on the board until early 1949, when he accepted the position of vice president of the New South Wales branch of the **Australian Aborigines' League**, a national body that arose after the Aborigines Progressive Association combined with **William Cooper**'s Australian Aborigines' League in Victoria.

After becoming disillusioned by the lack of response from both major political parties to end discriminatory legislation against Aboriginal people, Ferguson resigned from the Australian Labor Party to run unsuccessfully as an independent candidate for the rural New South Wales seat of Lawson in the December 1949 federal elections. He collapsed after making his final campaign speech and died at Dubbo, New South Wales, in January 1950.

FILM. Ethnographic film in Australia dates from 1898, when members of the Cambridge Anthropological Expedition used a Lumiere camera to record the cultural life of **Torres Strait** Islanders. It is the oldest ethnographic film in the world. In 1901, Walter Baldwin Spencer and Frank Gillen filmed the Arrernte people of central Australia, and in 1912, Baldwin Spencer made a series of short films featuring Aboriginal people at Oenpelli, the Flora River, and Bathurst Island in the Northern Territory. The supposed primitivism of the Aboriginal people and a widespread belief that they were destined to die out resulted in a number of efforts being made during the 1930s to document traditional Aboriginal social life and culture on film. Between 1930 and 1937, for example, the University of Adelaide and the South Australian Museum made a series of ethnographic films in central Australia. All were filmed by amateur cinematographers, and it was not until 1947 that the first Australian ethnographic film was finally produced by professionals. Entitled *Primitive*

People—The Australian Aborigines, it largely featured the Aboriginal people of **Arnhem Land**.

From 1950, the anthropologist and linguist Theodor Strehlow filmed more than 900 ritual acts in central Australia, principally among the Arrernte people. Following its establishment in 1961, the **Australian Institute of Aboriginal and Torres Strait Islander Studies** also became active in ethnographic film production, particularly after forming its own film unit in 1964.

Until the 1970s, there was only limited representation of Aboriginal people in fictional films. In some of the earliest productions, they were played by European actors with black makeup, and when Aboriginal people appeared at all, they were either incidental figures intended to reinforce the Australianness of the landscape or portrayed as hostile savages inhibiting the spread of European settlement. Only one film, *Bitter Springs* (1950), made any attempt to view the frontier conflict from an Aboriginal perspective. Two other major exceptions during the pre-1970 era were Francis Birtles's pioneering film *Coorab in the Island of Ghosts* (1922), an Aboriginal love story set on Melville Island, and Charles Chauvel's *Jedda* (1955), Australia's first feature-length color film. Starring Robert Tudawali (Marbuck) and Ngarla Kunoth (Jedda), *Jedda* engendered a tradition of fatalism in Australian films featuring Aboriginal people that continued into the following millennium.

In Nicolas Roeg's 1971 film *Walkabout*, the Aboriginal actor (**David Gulpilil**) rescues a European girl and her younger brother from the wilderness only to commit suicide when his affection for the girl is spurned. Fred Schepisi's *The Chant of Jimmie Blacksmith* (1978), a fictionalized account of the Aboriginal murderer Jimmy Governor (*see* BREELONG BLACKS) and itself based on Thomas Keneally's novel of the same name, ends dramatically with the death of the central character played by Thomas Lewis. This film was notable in that it deals with a historical episode from an Aboriginal perspective, just as Sue Milliken attempted to address contemporary issues from an Aboriginal viewpoint in *The Fringe Dwellers* (1987). In *Rabbit-Proof Fence* (2002)—Phillip Noyce's film based on the book by Doris Pilkington—fatalism reemerges with Gracie's recapture at Wiluna and, even more pertinently and much later, Molly's second removal from the Mardujara community of Jigalong with her own children.

There have also been a number of instances in which Aboriginal people have appeared in Australian films as stock comic characters, however subtle that might be. Examples can be seen in *Crocodile Dundee* (1986) and *Priscilla, Queen of the Desert* (1994). Direct Aboriginal participation in the film industry has, nevertheless, begun to correct the balance.

In 1982, the Boorooloola Aboriginal community in the Northern Territory worked closely with the Sydney Filmmakers Coop to produce *Two Laws*, an episodic film that examines historical and contemporary problems from the community's own understanding. Since then, Aboriginal film-makers, such as Tracey Moffatt and Ivan Sen, among a number of others, have made their mark well beyond Australian shores. More recently, in 2006 a collaboration between Rolf de Heer and Peter Djigirr resulted in the production of Australia's first full-length feature film—*Ten Canoes*—in an Indigenous **language**. This was followed in 2009 by Warwick Thornton's central Australian Aboriginal love story *Samson and Delilah*, which won the Camera d'Or for best feature film at the Cannes Film Festival before dominating the Australian Inside Film Awards with six wins.

FIRE-STICK FARMING. This phrase is used to describe Aborigines' use of fire in modifying the environment. Despite early observations of Aborigines utilizing fire in a range of ways, it was long held that Aborigines had minimal impact on the environment and that the condition of the continent was natural. It is now understood that throughout Australia, including Tasmania, Aborigines significantly modified their environment through judicious and purposeful firing of the country. Fire was used to keep tracts of country open, to burn off undergrowth to make for easier passage, to promote regrowth of flora, and to encourage green pickings for sought-after game, among other purposes. Rather than Australia being a natural wilderness, the environment was an anthropocentric artifact, maintained and nurtured by Aboriginal agency. Aboriginal land management practices, including the use of fire, are being increasingly integrated into the management of various ecosystems.

FORREST RIVER MASSACRE. The only mass murder of Aborigines to be investigated by a royal commission, the Forrest River **massacre** took place in June 1926 in an area northwest of Wyndham in Western Australia. It was an official response to the killing of Frederick Hay, part-owner of Nulla Nulla Station, who had been speared to death after whipping an Aboriginal man named Lumbia. Two police constables, Dennis Regan and James St. Jack, accompanied by Richard Jolly and Bernard O'Leary (who had been sworn in as special constables), Daniel Murnane (a visiting veterinarian and Gallipoli veteran), five Aboriginal police trackers, and an Aboriginal man named Charlie, who worked for O'Leary, spent weeks systematically killing small groups of Aborigines and burning their bodies.

Rumors of the killings reached Reverend Ernest Gribble of Forrest River **Mission**, whose Aboriginal deacon, James Noble, found charred human remains in the area. Largely through Gribble's efforts, the matter was investigated by Detective-Sergeant Manning from Perth and District Police Inspector William Douglas. Faced with overwhelming evidence of police illegalities, the Western Australian government appointed a Perth magistrate,

George Wood, to conduct an official inquiry into the actions of the party led by Regan and St. Jack. Although there were reports that up to 100 Aboriginal people had been killed by the police, the royal commission was only able to confirm 11 deaths, four of whom could be directly linked to Regan and St. Jack. The police officers were charged with murder, but at the committal hearing, the magistrate ruled there was insufficient evidence for the case to proceed. Regan and St. Jack were transferred to the southern districts of Western Australia. Regan subsequently left the police force, but St. Jack continued his policing career, eventually reaching the rank of sergeant before retiring in 1960. Lumbia was imprisoned on Rottnest Island and in Broome until 1935, when he became an open custody prisoner at Moola Bulla near Halls Creek. He died at Forrest River around 1950. *See also* CONISTON MASSACRE; MASSACRES; MYALL CREEK MASSACRE.

FREEDOM RIDE. In 1964, a group of students from the University of Sydney formed a protest group called Student Action for Aborigines, and emulating the freedom rides in the southern states of the United States, they organized a bus tour of northern New South Wales towns in February 1965 to survey the conditions under which Aboriginal people were living. Of the 29 students involved, only one, **Charles Perkins**, was Aboriginal, although they were joined later in the trip by Aboriginal activist Gary Williams. The students encountered widespread poverty and found that in a number of rural towns Aborigines were being denied access to public hospitals and schools. Where they were admitted at all, Aboriginal people were also segregated in cinemas, public baths, and hotels. The Freedom Ride received extensive national and international media coverage, the publicity contributing to the end of **segregation**, Aboriginal access to hospitals and schools, and a substantial increase in government funding for Aboriginal public **housing** in the worst affected towns.

FREEMAN, CATHERINE (CATHY) (1973–). Indigenous athlete. Born in Mackay, Queensland, Catherine Freeman is an Australian sporting icon. At the age of 17 she won gold at the 1990 Commonwealth Games in the 4 x 100-meter **women**'s relay team. Later that year, she was named Young Australian of the Year and, in 1991, Aboriginal Athlete of the Year. She won two gold medals at the 1994 Commonwealth Games in the 200- and 400-meter sprint events. Freeman created controversy after she won the 200-meter event when she carried both the **Aboriginal flag** and the Australian flag during her lap of honor. In 1997, she won gold at the World Championships in the 400-meter sprint and was named Australian of the Year in 1998. She won gold again in the 400-meter sprint at the 1999 World Championships. Freeman was chosen to light the Olympic Cauldron during the opening ceremony for the Sydney 2000 Olympic Games. She went on to win gold in the 400-meter event and again took the Aboriginal flag with her on her victory lap. The gesture of flying both flags at the Sydney Olympics was seen by many Australians as representing the spirit of **reconciliation**. She was made a Member of the Order of Australia (AM) in 2001. She announced her retirement from competitive **sport** in 2003 but remains a popular figure and role model. She uses this support to encourage young Indigenous Australians to pursue their goals, whether in sport or some other endeavor.

FRIENDLY MISSION. In 1829, with mounting concern in Tasmania over enduring murderous conflict between **Tasmanian Aborigines** (who were fighting for their land) and settlers and the failure of the **Black Line** to achieve its objective of driving surviving Aborigines onto the Forestier and Tasman peninsulas in the southeast, a "conciliator" charged with the task of "civilising" the Aborigines and effecting their removal to Flinders Island was appointed. The appointee, George Augustus Robinson, named this so-called "civilising mission" the "Friendly Mission." Between 1830 and August 1834, he made six expeditions on his Friendly Mission, traveling the length and breadth of Tasmania, including the remote west coast. Eschewing violence, Robinson was able to convince all but one family group to leave the Tasmanian mainland, with their ultimate destination **Wybalenna** on Flinders Island. How Robinson achieved this without force, and what inducements and incentives were offered, is the subject of contentious debate. Certainly, Aborigines were of the understanding that the transfer to Flinders Island would be temporary and that they would be provided safe access to land on the Tasmanian mainland.

Although Robinson did not write the book he intended, he did keep extensive journals of his Friendly Mission. Brian Plomley undertook the extraordinarily difficult task of transcribing and annotating them, and in 1966, the Tasmanian Historical Research Association published the journals under the title of *Friendly Mission*. A revised second edition was published by Quintus in 2008. *See also* ARTHUR, WALTER GEORGE; BLACK WAR.

FRONTIER. The notion of a frontier is used to describe the divide between black and white in early– to mid–Australian colonial history and also the boundary between those parts of the country settled or otherwise by Europeans and the land that lay beyond. The distancing of black and white implicit in many iterations of a frontier in Australia belies a more complex and nuanced relationship—one characterized at times and in places by intimacy, understanding, compassion, sensitivity, accommodation, friendship, and love, as well as enmity, discord, misunderstanding, hostility, aggression, and violence.

G

GARMA FESTIVAL. One of Australia's foremost annual Indigenous festivals, the Garma Festival is both a celebration of Yolngu culture (**dance**, song, **music**, **art**, and associated knowledge) and a sharing of that culture with other Indigenous and settler Australians. It is held by the Yolngu people in northeastern Arnhem Land in the Northern Territory on a site of great significance to them—the place where an **ancestral being** brought the *yidaki* (Gumatj word for **didgeridoo**) into existence.

GIBBS, PEARL (1901–83). Indigenous activist. Pearl Gibbs was born at La Perouse in Sydney shortly after her part-Aboriginal mother had left the town of Yass in southern New South Wales, where her father may have been a European blacksmith. Her mother returned to Yass before relocating to Bourke in northwestern New South Wales and marrying an Aboriginal man named Richard Murray. Gibbs first began work as a maid on grazing properties in that district before moving to Sydney with her sister Olga in 1917, where she found regular work as a domestic servant. She also came into contact with, and tried to assist, a number of young Aboriginal girls who had been forcibly removed from their families to work as domestic servants.

In 1923, she was briefly married to a British naval steward named Robert Gibbs. By the early 1930s, Pearl Gibbs was living with her mother and stepfather on the south coast of New South Wales, where all three engaged in itinerant work. At the same time, Gibbs attempted to improve conditions for local pea pickers and the residents of Wallaga Lake Aboriginal Reserve.

In 1937, she returned to Sydney and joined the **Aborigines Progressive Association**, serving as secretary in 1938–39. As an activist, Gibbs made full use of the media, and on 8 June 1941, she broadcast her own script on radio—the first Aborigine to do so—when she critiqued the injustices against Aborigines on stations 2GB Sydney and 2WL Wollongong.

Moving to the central New South Wales town of Dubbo, she became secretary of the local branch of the **Australian Aborigines' League** in 1950 and, two years later, served as organizing secretary of the New South Wales branch of the Council for Aboriginal Rights. From 1954 to 1957, she was an elected Aboriginal member of the government-run Aborigines Welfare

Board, but after being frustrated in her efforts to use official channels to improve conditions for Aboriginal people, she played an instrumental role in the establishment of the Aboriginal-Australian Fellowship in 1956. This organization drew together a number of leading Aboriginal activists and influential non-Aboriginal supporters, remaining a powerful force until the late 1960s. With financial assistance from the Waterside Workers' Federation, Gibbs also established a hostel in Dubbo for Aboriginal people receiving medical treatment. She continued to operate the hostel and campaign for Aboriginal rights until just before her death in April 1983. *See also* WOMEN.

GILBERT, EDWARD (EDDIE) (1905?–78). Indigenous sportsperson. Edward Gilbert was an Aboriginal cricketer born at Woodford, just north of Brisbane, around 1905. At the age of two, he was removed to Barambah (later Cherbourg) Aboriginal Reserve near Murgon, where he received a minimal primary school **education**. From an early age, he also excelled in sport—notably **cricket**—but it was not until the 1920s that he was coached as a fast bowler by the reserve school teacher, Robert Crawford, who was instrumental in having the local Aboriginal team included in the district competition.

Achieving local fame for his success in taking wickets, Gilbert was trialed in Brisbane by the Queensland Cricket Association in 1929 and chosen to play in the 1930 Queensland Country side. By the end of the season, he was playing for Queensland in the national Sheffield Shield interstate cricket competition, as he continued to do intermittently until 1937.

Although Gilbert has been rated as one of the fastest bowlers Australia has produced, his unique bowling action generated controversy throughout his playing career. While many contemporary cricketers claimed that he threw rather than bowled the ball, many others rallied to his defense. A combination of his bowling style, a number of strain injuries, and racial discrimination prevented Gilbert from being selected in an Australian test team. His most famous moment occurred in a Sheffield Shield match between Queensland and South Australia in November 1931, when he dismissed the great Don Bradman for naught.

After being forced out of first-class cricket in Queensland, Gilbert returned to Barambah, where he married and continued to work in menial occupations. Increasing mental illness resulted in his admission to a Brisbane psychiatric hospital in December 1949, and he remained there until his death in January 1978. *See also* SPORT.

GOOLAGONG-CAWLEY, EVONNE (1951–). Indigenous sportsperson. Born in Griffith, New South Wales, and raised nearby in Barellan, Evonne Goolagong-Cawley became one of the best known, most successful, and highly respected Aboriginal sportspersons, winning many major tennis titles, including the Wimbledon singles title twice (1971, 1980), the French Open (1971), the US Open runner-up four times (1973, 1974, 1975, 1976), and four times the Australian Championships singles winner (1974, 1975, 1976, 1977). She was, for a time, ranked number one **women**'s player in the world and was the winner of 14 Grand Slam titles (seven singles, six doubles, and one mixed doubles). She was inducted into the Women's Sports Hall of Fame (1989), the International Tennis Hall of Fame (1988), and the Australian Tennis Hall of Fame (1988) and was Australian of the Year in 1971. In 1972, she was made a Member of the Order of the British Empire (MBE). *See also* SPORT.

GOVE LAND RIGHTS CASE. In 1968, the federal government granted a 42-year lease to the mining company Nabalco to mine bauxite on the Gove Peninsula in northeastern **Arnhem Land** in the Northern Territory. This lease had formed part of the Arnhem Land Reserve, which had been declared in 1931. The traditional owners of the land, the Yolngu, had learned of the intention to excise their land from the reserve in the early 1960s and attempted to prevent this action by forwarding **bark petitions** to the federal government in Canberra. The petitions were in the form of two bark paintings enclosing texts written in one of the Yolngu languages and English. While the significance of these documents was recognized, they were ultimately unsuccessful, and the excision to the reserve was made. The Yolngu then lodged a claim in the courts against Nabalco and the federal government, arguing that they, the Yolngu, enjoyed sovereignty over their country and that the government had not acquired the property on "just terms," which they were obliged to do. They attempted to demonstrate to the court their ownership of their country and the manner in which that ownership was realized.

Their action was unsuccessful, with the Northern Territory Supreme Court handing down its decision in 1971. Justice Blackburn concluded that the traditional laws of the Yolngu did not confer a "proprietary interest" in the land and that the doctrine of communal **native title** was not part of any Australian law. While this decision was not appealed, it contributed to the activism that ultimately led to the legislative **Aboriginal Land Rights (Northern Territory) Act 1976**. It was not until 1982, when **Eddie Mabo** commenced legal proceedings, that courts would again be asked to make a determination on the existence of native title at common law. *See also* ABORIGINAL LAND RIGHTS COMMISSION; INDIGENOUS LAND USE AGREEMENTS; LAND CLAIMS; LAND OWNERSHIP; LAND RIGHTS; LINGIARI, VINCENT; MABO DECISION; NATIONAL NATIVE TITLE TRIBUNAL (NNTT); *TERRA NULLIUS*; WAVE HILL; WIK DECISION; WOODWARD INQUIRY.

GOVERNMENT RESERVES. Early Aboriginal reserves were an initiative of the British government that attempted to redress the dispossession of land. In 1850, approximately 50 reserves had been established in New South Wales, and by 1860, South Australia had gazetted 59 Aboriginal reserves. Victoria responded by setting up a number of government-run settlements by 1867, and the first Aboriginal reserve in Queensland was established near Mackay in 1875. While reserves also operated to segregate the Aboriginal population, part of the ideology was to create casual labor pools that could be drawn on by local European landholders.

In southeastern Australia, many Aboriginal reserves flourished, owing to their location on traditional territory and fertile soils, which allowed them to become virtually self-sufficient. As pressure for more farming land intensified in the latter half of the 19th and early 20th centuries, however, many of the reserves were closed down and thrown open for closer settlement by Europeans.

The Queensland situation altered considerably following the passage of the Aboriginals Protection and Restriction of the Sale of Opium Act in 1897, legislation which served as the blueprint for segregationist policies in Western Australia, South Australia, and later, the Northern Territory. Under the terms of the legislation, large numbers of Aboriginal people were forcibly moved from all parts of the state to centralized reserves, where their lives were totally controlled by government protectors.

While reserves did offer Aboriginal people some measure of protection from outside influences, their creation also served to undermine their basic civil rights and, at the same time, exposed the residents to a host of potentially fatal illnesses, resulting in high mortality rates.

GOVERNOR, JIMMY. *See* BREELONG BLACKS.

GULPILIL, DAVID (1953–). Indigenous actor, dancer, painter, and musician. Born at Ramingining, a Yolngu community in northeastern **Arnhem Land**, David Gulpilil's skill as a dancer led to his being cast in the lead role of Nicolas Roeg's 1971 **film** *Walkabout*. A succession of film appearances followed, including *Mad Dog Morgan* and *Storm Boy* (1976), *The Last Wave* (1977), *Crocodile Dundee* (1986), *Dead Heart* (1996), *Rabbit-Proof Fence* and *The Tracker* (2002), *Ten Canoes* (2006), and Baz Luhrmann's *Australia* (2008).

Gulpilil has also appeared in a number of television series, and in 1987, he led the Ramingining **dance** group on a national tour. In March 2004, he appeared at the Adelaide Arts Festival in a highly successful autobiographical stage production called *Gulpilil*. A talented painter, Gulpilil has also written the texts for two illustrated children's books based on traditional Yolngu beliefs. In 1988, he was made a Member of the Order of Australia (AM) for his contribution to the arts, but despite his fame and frequent international appearances, Gulpilil has remained firmly grounded in the culture of his Yolngu homeland.

GWION GWION. *See* BRADSHAW ART.

H

HALF-CASTE. *See* MIXED DESCENT.

HANSEN'S DISEASE. More commonly known as leprosy, this is a peripheral nerve disease recorded from ancient times that can result in skin ulceration, facial and physical deformity, loss of sensation, blindness, and death. It was unknown in Australia prior to British colonization, with the first recorded case being a Chinese resident of Brisbane in 1855. By the late 19th century, Hansen's disease was rampant throughout northern Australia and may have been introduced from two independent sources. Chinese immigrants are believed to have brought the disease into the Northern Territory and Western Australia, while Queensland infections may have emanated from either Papua New Guinea or New Caledonia.

Until the development of sulphone drugs in the 1940s, the only available treatment was ineffectual Chalmoogra oil. Fear of the disease spreading into the European population, relatively few of whom contracted it, led to a policy of isolating all patients, the majority of whom were Aboriginal, in lazarets. The first was built in the Northern Territory in 1884 on Darwin Harbour's Mud Island, a desolate mangrove island where inmates were largely neglected until the Channel Island Leprosarium opened in 1931.

Western Australia constructed a number of lazarets on Bezout, Bernier, and Dorre islands, and at Cossack, Beagle Bay, and finally, Derby in 1936. In Queensland, the first temporary lazaret was located on Dayman Island before being replaced in 1892 by new facilities on Friday Island in **Torres Strait** and at Dunwich on North Stradbroke Island in the south. These were replaced, in turn, by a lazaret on Peel Island in southern Queensland in 1910, where European patients continued to be treated until 1959, when they were transferred to Princess Alexandra Hospital in Brisbane. Between 1940 and 1973, all Aboriginal patients were confined on Fantome Island, off the coast of Townsville in northern Queensland.

Although the incidence of Hansen's disease has been dramatically reduced by sulphone drugs and educational programs, 28 new cases were reported from the **Kimberley region** of northwestern Australia between 1986 and 2002. *See also* HEALTH.

HEALTH. At the time of colonization in 1788, Indigenous Australians arguably enjoyed better physical and psychological health than many of their European counterparts. While injuries and some diseases took their toll, an extensive pharmacopoeia based on intimate knowledge of flora was available for treatment and remedy, as was a suite of traditional healing practices (*see* BUSH MEDICINE). Illness and death, except in the very young and old, were often attributed to spiritual causes or sorcery.

European colonization introduced infectious diseases that had a devastating impact on Indigenous Australians, ranging from the common cold, **smallpox**, influenza, measles, and whooping cough to sexually transmitted diseases such as syphilis. Because the Indigenous inhabitants had little or no resistance to infectious diseases or knowledge of their treatment, not only was the impact of these diseases exaggerated, but they frequently spread well in advance of European contact. Disease was one of the principal causes of the rapid population decline. Dispossession of land and increasingly restricted access to hunting and gathering grounds further exacerbated the decline into poor health.

Recognition of the need to extend primary health care to Aborigines and **Torres Strait** Islanders in the 1960s and 1970s resulted in the first sustained efforts to address a range of health issues. By then, lifestyle and other chronic diseases not experienced prior to colonization were also impacting on Indigenous Australians. Heart disease, diabetes, renal failure, trachoma, and ear and skin infections, among other illnesses, were and are prevalent. Substance abuse, such as **alcohol** consumption, tobacco smoking, and, in several remote communities, petrol sniffing, also contributes to a range of poor health outcomes. Suicide, which was either extremely rare or unknown prior to colonization, is now a serious problem, with Aboriginal youth and young adults particularly vulnerable. Environmental factors such as insufficient **housing** leading to overcrowding, inappropriate design, lack of reticulated potable water, other infrastructure shortcomings, and poor diet are problems experienced by many Aboriginal communities. Additionally, high unemployment rates not only affect individuals but also impact on overall community health.

Despite the need for better provision of primary health care, Aborigines were often reluctant to access the available services. In order to address the desperate need through services that were culturally appropriate, the first Aboriginal-community-controlled health service, the Redfern **Aboriginal Medical Service**, was established in Sydney in 1971. Aboriginal-community-controlled health services were quickly established throughout Australia. A number of these services in regional and remote Australia combine both Western-trained health practitioners and traditional healers. The health profile of Indigenous Australians remains a serious concern. *See also* HANSEN'S DISEASE.

HEISS, ANITA (1968–). Indigenous writer. Of the Wiradjuri people from inner western New South Wales, Anita Heiss works in a number of literary genres, including nonfiction, poetry, the novel, chick-lit, and children's books. Together with Peter Minter, Heiss coedited the significant *Macquarie Pen Anthology of Aboriginal Literature* (2008), the first comprehensive collection of Aboriginal writing, covering the period from 1796 to the early 21st century. *See also* LITERATURE.

HINDMARSH ISLAND. This small island near the mouth of the Murray River in South Australia came to national and international attention following a decision in 1991 to replace the cable-operated car ferry providing access to the island with a bridge. The bridge, mooted in late 1988 and early 1989, was linked to a development project expanding an existing marina and associated infrastructure including residential property. The state of South Australia agreed to both build the bridge and make a substantial contribution toward its costs.

The Ngarrindjeri know this area by the name of Kumarangk. While an earlier archaeological survey had found that a number of Aboriginal sites would be disturbed by the bridge's construction, in 1993, a group of Ngarrindjeri **women** opposed the bridge on the basis that it would interfere with and irrevocably damage sites pertaining to "secret women's business." These sites were held to be vital for Ngarrindjeri women's ongoing fertility, among other concerns. In December 1993, an application was made to protect the area under the South Australian Aboriginal Heritage Act 1988. In July 1994, on the basis of a commissioned report on the issue of Aboriginal sites and their potential damage, the federal minister for Aboriginal Affairs issued a 25-year ban on the bridge's construction. This protection order was overturned by the Federal Court in 1995.

Controversially, in May 1995, another group of Ngarrindjeri women proclaimed they knew nothing about "secret women's business" pertaining to the proposed bridge site—not even its existence as a category of knowledge. Moreover, they alleged the claim of "secret women's business" was a fabrication. On 8 June 1995, the South Australian government announced a formal inquiry—a royal commission—into the claims and counterclaims pertaining to the bridge site. Notwithstanding the fact that the Ngarrindjeri women seeking to have the site protected refused to give evidence before the commission, in December 1995, the commission released its findings that the "secret women's business" was a fabrication designed to halt construction of the bridge.

Following the passing of legislation seeking to remove consideration of Aboriginal heritage law in deliberations over the bridge's construction, a further attempt was made to halt it when Australia's High Court agreed to hear arguments against the legislation. In finding the legislative act constitutional, the High Court found against those Ngarrindjeri opposing the bridge. With all avenues of appeal seemingly exhausted, the path was open for the bridge to proceed. On 4 March 2001, the Hindmarsh Island bridge was opened.

HISTORY WARS. The history wars are a public debate that first emerged in the 1980s between conservative and progressive Australian historians, politicians, and the wider Australian public. Under dispute are the methodology, writing, and interpretation of Australia's history as a colonized country and the impact of colonization upon Indigenous people. The debate reflects underlying issues regarding national **identity** as well as scholarly, Indigenous, and amateur approaches to historiography.

Keith Windschuttle exacerbated the debate with the publication in 2002 of his book *The Fabrication of Aboriginal History, Volume One: Van Diemen's Land 1803–1847*, in which he challenged orthodox understanding and contemporary writings on the history of colonization in Tasmania. Windschuttle argued that many contemporary historians, rather than being objective and neutral, had politicized the interpretation of history by inaccurately claiming that Aboriginal people suffered grossly from various injustices during British settlement. He argued that many contemporary historians did this, for example, by exaggerating the number of Aboriginal deaths that occurred during the **Black War** and claiming that British settlers committed acts of genocide against Aboriginal people. Some scholars have argued further, as did Prime Minister John Howard, that these historians have adopted a "black armband" view of history. They argued that this view of history focuses unnecessarily on the negative aspects of Australia's past, overlooking the nation's considerable achievements.

Numerous academics and commentators have rebutted Windschuttle's arguments. Among the rebuttals, they argue that Windschuttle's claims to objectivity do not withstand scrutiny and that his history, too, reflects a highly politicized agenda—one that is right-wing and conservative and ignores the violence and dispossession that occurred as a result of British settlement. While waxing and waning, this debate, which is characteristic of settler societies, is ongoing.

HOUSING. As a hunter-gathering society, traditional Aboriginal housing was usually impermanent, although there was considerable regional variation in architectural styles. Temporary lean-to shelters consisting of layers of bark on timber supports were widespread across Australia. In more northern districts, the roof was often curved and the dwellings more substantially built, and in wet weather, domed huts were raised from the ground on stilts, allowing a fire to burn underneath and discourage mosquitoes. Domed huts, in fact, were a common design in cooler and wetter areas. In the rainforests of northeast Queensland, blady grass or palm fronds covered a rounded timber framework, with the outer covering attached with lawyer-cane ties. In western Tasmania, domed huts up to five meters in diameter were recorded by early European explorers. The inner covering was made of rushes, which acted as a bed for a thick layer of grass, with overlapping sheets of bark then forming the outer layer. A narrow entrance with a closing door ensured that these dwellings were completely rain- and wind-proof.

In central Australia, the *wiltja* was commonly made of arched boughs set firmly in the ground, with the framework covered with leafy boughs and spinifex. Again, the rounded shape resisted strong winds, while the outer covering functioned as both an insulator and a filter, which allowed only clean air to penetrate. The dark interior also served to discourage flies, which are a prolific pest in the inland regions of the continent. In the coastal areas of eastern and southern Australia, family huts were often constructed with a conical wooden framework waterproofed with layers of bark.

With the arrival of Europeans, new building materials were incorporated with traditional designs, and the fringe camps that were established on the outskirts of rural towns in the late 19th and 20th centuries regularly featured huts made from corrugated iron and packing material. In some of the more impoverished regions of rural and remote Australia, similar huts continue to house Aboriginal families.

The advent of the **assimilation** policy in the 1950s, nevertheless, saw increased Commonwealth and state government funding directed into the Aboriginal housing sector, the dwellings largely built to European designs. There have been a few exceptions to that rule, but the process of providing adequate housing for Aboriginal people across Australia is still far from complete, and home ownership has proved insurmountable for many. Only in Tasmania has Aboriginal home ownership exceeded 50 percent, although in urban centers on the mainland, the figures have improved since low-interest government housing loans were made available. That said, the majority of contemporary Aborigines remain dependent on public housing and, to a far lesser extent, on private rental. Community rental, whereby community-based Aboriginal organizations are funded to provide new houses and to renovate existing dwellings, remains insignificant.

In 2007, the Commonwealth government established the Strategic Indigenous Housing and Infrastructure Program as part of the **Northern Territory Emergency Response** with the intention of constructing new houses and renovating others in the most impoverished Northern Territory Aboriginal communities. The program was immediately beset with a raft of problems, not the least of which was the Northern Territory government's claim on 15 percent of the funding for administration purposes. The program finally began to function in 2010 when contractors and their workers, many of whom are Aboriginal, constructed the first houses in a number of widely separated communities.

HUMAN OCCUPATION. Thermoluminescence dating of hearths at Malakunanja II, an archaeological site in **Arnhem Land**, Northern Territory, has raised the possibility that the initial Aboriginal occupation of the Australian continent, or Sahul, as the ancient landmass is known, occurred at least 60,000 years ago. Core sediments extracted at Lake George in southern New South Wales, at Lynch's Crater on the Atherton Tableland in Northern Queensland, and on Queensland's Great Barrier Reef have revealed that around 130,000 years ago, charcoal fragments dramatically increased. A similar pattern emerged approximately 50,000 years ago, when fire-sensitive flora, such as southern beech, disappeared, to be replaced by fire-resistant species, prominent among which were the eucalypts. During an entire 700,000-year history, these charcoal patterns were unique and do not appear to have corresponded with any known climatic conditions.

Throughout human history, there has been no land bridge connecting the Australian continent with Asia (ancient Sunda), which means that the first humans to arrive must have done so by making transoceanic crossings. In the 1930s, American anthropologist Joseph Birdsell argued that physical variations among contemporary Aboriginal people indicated three distinct waves of migration in the past. His tri-hybrid theory was not supported by archaeological evidence, and ecological adaptation over a lengthy period could itself produce physical variation.

Alan Thorne, a physical anthropologist, later proposed that there had been two waves of migration, the first from Java being physically robust people whose skeletal remains were excavated at **Kow Swamp** in northern Victoria. According to Thorne's original theory, a more gracile people later entered Australia from China, evidenced by skeletal remains uncovered at **Lake Mungo** in southwestern New South Wales. More recent dating techniques have, nevertheless, revealed that the gracile remains actually preceded the more robust form, which is a complete reversal of human evolution elsewhere in the world. Australian prehistorians are in general agreement, however, that there were a number of migrations to Australia, evidenced by new and improved technologies, **art** styles, and the **dingo**, a placental mammal that entered Australia approximately 4,000 years ago.

Where the Aboriginal people originated remains open to speculation, as they lack blood groups B and A2, and attempts to link them with the Vedda of Sri Lanka or the Ainu of Japan have so far proved fruitless. Nor is it known how rapidly they occupied the continent after entering from the north. They may have dispersed throughout the continent as the prevailing climatic conditions were considerably cooler and moister than today. Alternatively, they may have followed the coast. It is known that they reached their southern limits in Tasmania by at least 35,000 years ago.

HUMAN RIGHTS AND EQUAL OPPORTUNITY COMMISSION (HREOC). Established in 1986, the HREOC is a Commonwealth statutory agency. The organization aims to promote understanding and awareness of human rights and the protection of individuals' human rights. Specifically, HREOC achieves this through **education**, advocacy, and public awareness—resolving complaints of discrimination or breaches of human rights under federal laws, developing policy and legislation, and undertaking research on discrimination and human rights issues.

The HREOC has an appointed president and five commissioners responsible for the following areas: **Aboriginal and Torres Strait Islander social justice**, race discrimination, human rights, disability discrimination, sex discrimination, and age discrimination.

HUNTER, RUBY (1955–2010). Indigenous singer-songwriter. Born near the Murray River in South Australia, Ruby Hunter was forcibly removed from her family when she was eight years of age and grew up in foster homes and government institutions. By her mid-teens, Hunter was destitute in Adelaide, where she met her future partner, **Archie Roach**, with whom she collaborated professionally. After contributing a single to Roach's first album in 1990, Hunter released her debut album, *Thought Within*, in 1994, becoming the first Australian Aboriginal **woman** to be signed by a major record label. A second album, *Feeling Good*, followed in May 2000, the same year she won her first Deadly Award for Female Artist of the Year. Two more Deadly Awards followed in 2003 and 2004, the last being for *Ruby's Story*, a concert based on her life. Hunter died suddenly in February 2010. *See also* MUSIC.

I

IAD PRESS. *See* INSTITUTE FOR ABORIGINAL DEVELOPMENT.

IDENTITY. Prior to British colonization in 1788, Aboriginal people throughout the continent expressed individual and group identity in terms of gender, age, clan and territorial affiliation, linguistic groupings, and placement within the **kinship** system. In the aftermath of colonization, local identity was subsumed under the generic term *Aborigines*, which itself was later subdivided in graded categories based on the perceived level of European-Aboriginal descent of individuals. It was not until 1972 that the United Nations Sub-Commission on the Prevention of Discrimination and Protection of Minorities insisted that identity should be recognized according to the perception and conception of Indigenous people themselves. That right was embraced by the Australian government the following decade, but it is relevant that at the very time the United Nations was establishing a universal right to Indigenous identity, a pan-Aboriginality had emerged in Australia as a means of contesting white political hegemony.

Largely owing to the fragmentation of Aboriginal societies, identity has also been expressed in regional terms. Queensland Aborigines readily identify as **Murris**, Victorian and New South Wales Aborigines regard themselves as **Kooris**, while in southwestern Australia, Aboriginal groups identify as **Nyungar** (or Noongar). There has also been a more recent trend in Australia to reestablish identity, where possible, in accordance with traditional geographical territories. *See also* MIXED DESCENT.

IMPARJA. *See* ABORIGINAL MEDIA.

INDIGENOUS LAND USE AGREEMENTS. The Commonwealth Native Title Act 1993 provides for Indigenous land use agreements between holders and/or claimants of **native title** and other interested parties. The agreements, once registered with the **National Native Title Tribunal**, are binding on all parties and stipulate such things as the management and uses of the relevant areas of land and sea. The agreements can be included as part of a native title determination or be negotiated separately. By August 2008, more than

340 Indigenous land use agreements had been registered by the Native Title Tribunal.

INITIATION. Once practiced (and with disparate degrees of adherence still practiced) throughout Australia, initiation rites are rites of transition. Initiation confers upon initiates a change of social status and roles and traditionally heralded the commencement of esoteric religious instruction, the transition from childhood to adulthood, and increasingly distinctive roles, obligations, and religious knowledge between young men and **women**. The nature of initiation rituals varied markedly from region to region: in the form the practices took, the type of procedures performed, the age at which initiation commenced, and in the significance and meaning adhering to specific aspects of initiation. The process of becoming fully adult, or fully instructed in religious esotery, could take many years and involve a number of different ordeals, many of which were painful and throughout which forbearance was expected. The first phase of initiation, therefore, heralded the commencement of a long process that might only cease in late middle or old age. Common features of many initiatory practices were that initiates were mostly passive. Their role was to endure things being done to them, rather than individually achieving goals set for them. Another common feature was that the novices would one day themselves become the initiators. Also, those initiators who played specific roles in an initiation would stand in a particular relationship with the novice in terms of social category and position in the **kinship** structure. In many desert societies, the male circumciser was expected to hand his daughter in **marriage** to the boy he circumcised when he was of appropriate age and initiatory status.

Many different initiatory rites were practiced across Australia, but not all these rites were practiced by all societies in all regions, and even where practices were similar, different significance and meanings were commonly applied. Among the rites were social isolation, where the novice would spend time alone in ritual preparation for the forthcoming procedure or during the period of recovery; tooth avulsion (the knocking out of a front tooth); circumcision (where practiced, often a rite to which considerable import is attached); subincision (the practice of cutting through the underside of the penis to the urethra—in the Western Desert, a male had to be both circumcised and subincised before being marriageable). Although the subincision rite was not as ritually significant as circumcision, it was of importance throughout one's life in subsequent ceremonies that involved the spilling of blood. For this purpose, the subincision scar would be scratched open. Cicatrices (or pronounced scarring across the back, shoulders, breasts, stomach, and/or thighs) was widely practiced. Hair removal (depilation), particularly of some but not all facial hair and sometimes pubic hair, was practiced in some regions routinely and, in other regions, for specific rites or ceremonies. Piercing of the nasal septum, through which an object might be inserted, was also a common practice.

Most initiatory practices are no longer adhered to, for example, tooth avulsion and subincision. Circumcision, however, is still practiced, and there is some evidence to suggest increasingly so. *See also* BODY DECORATION; *BORA*.

INSTITUTE FOR ABORIGINAL DEVELOPMENT. Established in Alice Springs in the Northern Territory in 1969 by the Uniting Church, the Institute for Aboriginal Development is now an independent Aboriginal-community-controlled adult **education** center. The institute houses an important **language** and culture center concerned with central Australian language maintenance and preservation. It also runs a national publishing house, IAD Press, which publishes a range of texts by Indigenous Australians, including dictionaries of central Australian languages.

ISLAND CO-ORDINATING COUNCIL (ICC). A statutory agency created under the Queensland Community Services (Torres Strait) Act 1984, the ICC advises the Queensland government on all matters and issues affecting **Torres Strait** Islanders. It also represents the interests of Torres Strait Islanders and coordinates and provides support services to Torres Strait Island councils.

J

JABILUKA. A name derived from the term for a billabong (a watercourse or large waterhole that runs after rain), Jabiluka is an area of 72 square kilometers containing one of four uranium deposits that were discovered in 1969–70 in the Alligator Rivers region 230 kilometers east of Darwin. The lease, currently owned by Energy Resources Australia, preceded the establishment of **Kakadu National Park** and was excised from the park when the park was established. The traditional owners of Jabiluka and adjacent areas are the Gagudju people, who have been and remain ambivalent over whether mining should proceed. (Two other nearby uranium deposits—Ranger, which abuts Jabiluka, and Nabarlek—are being mined.) Currently no mining is taking place at Jabiluka, and no further mining activities will take place without the traditional owners' consent.

JACKEY JACKEY (?–1854). Indigenous guide. An Aboriginal man from Muswellbrook in the Hunter Valley district of New South Wales, Jackey Jackey was chosen to accompany Edmund Kennedy's ill-fated expedition to **Cape York** in 1848. After landing at Rockingham Bay, Kennedy's party took five months to find a route inland and travel north, where they descended the northern foothills of the Great Dividing Range to Weymouth Bay. Leaving eight Europeans who were ill, Kennedy, the three remaining Europeans, and Jackey Jackey, who had proved himself the most capable member of the expedition, continued north to Shelburne Bay, where one of the Europeans accidentally wounded himself with a firearm. Desperate to make the scheduled rendezvous with a supply vessel near the tip of Cape York, Kennedy and Jackey Jackey carried on alone. At the Escape River and almost within sight of their goal, the pair was ambushed by Aborigines and Kennedy was speared to death. Although wounded, Jackey Jackey managed to elude his pursuers and reached the rendezvous two weeks later.

He led a relief party to the Shelburne River where no trace could be found of the three men left behind: two seriously ill survivors were rescued at Weymouth Bay. The following year, Jackey Jackey accompanied an expedition that attempted to locate Kennedy's body. Although unsuccessful, he managed to recover Kennedy's papers, and for his efforts on both occasions, Jackey

Jackey was rewarded with a silver **king plate** (also known as a breast plate) and a government gratuity of £50. By then, he had also become addicted to **alcohol**, and in 1854, Jackey Jackey burned to death after falling into a campfire while intoxicated.

JANDAMARRA (c. 1870–97). Indigenous tracker and resistance fighter. Also known as Pigeon, Jandamarra led an organized resistance campaign against European settlers in the **Kimberley region** of northwestern Australia between 1894 and 1897. Jandamarra initially worked for the Europeans as a stockman and police tracker, and it was in the latter capacity that he assisted Constable William Richardson to capture a group of his own people wanted for spearing stock. Among them was an elder named Ellemarra, who convinced Jandamarra to join them. Richardson was shot dead by Jandamarra as he slept, and using police firearms, he led an attack on five Europeans overlanding livestock through Windjana Gorge in November 1894. Two Europeans were killed in the clash—the first time Aborigines on mainland Australia had used firearms in organized resistance.

Fearing a general uprising, at least 30 well armed police and settlers set out from Derby in pursuit, the punitive expedition allegedly killing a large number of innocent Aborigines near Fitzroy Crossing before fighting a pitched battle against Jandamarra's followers at Windjana Gorge. Ellemara was among those killed; although wounded, Jandamarra managed to escape through a labyrinth of subterranean passages in the Napier Range. For the next three years, Jandamarra continued to lead attacks against European settlers and their livestock until he was finally tracked to his hideout in the Napier Range by an Aboriginal police tracker named Micki and killed in a running duel.

K

KADAITCHA. An Arrernte Aboriginal term from central Australia, *kadaitcha* usually refers to individuals or small parties of men who were instructed by elders to kill serious transgressors of **customary law** or exact revenge against sorcerers and outside groups. A highly ritualized procedure, the term *kadaitcha* was also applied to the special footwear of the avengers, the soles of which were made from emu feathers bound together with blood, with the uppers consisting of human hair or animal fur. This footwear, together with the application of ochre and feather-down on the body and face, was intended to disguise the true **identity** of individuals. *Kadaitcha* was an important means of social control across a wide area of central Australia, from northeastern South Australia through the Tanami Desert in the Northern Territory to the Pilbara and southern **Kimberley region** of Western Australia.

KAKADU NATIONAL PARK. Australia's largest national park, comprising an area greater than 19,000 square kilometers, is situated in the Northern Territory to the east of Darwin and adjoining the **Arnhem Land** escarpment. Satisfying the criteria for both natural and cultural values, the park was listed on the World Heritage List in 1992, and it is listed with the Ramsar Convention on Wetlands because of the international significance of its wetlands. The name Kakadu is derived from Gagudju, one of the Aboriginal **language** groups of the region. Aborigines have been living in the region for at least 40,000 years, and descendants of the original groups inhabiting the region still live there. Over this period, the regional environment has changed considerably due to rising sea levels, changing from an inland freshwater environment to a rich estuarine one dominated by extensive wetlands refreshed by seasonal flooding.

The long period of Aboriginal occupation has left a rich artistic heritage in magnificent painted rock galleries. A continuous tradition of painting dating back at least 20,000 years BP is evident, with a number of stylistic changes reflecting in part the changing environment occurring over this period. The best known is the **x-ray** style **art**, which dates from the later period (approximately 4,000 to 3,000 years BP). This work was still being produced in the early 1960s, and it draws many visitors to the national park.

More than 50 percent of the park has been returned to Aboriginal ownership under the **Aboriginal Land Rights (Northern Territory) Act 1976**. The traditional owners have, in turn, leased their lands to the Director of National Parks. The park's management structure establishes comanagement of the park between the traditional owners and Parks Australia. **Uluru–Kata Tjuta National Park** and Nitmiluk (Katherine Gorge) National Park in the Northern Territory are two other major tourist destinations that have been returned to the traditional owners under a similar management scheme.

KATA TJUTA. *See* ULURU.

KIMBERLEY LAND COUNCIL. Established in 1978, this is the peak Aboriginal regional community organization in the **Kimberley region** of northwestern Australia. It is the representative body for **native title** for the region, assists traditional owners in land and sea management, and undertakes advocacy for Aboriginal peoples.

KIMBERLEY REGION. The far northwestern corner of Australia, situated in the state of Western Australia, is known as the Kimberley. To the north and west it is bounded by the sea, while to the south it is bounded by desert. Climatically, it experiences two predominant seasons: a dry winter period and, during summer, flooding rains (the wet season). Because of its remoteness, settler impacts in the Kimberley were few until the 1880s, when pastoralists assumed extensive land holdings. It contains a rich Aboriginal presence. The striking **Wandjina** appears only in the Kimberley, as does **Bradshaw art**. Several distinct Indigenous **language** groups occupy the region, and more than 20 languages are spoken. Traditionally, the Kimberley was a focal point for much trading activity in material objects, ritual, and myth. Pearl shell from the Kimberley was widely sought, and it traveled many hundreds of kilometers inland along various trade routes. *See also* ART.

KING PLATES. Also known as breast plates, these objects are inscribed metal, crescent-shaped, flat plates worn around an individual's neck on a chain. Governor Lachlan Macquarie, who commenced his commission as governor of New South Wales in January 1810, began some years later bestowing these plates upon those Aborigines who the colonizers felt exemplified traits of leadership among their **tribe**. These plates were engraved with titles such as "King," "Queen," "Prince," "Duke," or "Chief." The practice quickly became widespread, and plates were issued not only to supposed leaders but also to Aborigines who were particularly helpful to the colonists and settlers. The national museum of Australia holds a significant collection of these plates.

KINSHIP. Kinship is at the very core of Aboriginal society, with relationships defining individuals and the way they interact with others. As a consequence of **marriage** to outside groups, the breadth of Aboriginal kinship can be quite extensive because everyone must be placed within the kinship system and have some form of relationship to the individual, just as if he or she were a member of that person's immediate family. The Aboriginal system is a classificatory kinship system: terms used to classify consanguine relatives are also applied to people who may be only distantly related or, in some cases, not related at all.

The Aboriginal kinship system has two guiding principles. One is that same-sex siblings are classified equally. A mother's sisters are recognized as mothers, although a mother's brothers are termed uncles. Similarly, a father's brothers become fathers, although a father's sisters are termed aunts. Same-generation children of different mothers and fathers, therefore, become brothers and sisters. The second principle underlying Aboriginal kinship is its remarkable flexibility, which allows outsiders who have spent time in the community to be incorporated. At the same time, however, a number of relationships require avoidance, one of the most common being that between son-in-law and mother-in-law. All relationships, nevertheless, dictate the expected behavior between individuals, whether they must be maintained at a strictly formal or quite casual level.

Across much of Australia, Aboriginal societies are split by two kinship divisions, or moieties, based on either patrilineal or matrilineal descent. All children born to a couple must be placed within the moiety of one parent only, which means that upon reaching marriageable age themselves, they must choose a partner from the opposite moiety. In some areas of Australia moieties are further subdivided into four sections or eight subsections (skins), though this appears to be a relatively recent phenomenon and has no bearing on marriage. Importantly, the traditional Aboriginal kinship system was not only designed to ensure correct marriages but also regulated broader social relations, including access to resources.

KNGWARREYE, EMILY KAME (c. 1910–96). Indigenous artist. Emily Kngwarreye was a founding member of the Utopia Women's Batik Group (1977) in the Northern Territory community of Utopia, 200 kilometers northeast of Alice Springs. It is not uncommon for Aboriginal artists to take up painting later in life, and uninformed commentators sometimes categorize the work of such individuals as naïve, untutored, and intuitive, albeit gifted. Yet although Kngwarreye did not start painting on canvas until her late 70s, and critical acclaim was not immediate, her assured, striking yet subtle style soon attracted international recognition. Her paintings drew on a rich heritage of artistic production for communal and ritual purposes, such as sand drawings and body painting. Designs and styles used in batiks from Utopia were also recognizable in her canvasses. *See also* ART; PAPUNYA TULA; TJAPALTJARRI, CLIFFORD POSSUM; WESTERN DESERT ART.

KOORI. This Aboriginal word meaning "aborigine" is used by Aboriginal people in New South Wales and Victoria to refer to themselves. It originated in the Awabakal **language** in the Newcastle region and is shared by neighboring languages. Some Aboriginal people prefer to use "Koori" rather than "Aboriginal" or "Aborigine," as the latter words were introduced by British colonizers. "Koori" is used as a term that expresses pride in Aboriginality. Not all Aboriginal people identify with the term "Koori," however, for it does not represent some Aboriginal groups, such as the **Murri** in Queensland or **Nunga** in South Australia. *See also* NYUNGAR.

KOW SWAMP. This significant archaeological site is located near the Victorian town of Leitchville on the Murray River, approximately 262 kilometers north of Melbourne. Between 13,000 and 9,000 years BP, Kow Swamp was a freshwater lake. As with **Lake Mungo**, sand dunes called *lunettes* formed a boundary on one side of the lake. Following a chance find of skeletal remains by irrigation canal diggers, archaeological excavations in 1968 revealed the former lake bed silt and sand lunette contained a cemetery holding many shallowly dug graves.

A significance of the remains at Kow Swamp is that the skulls are far more robust than those of modern humans and far more robust than the gracile remains found at Lake Mungo. These robust remains suggest a more "archaic" form, yet they are only 13,000 to 9,500 years old. Hence, the apparently more archaic forms are actually more recent than the lightly built gracile Lake Mungo remains. Some researchers suggest that sexual dimorphism explains the differences in build, but others argue the evidence points to the coexistence of two different human groups occupying Australia. There is also debate over whether the Kow Swamp skulls had been artificially deformed through the practice of infant head-pressing, resulting in a more sloping forehead.

The Museum of Victoria returned all the Kow Swamp material to the local Aboriginal community in 1990. *See also* HUMAN OCCUPATION.

L

LAKE MUNGO. This significant archaeological site is located in New South Wales, approximately 966 kilometers west of Sydney. It is one of a series of 13 now dry lakes in a semiarid zone within the Willandra Lakes World Heritage Area. For some 30,000 years during the Pleistocene period, these shallow lakes contained fresh water and were rich in aquatic foods. They provided a salubrious environment for an intensive Aboriginal population over a long period of time, commencing 45,000 years BP. Approximately 30,000 years BP, the lake system began drying, and from 15,000 years BP to the present, the lakes have been dry. Some 15,000 years BP, human occupation, other than more transitory visits, ceased.

On the eastern shoreline of the lakes, large, crescent-shaped sand dunes known as lunettes formed. The Lake Mungo lunette was up to 40 meters high and 24 kilometers long. The lunettes provided protected campsites for Aborigines, and extensive erosion has revealed stone artifacts, mussel shells, fire hearths, and skeletal remains.

The first set of remains—those of a female known as Mungo I—initially dated to 24,710 ± 1,270 years BP have now been dated to c. 44,000 years BP. It is Australia's and, to date, the world's oldest known cremation. Ochre pellets were also present in the grave, suggesting the practice of elaborate burial rites. A second set of remains—this time the complete skeleton of a male—was located close by and has been dated to around the same age. The grave-fill was stained pink, indicating that the body had been extensively ochred prior to burial, further pointing to elaborate burial practices.

The remains of Mungo I are now in the custody of the local Aboriginal people. *See also* HUMAN OCCUPATION; KOW SWAMP.

LAND CLAIMS. In 1972, after winning the election on the platform of Aboriginal **land rights**, the federal government, under Prime Minister Gough Whitlam, introduced a bill into parliament that would create, for the first time in Australian law, a statutory land claims process. The bill became the Commonwealth **Aboriginal Land Rights (Northern Territory) Act 1976 (ALRA).** The ALRA enabled reserve and mission lands in the Northern

Territory that had previously been held by the Crown to be transferred to Aboriginal land trusts. There are now similar statutory land claim schemes in the Northern Territory, Queensland, New South Wales, South Australia, and Victoria.

A land claim is distinct from **native title**. Land claims are claims for a grant of title from the government. In contrast, native title is a bundle of rights originating from Aboriginal peoples' traditional laws and customs. Native title is not a right granted by the government but is a burden on the Crown's radical title. As with native title, under statutory land claim schemes, title to land is a form of communal title. An individual cannot hold title to land. There are statutory restrictions in land claim schemes on how this title may be dealt with. For example, as inalienable land, it cannot be bought, acquired, or forfeited. *See also* ABORIGINAL LAND RIGHTS COMMISSION; GOVE LAND RIGHTS CASE; LAND OWNERSHIP; LINGIARI, VINCENT; *TERRA NULLIUS*; WAVE HILL; WOODWARD INQUIRY.

LAND COUNCILS. *See* ABORIGINAL LAND RIGHTS (NORTHERN TERRITORY) ACT 1976 (COMMONWEALTH) (ALRA).

LAND OWNERSHIP. Indigenous people are the traditional owners of their lands and this ownership is recognized in Australian law through statutory **land claims** and **native title**. Under existing statutory land claims schemes, such as the Commonwealth **Aboriginal Land Rights (Northern Territory) Act 1976**, and native title, land ownership is held communally, reflecting Indigenous peoples' traditional customs and laws. *See also* ABORIGINAL LAND RIGHTS COMMISSION; GOVE LAND RIGHTS CASE; LAND RIGHTS; LINGIARI, VINCENT; MABO DECISION; MABO, EDDIE ("KOIKI"); NATIONAL NATIVE TITLE TRIBUNAL (NNTT); *TERRA NULLIUS*; WAVE HILL; WIK DECISION; WOODWARD INQUIRY.

LAND RIGHTS. With the application of the doctrine of *terra nullius* and the Crown's assertion of sovereignty over the continent in 1788, Indigenous peoples were not recognized as having any proprietary rights to the land they had traditionally owned. This approach justified the Crown acquiring absolute beneficial ownership of all lands. Indigenous and non-Indigenous peoples have fought for recognition of Indigenous peoples' land rights based upon their laws and customs. The enactment of the Commonwealth **Aboriginal Land Rights (Northern Territory) Act 1976** created, for the first time in Australian law, the recognition that Aboriginal peoples have rights to traditional lands, and it established a statutory framework for making **land claims**. In 1992, the **Mabo Decision** of the High Court of Australia overturned the legal doctrine of *terra nullius* and recognized the existence of **native title**. *See also* ABORIGINAL LAND RIGHTS COMMISSION; GOVE LAND RIGHTS CASE; LAND OWNERSHIP; LINGIARI, VINCENT; MABO, EDDIE ("KOIKI"); NATIONAL NATIVE TITLE TRIBUNAL (NNTT); WAVE HILL; WIK DECISION; WOODWARD INQUIRY.

LANGTON, MARCIA (1951–). Aboriginal academic. Marcia Langton was born in Brisbane and grew up in southwestern Queensland. In 1969, she enrolled in an arts-law degree course at the University of Queensland, but her wide interests in Aboriginal and **Torres Strait** Islander affairs frequently interrupted her academic pursuits. In 1970, she joined the **Aboriginal Medical Service** in Sydney, where her main focus was on the improvement of nutrition. Langton also worked in publishing and appeared in stage and television productions. In 1983, she represented the Federation of Aboriginal **Land Councils** at the United Nations International Working Group for Indigenous Affairs held in Geneva. The following year she graduated with first-class honors in anthropology at the Australian National University in Canberra, from where she took up the position of senior anthropologist with the Central Land Council in Alice Springs.

In 1989, Langton was appointed to the Northern Territory section of the **Royal Commission into Aboriginal Deaths in Custody**. Two years later, Langton accepted a lectureship in anthropology at Macquarie University in Sydney, before moving to Darwin in 1995 and teaching Aboriginal and Torres Strait Islander studies at the then University of the Northern Territory (now Charles Darwin University). In 2005, Langton completed her doctorate in geography at Macquarie University and is currently foundation chair in Australian Indigenous studies at the University of Melbourne.

LANGUAGE. At the time of colonization (1788), some 250 discrete Aboriginal languages were spoken across Australia, with a greater number of corresponding dialects—perhaps as many as 700. The languages can be clustered into approximately 26 related groups, with one group alone spanning most of the continent. All languages appear to stem from a common ancestral language. Tasmania is a possible exception. To date, the Tasmanian languages have not been conclusively linked to the mainland languages, but this work is ongoing. Similarly, it is not known conclusively whether **Tiwi**, the language of Melville Island in Australia's north, is related to the mainland languages. Because of the rapid depopulation of Tasmania, much knowledge of precolonial Aboriginal life was lost, including information pertaining to the languages spoken. However, there were at least three and possibly up to 16 Tasmanian Aboriginal languages.

There are approximately 30 extant Aboriginal languages, and very few people use these as their main means of communication. Of those that are still spoken, the majority have less than 100 speakers. Northern and central Australia are the stronghold of Aboriginal languages, with some 20 languages in these regions still forming the principal means of communicating, and children are still acquiring these languages naturally.

A form of Creole, known as Kriol, is spoken across northern Australia, and it too has a number of regional dialects. A widely spoken dialect of English is Aboriginal English. This is spoken across Australia, with regional variation.

As for many other Indigenous people and minority groupings, language has become a salient marker of **identity**. Its loss is considered a form of cultural dispossession. The preservation and maintenance of language, therefore, is a political issue as much as anything else. For example, in the state of Tasmania, the Palawa Kani Languages Program is attempting to develop a composite Tasmanian Aboriginal language from fragmentary vocabularies from a number of the former languages. Complicating this task further is lack of information on the grammar of the Tasmanian languages. Nevertheless, while still under development, Palawa Kani is being learned, and there is a small but growing number of users.

LEGAL SERVICES. *See* **ABORIGINAL LEGAL SERVICES.**

LEPROSY. *See* HANSEN'S DISEASE.

LINGIARI, VINCENT (1908–88). Aboriginal activist. A member of the Gurindji people from the Northern Territory, Vincent Lingiari led a walk-off at **Wave Hill** Station in the Northern Territory on 23 August 1966 in protest against the poor conditions and wages paid to its Aboriginal workers. The walk-off became a protest for the return of their traditional lands. The strike lasted seven years.

In 1972, a federal Labor government was elected on the platform of legislating to recognize Aboriginal **land rights**. In 1975, following the **Woodward Inquiry** into Aboriginal land rights, Prime Minister Gough Whitlam held a ceremony at Daguragu (Wattie Creek) at which the traditional lands of the Gurindji people were returned to them. Prime Minister Whitlam formally handed Lingiari the deeds to his people's land and symbolically poured sand into Lingiari's hands, affirming that the lands belonged to the Gurindji.

In 1976, Lingiari became a Member of the Order of Australia (AM). His achievements have been honored in the song "From Little Things Big Things Grow," written by Paul Kelly and **Kevin Carmody**. The Lingiari Foundation was established in 2001 with the aim of continuing Lingiari's legacy by advancing Indigenous rights, promoting reconciliation, and developing Indigenous leadership. The founding chairperson is **Patrick Dodson**. *See also* ABORIGINAL LAND RIGHTS COMMISSION; ABORIGINAL LAND RIGHTS (NORTHERN TERRITORY) ACT (COMMONWEALTH) (ALRA); GOVE LAND RIGHTS CASE; LAND CLAIMS; LAND OWNERSHIP.

LITERATURE. Traditionally, Indigenous Australian literature was oral. Much of this literature, particularly that which carried information essential to survival, **social organization**, and conduct, was conveyed in **Dreaming** stories, which told of mythic events. While many such stories were narrated, many were also told through song. Oral literature expressed the profound and was an integral component of ceremony and ritual. The visual **arts**, too, conveyed the esoteric knowledge contained within oral literature. Storytelling and singing was also a mundane activity, providing relaxation and entertainment. Song cycles comprising verse telling of the exploits of **ancestral beings** could be extensive, their recitation in full taking many hours. Some song cycles traversed territorial and linguistic boundaries, with each group responsible for the verses applicable to the land for which they had primary responsibility. Distant groups might be unaware of the detail of each other's verses, while near groups had varying familiarity.

Examples of Aboriginal writing, in the form of journalism and a protest letter, date from the 1830s and 1840s. Nevertheless, it was the 1970s and 1980s that saw the emergence of what quickly became a large body of Aboriginal literature. Plays and searing political critiques were among the early work of this period, but it was the memoir that attracted wide readership. **Sally Morgan**'s *My Place* is the best known of this genre. A number of Aboriginal poets have been published, including perhaps most notably **Oodgeroo Noonuccal**, who was known for much of her life as Kath Walker. Increasingly, contemporary Indigenous novelists, such as award winners **Kim Scott** and **Alexis Wright**, are receiving critical acclaim, successful screenplays are being produced, and children's books by Indigenous authors, such as **Melissa Lucashenko** and **Anita Heiss**, are winning awards. In addition, a growing number of Indigenous intellectuals are not only contributing to scholarship but also to national debates concerning Indigenous affairs. Notable contributors include **Noel Pearson** and **Marcia Langton**. *See also* ABORIGINAL MEDIA.

LITTLE, JAMES OSWALD (JIMMY) (1937–). Indigenous singer, musician, and actor. Born at Cummeragunja on the Murray River in southern New South Wales, Jimmy Little followed in the footsteps of his father, also named

James—a song and **dance** man who traveled the vaudeville circuit in the 1930s and 1940s. After learning guitar at the age of 14, Jimmy Little Jr. began performing as a hillbilly singer, and in 1953, he appeared on the *Australia's Amateur Hour* radio program. His first recording, "Mysteries of Life," appeared in 1955, but it was not until November 1963 that his name became widely known through the hit single "Royal Telephone," which earned him two gold records and a gold album.

His all-Aboriginal band remained together for three decades, with further successes coming in 1974 with "Baby Blue," followed by "Beautiful Woman" in 1983. In 1995, Little released an independently produced album, *Yorta Yorta Man*, based on his life story. Festival Records released *Messenger* in 1999, the album going gold and winning two Australian Recording Industry Association (ARIA) Awards. Little was inducted into the ARIA Hall of Fame the same year.

Little has appeared on television and in a number of Australian **films**. Since 1985, he has worked as a **music** tutor at the Redfern Eora Centre in Sydney, and his work with the wider Aboriginal community has been recognized with a host of awards and honors. In 1990, Little was named **National Aboriginal and Islander Day Observance Committee** Aborigine of the Year and has received an honorary doctorate from the Queensland University of Technology for his contributions to Australian music and Aboriginal **education**.

In 2004, the year Little released his 34th album and was named as an Australian Living National Treasure, he was diagnosed with kidney failure. After undergoing a successful kidney transplant in 2006, he launched the Jimmy Little Foundation to assist other Indigenous Australians suffering from similar medical problems.

LITTLE CHILDREN ARE SACRED REPORT. *See* NORTHERN TERRITORY EMERGENCY RESPONSE.

LUCASHENKO, MELISSA (1967–). Indigenous novelist, poet, and essayist. Melissa Lucashenko is of Ukrainian, Yugambeh, and Bundjalung heritage. Her novels include *Steam Pigs* (1997), which was the winner of the Dobbie Prize for Australian **women**'s fiction, *Hard Yards* (1999), and for teenagers, *Killing Darcy*, which, in 1998, won the Royal Blind Society Talking Book of the Year Award in the young people's category. *Too Flash* (2002) is also a novel for teenagers. *See also* LITERATURE.

M

MABO, EDDIE ("KOIKI") (1936–92). Indigenous activist. Eddie Mabo initiated legal proceedings in 1982, together with other Meriam claimants, that ultimately became known as the **Mabo Decision**. The claimants were seeking formal recognition of their proprietary interests in their lands and acknowledgment of their traditional ownership of the lands. Mabo was born on Mer Island in the **Torres Strait** and died only months before the High Court of Australia handed down its decision on 3 June 1992. *See also* GOVE LAND RIGHTS CASE; LAND OWNERSHIP; LAND RIGHTS; NATIONAL NATIVE TITLE TRIBUNAL (NNTT); NATIVE TITLE; *TERRA NULLIUS*; WIK DECISION.

MABO DECISION. This is a decision of the High Court of Australia that, for the first time, rejected the doctrine of *terra nullius* and found that the five claimants, including **Eddie ("Koiki") Mabo**, held **native title** to their traditional lands on Mer Island in the Torres Strait. The decision, which was handed down by the High Court on 3 June 1992, transformed Australian jurisprudence. It held that the Crown did not acquire absolute beneficial ownership of all lands over which it asserted sovereignty in 1788. Rather, the High Court recognized that the Crown acquired radical title—that is, title that is subject to native title rights where native title has not been validly extinguished. The federal government enacted the Commonwealth Native Title Act 1993 as a result of the decision. Subsequent High Court decisions have further clarified the High Court's interpretation of native title and the nature and extent of native title rights. *See also* ABORIGINAL LAND RIGHTS (NORTHERN TERRITORY) ACT 1976 (COMMONWEALTH) (ALRA); ABORIGINAL LAND RIGHTS COMMISSION; GOVE LAND RIGHTS CASE; INDIGENOUS LAND USE AGREEMENTS; LAND CLAIMS; LAND OWNERSHIP; LAND RIGHTS; LINGIARI, VINCENT; NATIONAL NATIVE TITLE TRIBUNAL (NNTT); WOODWARD INQUIRY.

MACASSANS. Fishermen from the city of Macassar on the island of Sulawesi in Indonesia, the Macassans made annual voyages to northern Australian shores during the monsoon season to exploit sea slugs, or bêche-de-mer, for the Chinese market. Contact between the Macassans and the Aboriginal people lasted from the 18th century until 1906, when their entry was prohibited by the Australian government. Their influence on coastal Aboriginal people from the Gulf of Carpentaria to the **Kimberley region** of Western Australia was considerable. In exchange for sea slugs, pearl shell, pearls, turtle shell, shark fins, clam meat, sandalwood, and, later, buffalo horns, the Macassans traded iron, axes, tomahawks, knives, glass, cloth, dugout canoes, cooked rice, **alcohol** (arak), and tobacco. In turn, Macassan goods were traded south across an area of approximately 80,000 square kilometers.

Macassan influence extended to **language** (Malay being the universal language spoken among the composite crews of Macassan praus), many words of which were incorporated into Aboriginal vocabularies. They also influenced Aboriginal burial practices, **art**, and **totemism**, although the Islamic **religion** was apparently rejected by the Aboriginal people in this region. Intermarriage was not uncommon, and a considerable number of Aboriginal men and **women** are known to have traveled to Macassar and elsewhere throughout Southeast Asia. It appears likely that the Macassans also introduced **smallpox** into northern Australia, while another serious consequence of their visits exists today in the form of Machado-Joseph disease, a debilitating and often fatal genetic disorder found within one large extended Aboriginal family on Groote Eylandt and adjacent areas of **Arnhem Land**.

MACQUARIE PEN ANTHOLOGY OF ABORIGINAL LITERATURE. *See* HEISS, ANITA; LITERATURE.

MAKARRATA. This Yolgnu word (a word of the people of northeastern Arnhem Land) signifies the ceremonial practice of formally ending a dispute and the recommencement of community accord. The negotiation of a treaty between the Australian government and Aborigines was one of the early initiatives of the National Aboriginal Conference, an elected representative body formed in 1977 by the federal government to provide advice to the government on Indigenous concerns. They chose an Aboriginal word, *makarrata*, for the desired treaty. Despite support by an Aboriginal treaty committee that comprised some high-profile spokespeople and a 1981–82 Senate committee inquiry, the impetus for the *makarrata* lapsed. It was briefly reinvigorated in the mid-1980s by Prime Minister Robert Hawke, who spoke of a "compact" between Aborigines and the government, not *makarrata* or treaty. Rather than a compact, however, in 1991, the **Council for Aboriginal Reconciliation** was formed. Today, there remains strong support among many Aborigines for a treaty between Aborigines and the broader settler population.

MANSELL, MICHAEL (1951–). Indigenous lawyer and activist. **Tasmanian Aborigine** Michael Mansell left school at the age of 15 and spent a decade working in laboring occupations. In 1978, he enrolled as a law student at the University of Tasmania, graduating in 1982. He was admitted as a barrister and solicitor of the Supreme Court of Tasmania in 1984 and is principal legal adviser to the Tasmanian **Aboriginal Legal Service** and legal director of the Tasmanian Aboriginal Centre.

Actively campaigning for Tasmanian Aboriginal rights since the early 1970s, Mansell's tactics have often been controversial. In 1987, the year he was named Aborigine of the Year, Mansell attended the World Conference on Zionism, Racism and Imperialism in Libya, returning the following year with a delegation to discuss trade sanctions against Australia with Colonel Muammar al-Gaddafi. At the same time, Mansell's alternative Aboriginal passport was officially recognized by Libya. In 1990, he was elected as a member of the newly formed Aboriginal Provisional Government (APG), of which he is the current secretary. Never garnishing wide support, the APG nevertheless exists as a national body engaged in advocacy. Its founding premise was that Aborigines are a sovereign people entitled to self-government with vested powers. Among many demands, it has provocatively called for Aborigines to enter their own national team in Olympic Games. Mansell continues to have a high profile as a spokesperson on Aboriginal issues.

MARALINGA. During the 1950s, the British government conducted atomic tests at Maralinga, South Australia, on the traditional land of the Maralinga Tjarutja. The closest Aboriginal mission, Ooldea, was closed in 1952 shortly before the tests began, and many of the traditional owners were moved to Colona and, eventually, Yatala. From 1952 to 1981, they were denied access to their land. The testing included both major tests and minor trials. In the major tests, nine nuclear bombs were exploded in Maralinga and the nearby town of Emu, seven of which were detonated at Maralinga itself. About 200 minor trials were also conducted between 1953 and 1963, and while they did not involve nuclear explosions, radioactive materials were used with conventional high explosives, causing plutonium to contaminate surrounding soil.

The sites, which were severely contaminated by these tests, were rehabilitated by the British from 1963 to 1967, but this did not meet current standards and left the land unsafe for access or occupation. In 1984, the South Australian government handed back some land to the Maralinga Tjarutja under the South Australian Maralinga Tjarutja Land Rights Act 1984 but retained those sections that were still dangerously contaminated. In 1985, a royal commission recommended that the land be rehabilitated so that it would be fit for unrestricted occupation by the traditional owners. The federal and South Australian governments worked with the Maralinga Tjarutja to develop the rehabilitation plan. A compensation settlement was also agreed upon, involving training opportunities in the rehabilitation project as well as $AUD13.5 million to be paid to the traditional owners. The rehabilitation project commenced in 1996 and concluded in 2000. Under the rehabilitation plan, it was agreed that the decontamination would allow unrestricted access to all but 120 square kilometers of the 3,200 square kilometer test site. The final area could not be decontaminated without causing further environmental damage. All but this remaining section of land has been returned to the Maralinga Tjarutja, but negotiations to finalize the handing back of this land continue.

MARIKA, WANDJUK (1927–87). Indigenous artist, musician, and advocate. Born in northeastern **Arnhem Land** and belonging to the Yolgnu people, Wandjuk Marika inherited a ritual leadership position from his father, and his expertise and knowledge were widely respected. He was the ritual custodian of the beach where the creator **ancestral beings** landed, as well as the upholder of traditional law. He oversaw ceremonial activities, ensuring they were conducted appropriately and in accordance with **Dreaming** lore, and ensured the maintenance and care of **sacred sites**. Taught traditional painting by his father from an early age, Marika became an accomplished artist whose work is held in major national collections. He was also an accomplished musician, and player of the **didgeridoo**. Widely traveled internationally, Marika was an effective advocate for his people. **Land rights** and the need to recognize Aboriginal copyright—the latter still a burning issue—were among the issues Marika pursued. He was a central figure in negotiations over the **Gove land rights case** and a founding member of the Aboriginal Arts Board, serving as its chairperson from 1976 to 1979. *See also* ART; MUSIC.

MARRIAGE. Marriage practices varied considerably throughout Australia and were characterized by great complexity. Some features, however, were reasonably widespread. Traditionally, the range of eligible marriage partners was circumscribed and individual choice limited or nonexistent. Who one could marry was determined by one's position in the **kinship** system and one's social category, the latter determined by descent from mother or father, age, and gender. While kinship systems, social categories, and, hence, marriage rules varied across Australia, societies were typically cleaved into two fundamental halves, or moieties. Moieties were exogamous in that eligible marriage partners were to be found in the opposite moiety, not the moiety to which one belonged. In contrast, however, most social categories were endogamous, with eligible marriage partners belonging to the same social category. For example, one common social division was generational, whereby those of the same and alternate generations would belong to the same social category. Hence, an individual was in the same generational category as his or her age group, grandparents, and grandchildren, but in a different category to parents and children.

Even though the classificatory kinship system extended one's close "relatives" considerably and prescribed the basis of the relationship one had with all other members of the society, marriage formed the basis of family and social life. It was rare for anyone not to be married, and for men, absence of a partner generally indicated absence of a female in the appropriate marriageable category. An unmarried woman was even rarer, and in some societies, unknown. In others, severe disability was a reason for a woman to be unmarried. In the eventuality of the death of a spouse, unless very old, a woman would remarry. While eloping with a proscribed partner was a serious, sometimes capital offence, premarital and extramarital affairs were generally not prohibited, but the choice of one's sexual partner was, like marriage, constrained by position in the kinship system and social category, with varying prohibitions and sanctions.

Infant betrothal of **women** was practiced by many Aboriginal societies. Until the infant was of marriageable age, the husband-to-be was required to regularly pay dues to the family of the child through such gifts as the sharing of food or, more recently, money and purchasable commodities. So-called promissory marriages are still sometimes practiced under customary law in some communities but have come under pressure by women seeking to exercise choice of partner or choosing not to marry. On occasion, such marriages have also come to the attention of law enforcement agencies when sexual relations in a marriage sanctioned under customary law have occurred with a woman deemed underage (under 16) by Australian law.

It was not uncommon for a man to have more than one wife (polygyny). In most societies, such arrangements were in the minority, but in some societies, up to 40 percent of men had two or more wives. A man was normally of at least middle age, often significantly older, before having the capacity to take more than one wife. Before being able to take a wife, a man had to be of a certain initiatory status and to have acquired a requisite level of customary knowledge. Having more than one wife conferred status, economic benefits (for women were the primary gatherers of food), and increased one's sphere of political influence through the more extended kin network obtained through additional wives. In meeting his obligations to the family of his wives, a husband could build strategic alliances. Not all wives under such arrangements were sexual partners, with some considered too old and others too young. They, nevertheless, were considered married or at least betrothed in the case of the young. The restriction of the number of eligible women available for marriage to younger men where polygyny was practiced was a source of jealously and conflict.

Marriage was usually not a cause for elaborate ritual celebration, although practices Australia-wide did vary markedly. Simply cohabiting, so long as one's partner was from an eligible category, was in many instances sufficient indication that marriage had occurred and of its acceptance. Divorce for a man was informal and was enacted by his leaving his wife. A woman, however, remained wedded to her husband until such time as he relinquished his claim, even if she had moved away from the family group or was living with another partner.

Customary marriages still occur throughout much of northern Australia; however, infant betrothal and polygyny are increasingly rare. Aboriginal women and men now share an interest in exercising individual choice in these (and other) matters, traditional practices are no longer as rigidly enforced, and many have been influenced by Christian doctrine and Western notions of the nuclear family. Furthermore, recent census data indicated that Australia-wide, 69 percent of couples with an Aboriginal partner were unions with a non-Aboriginal person. In capital cities this was 87 percent.

MASSACRES. This emotive word conjures up visions of Aboriginal people as passive victims of colonization in Australia, and by doing so it either belittles or completely ignores the often stout Aboriginal resistance on the Australian frontier. Until the 1850s, Aboriginal weaponry was actually superior to that of their European opponents, exemplified during Tasmania's **Black War** from the late 1820s to the early 1830s. Cessation of hostilities resulted from disease, overwhelming numbers, limited resources, exhaustion, and conciliation: the **Tasmanian Aborigines** were not defeated by force of arms.

Despite attempts in recent decades to deny the high level of violence on the Australian frontier, there is ample evidence in diaries, official reports, reminiscences, and oral histories that considerable numbers of Aboriginal people were killed during the struggle for land and resources. Exact figures have proved elusive for a number of obvious reasons. At times, the perpetrators were not concerned with recording the number of Aboriginal casualties or simply did not know the true figure. Avoidance was also a means of soothing troubled consciences or was motivated by fear of retribution from the authorities. Legally, Aboriginal people were British subjects and cold-blooded killing was murder. That was made poignantly clear after seven Europeans were executed for their part in the 1838 **Myall Creek Massacre** in northern New South Wales.

Massacres were not always effected through the use of firearms or other weapons. Reports of mass poisonings are known from many parts of Australia even though few can be substantiated. One that definitely occurred, in February 1842, on Kilcoy Station in southern Queensland, resulted in a large number of Aboriginal deaths. Conversely, Europeans were occasionally massacred by Aborigines, two of the best-known examples being from Queensland, where 10 Europeans were killed at Hornet Bank Station in 1857 and 19 at Cullin-la-Ringo in 1861. Both incidents, nevertheless, resulted in even more violent reprisals against local Aboriginal people.

Those responsible for the massacre of Aboriginal people ranged from individual settlers to vigilante groups, soldiers, and police. The most deadly group of all was the **Native Police**, a paramilitary force commanded by European officers. Importantly, massacres of Aboriginal people occurred in many regions of Australia and are known to have taken place from the 1790s right up until 1926, at **Forrest River** in Western Australia, and 1928, at **Coniston** in the Northern Territory. There is a distinct possibility that the mass killing of Aboriginal people continued into the 1930s and possibly even the 1940s in the more remote areas of northern Australia.

MAYNARD, FREDERICK. *See* AUSTRALIAN ABORIGINAL PROGRESSIVE ASSOCIATION (AAPA).

MCGINNESS, JOSEPH (JOE) (1914–2003). Aboriginal activist. Joseph McGinness was born at a tin mine operated by his Irish father and Aboriginal mother approximately 50 kilometers south of Darwin, Northern Territory, in 1914. Following his father's death in 1918, McGinness was removed to the Kahlin Aboriginal Compound in Darwin, where he received an elementary **education** before entering the workforce at the age of 13. During the economic depression of the 1930s, McGinness protested the prevailing mass unemployment and began agitating for Aboriginal rights. He served in a field ambulance unit during World War II and, after demobilization, became a stevedore at Thursday Island in the **Torres Strait**, where he joined the Waterside Workers' Federation in 1949.

Two years later, McGinness moved to Cairns and was elected to the executive committee of the union, a position he used to resume his campaign for Aboriginal rights. In 1958, McGinness was elected secretary of the newly formed Cairns Aboriginal and Torres Strait Islander Advancement League, which affiliated with similar organizations the same year to form the Federal Council for Aboriginal Advancement (later the **Federal Council for the Advancement of Aborigines and Torres Strait Islanders**). McGinness became the first Indigenous president of this national body in 1961, a position he continued to hold until 1973. He played a prominent role in the 1967 **referendum**. After stepping down as president, McGinness briefly joined the Department of Aboriginal Affairs before becoming the Cairns regional manager of Aboriginal Hostels Limited. He was instrumental in the establishment of a number of Aboriginal and Torres Strait Islander organizations in northern Queensland.

MCKENZIE-HATTON, ELIZABETH. *See* AUSTRALIAN ABORIGINAL PROGRESSIVE ASSOCIATION (AAPA).

MCRAE, TOMMY (1836–1901). Indigenous artist. Tommy McRae lived most of his life in the Wahgunyah Corowa region along the Murray River on the border of New South Wales and Victoria. Before starting to paint in the 1860s, he worked at odd jobs, such as station hand, drover, fisherman, itinerant rural worker, and maker and seller of artifacts. His distinctive style was characterized by images drawn as if in silhouette, and his subject matter included details on hunting techniques, episodes from his travels, ceremonial **dance**s, and fights. He was a keen observer, and many of his drawings were of things he remembered from the past, such as the pig-tailed Chinese who swept through the area on their way to the gold fields and early squatters who are depicted in their tails and top hats. McRae also produced a series of images concerning the escaped convict William Buckley. Sentenced to transportation for life, Buckley escaped when Lieutenant Governor David Collins attempted to establish a colony at Sorrento on Port Phillip, New South Wales (now Victoria). Buckley then lived with Aborigines for 32 years, eventually giving himself up to a party of surveyors in 1835. McRae inverts colonial depictions of Buckley, which mostly emphasize his return to white civilization, by illustrating Buckley's entry into the welcoming and rescuing embrace of Aborigines.

Because McRae sold his paintings for cash, becoming relatively affluent for an Aboriginal person of that era, and insisted on the right to spend his money outside the controls and strictures then placed on Aborigines, he is sometimes regarded as a forerunner to the Arrernte watercolorists of the mid-20th century. *See also* ART; BARAK, WILLIAM; NAMATJIRA, ALBERT.

MEDIA. *See* ABORIGINAL MEDIA.

MEGAFAUNA. This term refers to a range of large animal species, including macropods (e.g., *Procoptodon*, which stood up to three meters tall), a marsupial lion-type carnivore called *Thylacoleo*, a *Diprotodon* (at over two tons, Australia's largest ever marsupial), birds, and reptiles, the majority of which became extinct between c. 46,000–47,000 years BP. There is considerable debate as to whether their extinction was caused by humans (through hunting and/or habitat change through **fire-stick farming**) or other factors, such as climate change. While the debate continues, there is growing consensus that the extinction was caused by a complex of interrelated factors, including anthropogenic hunting and modification of habitat and a range of environmental transformations precipitated by climate change.

MIDDENS. Sites where the discarded shells of shellfish and other foodstuffs have accumulated over time and been preserved are called middens. They can reveal much about traditional Aboriginal cultural practices. The sites may include shellfish remains, bones of birds, fish, and mammals, charcoal from campfires, and traditional tools.

MILITARY SERVICE. While it is believed that Aboriginal people may have served as scouts in Australian colonial units during the South African War of 1899–1902, perhaps as many as 400 Indigenous Australians are known to have enlisted in the Australian Imperial Force during World War I. Military authorities initially showed great reluctance to recruit Indigenous Australians, and many who joined up claimed either Maori or Indian descent. After the failure of the conscription referendum in 1916 and mounting casualties on the Western Front, an amendment to military regulations in May 1917 permitted Indigenous Australians to enlist if they could prove that at least one of their parents was of European origin.

Having entered military service, Indigenous soldiers were treated on an equal footing with European personnel. A number of Indigenous servicemen were also recommended for bravery awards, including Private William Rawlings, who led a bombing attack on a German communication trench in July 1918 and was posthumously awarded the Military Medal after being killed at the Battle of Amiens the following month. A number of other Indigenous Australians served in Palestine, where a unit of the 11th Light Horse Regiment, known as the Black Watch, was composed almost solely of Queensland Aborigines.

The outbreak of World War II in 1939 divided the Indigenous community. Many veterans from the first global conflict were bitter about their treatment after returning to Australia following the Armistice. Others believed that war service could assist the campaign for **citizenship** and equal rights. Military authorities welcomed the enlistment of Indigenous Australians until 1940, when it was suddenly decided that they were neither necessary nor desirable.

It was not until Japan entered the war in December 1941 that restrictions were again relaxed.

It has been estimated that as many as 3,000 Indigenous Australians served in the Australian armed forces between 1939 and 1945, including 500 members of the **Torres Strait** Light Infantry Battalion. Another 150 served in irregular units, such as the Northern Territory Special Reconnaissance Unit and the North Australia Observer Unit, forerunner of the North West Mobile Force (Norforce).

The son of a World War I veteran, **Reginald (Reg) Saunders** became the Australian Army's first Indigenous commissioned officer when he was promoted to lieutenant in November 1944. It is not known how many Indigenous Australians served in the Royal Australian Navy or Royal Australian Air Force, though Leonard Waters is recognized as having been Australia's only Indigenous fighter pilot in the Second World War. Waters flew 95 sorties in the southwestern Pacific and was promoted to flight-sergeant in 1945. He was discharged from the air force the following year with the rank of warrant officer.

Between 1939 and 1945, an estimated 3,000 Indigenous men and **women** were also employed in labor units, auxiliary services, or industries essential to the war effort. Indigenous Australians continued to serve in later conflicts, including the Korean War and the Vietnam War. Today, they are represented in all branches of the Australian Defence Force as well as comprising an important component of Norforce, a special Army Reserve surveillance unit formed in the Northern Territory in 1981.

MILURRPUM AND OTHERS V. NABALCO AND THE COMMONWEALTH OF AUSTRALIA. *See* GOVE LAND RIGHTS CASE.

MISSIONS. Torres Strait Islanders found Christianity compatible with their own **religion**s and readily embraced it following the arrival of the London Missionary Society in 1871. The expansion of Christianity throughout the islands was also facilitated by the deployment of South Sea Island lay preachers, a process that would not have been of any use on the Australian mainland. Indeed, even today, Christianity has found a mixed reception among the Aboriginal people.

Initially, there was little attempt to spread the gospel among the Aboriginal people, as early missionaries held Polynesians to be at a more advanced level of civilization and accordingly focused their attention on the Pacific Islands. The first Christian missions in Australia were not established until the 1820s. The most significant of these was run by Reverend Lancelot Threlkeld at Lake Macquarie on the central coast of New South Wales between 1825 and 1841. In 1831, the Church Missionary Society established a mission in the Wellington Valley that lasted until 1856, but none of the early missions achieved any real success. Aboriginal people resisted settling in one place, and few cared to cultivate the soil in the European fashion. Nor did the Aborigines take kindly to the institutionalization of their children.

The spread of European settlement in the latter half of the 19th century and a widespread social Darwinist belief that the Aboriginal people were destined to die out encouraged missionaries to direct their attention to the more remote regions of northern, western, and central Australia. By the 1920s, more than 20 Christian missions were scattered across northern Australia, chiefly on the coast and islands, with a small number in the arid inland areas. While some of them became important sanctuaries as graziers and other European adventurers encroached on traditional Aboriginal homelands, others were ideally located to serve as temporary campsites during seasonal migrations. Their attraction was further enhanced by the issue of rations and luxury goods such as tobacco.

Missionaries were often ranked with traditional sorcerers, partly owing to their lack of firearms and partly through the curative powers of their medicines. In many instances, however, the missions remained only at the discretion of the Aboriginal landowners. In 1917, Presbyterian missionary Robert Hall ignored Aboriginal demands to leave Mornington Island in the Gulf of Carpentaria and was fatally speared.

During the first half of the 20th century, a small cadre of missionaries attempted to run their missions in accordance with Aboriginal expectations. In 1927, Robert Love managed to gain a few Christian converts at the Kunmunya Mission in Western Australia after bringing the **segregation** of Aboriginal children in dormitories to an end. In the 1930s, George and Sally Goldsmith undertook similar measures on Goulburn Island in the Northern Territory, while Ernabella Mission, established by Charles Duguid in the Musgrave Ranges of central Australia in 1936, developed protocols that were acceptable to the local Pitjantjatjara people.

Although conversion to Christianity was a major underlying purpose of the missions, none was ever overwhelmed with converts. Their role also began to alter markedly in the years following World War II, a trend that has continued to the present day. When many missionaries began training in anthropology, greater emphasis was placed on assisting Aboriginal people in practical rather than theological terms. It was only after they became proactive in the preservation of Aboriginal cultures and joined the push for **land rights** and **self-determination** that the efforts of the missionaries finally found more ready acceptance.

MIXED DESCENT. This term refers to people with parents or grandparents from different cultural and/or ethnic backgrounds, such as Indigenous and European ancestry. In Australia, various names were used to differentiate people with both Indigenous and European heritage, but the most common term used was "half-caste." Individuals with mixed heritage were defined in contrast to those Indigenous people regarded as "full blooded."

The colonizers' societal norms maintained that physical and mental attributes as well as social status were largely biologically determined and, hence, inherited and, further, that they were carried through the blood line. Individuals with mixed descent were, therefore, seen to have "mixed blood." While such people were seen to be racially and socially "impure," it was thought that "mixed blood" people, with traces of European blood, were slightly more "advanced" or more educable than their "full blooded" relatives. It was believed that with more European "blood" and increasing physical and mental attributes resembling European ancestry, people of mixed descent could ultimately blend into European society. Such theories justified the **assimilationist policies** of the **Aboriginal Protection Board**, including the forcible removal of children from their families that resulted in the **Stolen Generations**.

The belief that **identity** is locatable in an individual's biology or blood continues to inform dominant discourses and government policy. This is despite the fact that the majority of couples in which at least one partner is Aboriginal are intermixed. Data from the 2001 census revealed that an overall 69 percent of Aboriginal partnerships were with a non-Aboriginal person. In capital cities, the rate was 87 percent. The majority of children from mixed marriages identify as Aboriginal.

MOFFATT, TRACEY. *See* FILM.

MORGAN, SALLY (1951–). Indigenous author and artist. Sally Morgan was born in Perth, Western Australia, and grew up believing she was of Indian descent. After graduating from the University of Western Australia in 1974 and gaining postgraduate qualifications in a number of fields, Morgan began investigating her family background. She traced her Aboriginal origins to the Pilbara region of Western Australia, the results being published as *My Place* (1987), a work that won a number of important literary awards. Following the success of her autobiography, Morgan published three biographies and seven children's books, in addition to a number of edited works. Her other major interest is painting. Since holding her first solo exhibition at Fremantle, Western Australia, in 1989, Morgan has gained a national reputation for her unique style, which incorporates aspects of traditional Aboriginal **art**.

Many of her works are now held in major public collections in Australia and overseas. *See also* LITERATURE.

MURRI. This term is used by Aborigines of Queensland (not including the **Torres Strait** Islanders) and far northern New South Wales to collectively identify themselves. *See also* KOORI; NUNGA; NYUNGAR.

MUSIC. Indigenous music today crosses most genres, including country and Western, jazz, hip-hop, opera, rock and roll, heavy metal, pop, choir, gospel, soul, and blues.

Traditionally, much Australian Indigenous music was expressed through song. Together with **dance**, songs formed an integral part of the ceremonial, sacred, and ritual inventory and were also a form of everyday expression. Singing could be in groups, involving both men and **women**, as social entertainment or more formal ceremonial events; as a family activity, such as gathering around the evening campfire; or as a form of everyday individual expression in which individuals simply sang to themselves when the desire called. Much singing was unaccompanied by other instruments, but depending on circumstances and occasion, a range of instruments was often employed.

Clapsticks were a common percussive instrument and were used throughout much of Australia. Drum-like instruments were also in use, varying from region to region. These ranged from hollow logs that were tapped, to tightly bound animal skin rugs, some of which were also stuffed with assorted fibers, to an actual hand drum introduced into **Cape York** Peninsula in Queensland from New Guinea. In some regions, wooden clubs were struck against the ground, feet stomped, and thighs slapped for percussive effect. Performers deployed various rattles and also bound dried or fresh leaves to their limbs, not only to enhance the visual spectacle but also for the rustling sound this created, particularly in association with the synchronized movement of dancers. Originally, in northern Australia and now throughout the continent, the **didgeridoo**—an aerophone—was/is a principal instrument. As with singing, its function could be formal and restricted or more casual. Another aerophone—the gum leaf—served as a powerful expression of Aboriginality during the first half of the 20th century, with numerous troupes of gum leaf musicians touring extensively throughout Australia.

Whether accompanied or unaccompanied, song in its formal context was (and is) linked inextricably to the **Dreaming** and the activities of the **ancestral beings**. Through the singing of songs (and associated activities), not only are the Dreaming and the exploits of the ancestral beings reinvigorated in the present, but also important cultural knowledge is imparted.

While distinctive occasions helped to mark musical events and to distinguish between entertainment and formal ceremony, such a disjuncture was not inevitable. As with **art**, a musical performance in whatever form could be multilayered, with a person's understanding of the performance dependent upon age, gender, initiatory status, and place within the **kinship** system. Thus, in a single performance, what might be entertainment for some (children for example) could be privileged esotery for others. *See also* BLAIR, HAROLD; CARMODY, KEVIN (KEV); HUNTER, RUBY; LITTLE, JAMES OSWALD (JIMMY); ROACH, ARCHIBALD (ARCHIE); YOTHU YINDI.

MUSQUITO (c. 1780–1825). Indigenous resistance fighter and outlaw. Possibly from the Broken Bay area north of Sydney in New South Wales, Musquito was involved in raids on British settlers in the Hawkesbury and Georges River districts and may have murdered an Aboriginal **woman**. In July 1805, he was captured by local Aboriginal people and handed to British authorities, who exiled him to Norfolk Island. He remained there until January 1813, when he was transported to Tasmania and granted a ticket-of-leave—a pass granted to well behaved convicts that allowed them to work for wages. By February 1818, Musquito was employed by prominent landowner Edward Lord, but he was also hired by the government to track down outlaws, the success of which brought the promise of repatriation to Sydney. When it became evident that he was not going to be returned home, Musquito joined a group of displaced **Tasmanian Aborigines** known as the Tame Mob and organized a series of raids on pastoral properties during 1823–24, in which several Europeans were killed or wounded. Captured in August 1824, Musquito and a Tasmanian Aborigine named Black Jack stood trial for murder the following December. While there are a number of doubts over the legality of the court proceedings, both men were found guilty and executed in February 1825. A number of contemporaries believed that the death of the two men marked the beginning of Tasmania's **Black War**.

MYALL CREEK MASSACRE. In June 1838, a group of 10 stockmen and hut-keepers—mostly convicts—arrived at Henry Dangar's property on the Gwydir River in northern New South Wales, ostensibly in search of Aborigines who had been spearing cattle on properties further south. They tethered together 28 Aborigines who were camped there, most of whom were **women** and children, and joined by one of Dangar's own convict stockmen, they took their captives a short distance into the bush, killed them with cutlasses and muskets, and mutilated the bodies. An attempt was later made to burn the remains. Their murder was reported by Dangar's overseer, William Hobbs, and thoroughly investigated by police magistrate Edward Day. Importantly, the massacre of innocent Aborigines gave Governor George Gipps an opportunity to reassert British law on the distant frontier.

The perpetrators were charged with murder and conveyed to Sydney, where they were tried in November 1838. Following their acquittal by a sympathetic jury, Gipps ordered seven of the offenders to be retried using the same evidence, and on this occasion, all were found guilty and sentenced to death. Despite widespread calls for their release, the men were hanged the following month—the first time Europeans had been executed for killing Aborigines and a precedent that was never to be followed. Nor did their execution prevent further bloodshed on the frontier, where the punitive actions of Europeans simply became more covert. *See also* CONISTON MASSACRE; FORREST RIVER MASSACRE; MASSACRES.

N

NAMATJIRA, ALBERT (1902–59). Indigenous artist. Australia's most famous Aboriginal artist, Albert Namatjira, was born and educated at Hermannsburg **Mission** in central Australia. Initiated at the age of 13, he married five years later and worked in a variety of rural occupations. As a sideline, he regularly produced traditional artworks in a range of genres. Following an exhibition of paintings at Hermannsburg in 1934 by European artists Rex Battarbee and John Gardner, Namatjira became interested in watercolors as a medium. Two years later, he received tuition from Battarbee while working as the latter's cameleer during an eight-week painting expedition through the Macdonnell Ranges. It was the only formal training in **art** that Namatjira ever received. Encouraged by Battarbee and mission superintendent Pastor Friedrich Albrecht, Namatjira began exhibiting his paintings. Although there were numerous critics of his style and medium, the demand for Namatjira's work grew rapidly, until he was receiving both national and international recognition.

Namatjira's success masked inner torment. As an initiated Arrernte man, customary obligations prevented him from accumulating material wealth, and his personal ambition was often frustrated by racial discrimination. In 1951, he established a camp at Morris Soak on the outskirts of Alice Springs after being refused permission to purchase a block of land in the town on which he intended to build a house. Six years later, Namatjira was granted **citizenship**, which, among other things, allowed him to purchase and consume **alcohol**. In 1958, he was sentenced to six months' imprisonment for supplying alcohol to a fellow artist who was legally a ward of the state. After widespread public outcry and two legal appeals, the sentence was reduced to open detention on Papunya settlement. On 8 August 1959, just three months after completing his sentence, Namatjira died from heart failure.

NAMOK, BERNARD. *See* TORRES STRAIT ISLANDER FLAG.

NATIONAL ABORIGINAL AND ISLANDER DAY OBSERVANCE COMMITTEE (NAIDOC). This week-long event is held throughout Australia in the first week of July to celebrate Aboriginal and Torres Strait

Islanders' history, culture, and achievements. While originally a term referring to the organizing committee, "NAIDOC" is now used to refer to the week itself.

The event originates in the 1920s and 1930s, when Aboriginal and non-Aboriginal people fought for recognition of the injustices Aboriginal people suffered, such as lack of citizenship and poor living standards. On 26 January 1938, more than 1,000 Aboriginal people attended a National Day of Mourning Conference and proposed a national policy for Aboriginal people. This was presented to Prime Minister Joseph Lyons but was rejected because the federal government did not have constitutional power to legislate on Indigenous affairs. An advocate for Aboriginal rights pushed for a national day of mourning or Aboriginal Sunday, which would be an annual day to remember those Aboriginal people who had died during British settlement and to reflect upon the injustices still suffered. In 1957, with the support of the federal and state governments, a National Aborigines Day Observance Committee (NADOC) was formed to promote this national day. In 1975, following the 1967 **Referendum** and with the **land rights** movement gaining momentum and national attention, the national day for Aboriginal people was extended to National Aborigines Week.

In 1988, NADOC recognized Torres Strait Islanders and changed its name to NAIDOC. Responsibility for organizing NAIDOC was transferred to the **Aboriginal and Torres Strait Islander Commission** (ATSIC) from 1997 until ATSIC was abolished in 2004. In 2005, Indigenous leader and former senator Aden Ridgeway became NAIDOC's custodian. He continues as chairperson of the national committee.

NATIONAL ABORIGINAL AND TORRES STRAIT ISLANDER ART AWARD (NATSIAA). The Northern Territory Museum and Art Gallery in Darwin first established this award in 1984. It quickly became the premier Australian Indigenous **art** award. It accepts entries of both traditional and contemporary works from Indigenous artists working in varied media. There is an overall major prize and awards in an additional four categories: the general painting award, the bark painting award, the work-on-paper award, and the **Wandjuk Marika** 3D Memorial Award. Since 1992, the awards have been sponsored by Telstra, and each award now bears this corporation's name.

NATIONAL ABORIGINAL CONFERENCE. *See MAKARRATA.*

NATIONAL ABORIGINAL CONSULTATIVE COMMITTEE. *See* FEDERAL COUNCIL FOR THE ADVANCEMENT OF ABORIGINES AND TORRES STRAIT ISLANDERS (FCAATSI).

NATIONAL ABORIGINES DAY OBSERVANCE COMMITTEE (NADOC). *See* NATIONAL ABORIGINAL AND ISLANDER DAY OBSERVANCE COMMITTEE.

NATIONAL CONGRESS OF AUSTRALIA'S FIRST PEOPLES. Launched on 2 May 2010, this is the first formal representative Indigenous body at the national level since the axing of ATSIC on 24 March 2005. It comprises an appointed eight-member executive board and 120 elected members.

NATIONAL DEATHS IN CUSTODY PROGRAM. *See* ROYAL COMMISSION INTO ABORIGINAL DEATHS IN CUSTODY (RCIADIC).

NATIONAL NATIVE TITLE TRIBUNAL (NNTT). The NNTT is a Commonwealth statutory agency established under the Commonwealth Native Title Act 1993. It is responsible for mediating **native title** claims. The NNTT may become involved in assisting parties to reach agreement about future developments, such as mining projects, on lands over which there are native title claims, or where determinations of native title have been made. The NNTT may assist in the negotiation of agreements, such as **Indigenous Land Use Agreements**. The NNTT may also act as an arbitrator where an agreement cannot be reached between interested parties. *See also* ABORIGINAL LAND RIGHTS COMMISSION; ABORIGINAL LAND RIGHTS (NORTHERN TERRITORY) ACT 1976 (COMMONWEALTH) (ALRA); AUSTRALIANS FOR NATIVE TITLE AND RECONCILIATION (ANTaR); GOVE LAND RIGHTS CASE; LAND CLAIMS; LAND OWNERSHIP; LAND RIGHTS; LINGIARI, VINCENT; MABO DECISION; MABO, EDDIE ("KOIKI"); *TERRA NULLIUS*; WAVE HILL; WIK DECISION; WOODWARD INQUIRY.

NATIONAL SORRY DAY. One of the recommendations of the report ***Bringing Them Home*** was that a National Sorry Day be held each year on 26 May to remember the government policy that resulted in the **Stolen Generations** and the ongoing impacts of this policy. Until the new Labor government led by Kevin Rudd issued an apology on 13 February 2008, the federal government had refused to issue a formal apology, maintaining that it was inappropriate for current generations to assume responsibility for past wrongs. Despite this, many state governments issued formal apologies, and a community-based National Sorry Day Committee was formed. The first National Sorry Day was held on 26 May 1998.

At this first National Sorry Day, Sorry Books were presented to representatives of Aboriginal communities affected by this policy. One thousand

Sorry Books had been circulated throughout Australia before the event, and individuals around the country had signed the books to personally apologize to Aboriginal people for the policy that had resulted in children being taken away from their families.

Wider public support and the willingness to apologize for past injustices was a pivotal gesture in the **reconciliation** process. This support for reconciliation reached a climactic moment when, on 28 May 2000, more than 250,000 people participated in the People's Walk for Reconciliation in Sydney and, as a symbolic gesture of bridging the divide, walked across the Sydney Harbour Bridge. Many thousands of the participants openly carried signs saying "sorry" and called on the Howard government to apologize on behalf of the nation. A skywriter wrote "sorry" in the sky. Prime Minister John Howard did not participate in the march.

NATIONAL TRIBAL COUNCIL. *See* FEDERAL COUNCIL FOR THE ADVANCEMENT OF ABORIGINES AND TORRES STRAIT ISLANDERS (FCAATSI).

NATIVE POLICE. A paramilitary force first used in the Port Phillip district (Victoria) in 1837, Native Police units were later established in New South Wales and, after separation in 1859, in Queensland, where they acquired a particularly brutal reputation. Detachments consisted of up to twelve Aboriginal troopers with one or two European officers. Their official purpose was to pacify districts where conflict had erupted between European settlers and local Aborigines, and in the more violent districts, Native Police patrols frequently overlapped. Unofficially, they were search-and-destroy units sent out to eliminate Aboriginal opposition wherever it could be found, and there are numerous documented accounts from Queensland where entirely innocent groups of Aboriginal people bore the brunt of Native Police aggression.

Aboriginal troopers could never aspire to any rank above corporal, and the pay was low, the work dangerous, and discipline harsh. Yet there were many reasons why Aboriginal men chose to enlist in the Native Police. They were generally deployed to areas far removed from their home territories to discourage fraternization and desertion, but due to the low caliber of many European officers, the troopers were often able to exercise a considerable degree of independence while on patrol. They were paid regular wages and reasonably well fed, clothed in uniforms, and armed with modern European weaponry. From 1870, Queensland Native Police were equipped with lethal rapid-firing Snider carbines. The force was never particularly large, and the number of Aboriginal troopers fluctuated from a maximum of 250 in the 1860s to a low of 106 during the 1880s. They operated in all parts of

Queensland, being deployed wherever the need arose. Although a journal was kept of duties performed in camp, it is perhaps relevant that there was no written record of activities undertaken while on patrol. The Native Police continued to operate in Queensland until the outbreak of World War I.

NATIVE TITLE. The recognition in Australian law that Indigenous people continue to have rights to traditional lands and waters is known as native title, which is characterized by a bundle of associated rights and interests. Because native title is derived from Indigenous people's traditional laws and customs, its scope and nature will vary according to the traditional laws and customs of the particular native title holders. Native title rights may include the right to possess and occupy an area to the exclusion of others. Such rights can only exist on particular areas of land, such as unallocated Crown land or reserve land. Native title does not give rights to minerals, gas, or petroleum. Native title continues to exist unless it is abandoned or surrendered by the traditional owners, lost through extinction, or extinguished by the Crown through clear and unambiguous legislation or by inconsistent grant, such as a grant of freehold title.

Native title was first recognized in Australian law in 1992 as a result of the **Mabo Decision**. The Commonwealth Native Title Act 1993 (NTA) was enacted to create a statutory framework for making claims of native title and resolving disputes between conflicting proprietary interests. Substantial amendments to the NTA were made in 1998 by the federal government. These amendments included introducing **Indigenous Land Use Agreements**. On a case-by-case basis, decisions of the High Court of Australia continue to interpret the nature and scope of native title. *See also* ABORIGINAL LAND RIGHTS COMMISSION; ABORIGINAL LAND RIGHTS (NORTHERN TERRITORY) ACT 1976 (COMMONWEALTH) (ALRA); AUSTRALIANS FOR NATIVE TITLE AND RECONCILIATION (ANTaR); GOVE LAND RIGHTS CASE; LAND CLAIMS; LAND OWNERSHIP; LAND RIGHTS; LINGIARI, VINCENT; MABO, EDDIE ("KOIKI"); NATIONAL NATIVE TITLE TRIBUNAL (NNTT); *TERRA NULLIUS*; WAVE HILL; WOODWARD INQUIRY.

NEIDJIE, BILL ("BIG BILL") (c. 1912–2002). Indigenous elder and environmental advocate. A member of the Gagudju people, who became widely known as "Kakadu Man," Bill Neidjie was born on the East Alligator River in the Northern Territory and spent a number of his early years living in the bush. He subsequently took on a variety of jobs, including working in timber mills and as a domestic cleaning houses and mowing lawns in Darwin. Often, Neidjie was paid with flour, tea, tobacco, and the like instead of wages. He was renowned for his strength, which, for approximately 30 years, he put to use loading and unloading a lugger that plied the northern coastline. Then, in 1979, he moved back to the country of his birth in the **Kakadu** region. The last fluent speaker of the Gagudju **language**, Neidjie became internationally known through his work supporting the successful nomination of Kakadu National Park for World Heritage status for both its cultural and natural significance. He had extensive traditional knowledge of the region and profound knowledge of the environment. Following the proclamation of Kakadu National Park, for which Neidjie provided crucial evidence, he worked as a park ranger and subsequently as a cultural advisor. In these capacities and through books and **film**s, he shared his knowledge of country, of traditional beliefs, and philosophy on life.

NEMARLUK (c. 1911–40). Indigenous resistance fighter. From the central Daly River district of the Northern Territory, Nemarluk led a small band of resistance fighters who speared cattle and horses as well as attacking lone European travelers. In July 1931, Nemarluk was involved in the killing of three Japanese fishermen near the mouth of the Fitzmaurice River and was almost certainly complicit in the fatal spearing of two European prospectors in the same area during November the following year. Although all other members of his band had been captured and tried for murder in March 1933, Nemarluk remained at large until the following May. He escaped from Darwin's Fanny Bay Jail while awaiting trial and managed to evade police search parties for a further six months before being tracked down on Legune Station by an Aboriginal tracker known as Bul-Bul. Nemarluk's death sentence in April 1934 was commuted to life imprisonment, but after contracting tuberculosis, he died in August 1940.

NICHOLLS, DOUGLAS ("PASTOR DOUG") (1906–88). Indigenous sportsperson and advocate. Grand-nephew of **William Cooper**, Doug Nicholls was born in 1906 on the Cummeragunja Aboriginal Reserve near Moama in southern New South Wales. From the age of 13, he worked in shearing sheds and other menial occupations until he became a professional sportsman. From 1929, Nicholls won a number of professional running events in Victoria, and in the same year, he played for the Northcote Football Club, an Australian rules team, which won the Victorian premiership. Nicholls was also a boxer in Jimmy Sharman's traveling troupe. From 1933 to 1936, he played Australian rules with the Fitzroy Football Club, with his playing career continuing until 1939, when knee injuries forced his retirement. In 1940, he briefly rejoined his old Northcote club as a nonplaying coach.

A convert to the Church of Christ in 1932, Nicholls was practicing as a lay preacher by 1935. He was ordained in 1939 and, two years later, enlisted in the Australian Army. He was released from military service in 1942 at the request of the Victorian police, who recognized his value as a social worker among the Aboriginal community in the Melbourne suburb of Fitzroy.

Following in the footsteps of his granduncle, Nicholls was also an active crusader for Aboriginal rights. In 1957, he was a founding member of the **Aborigines Advancement League** and became the organization's first field officer. He played a prominent role in establishing hostels for Aboriginal children and a holiday home at Queenscliff. In 1958, Nicholls became a founding member and Victorian secretary of the **Federal Council for the Advancement of Aborigines and Torres Strait Islanders** (at that time, the Federal Council for Aboriginal Advancement). In 1968, Nicholls joined the Victorian Ministry of Aboriginal Affairs, and the following year, he became chairperson of the National Aboriginal Sports Foundation.

In 1957, Nicholls was appointed a Member of the Order of the British Empire (MBE), becoming an Officer of the Order (OBE) in 1968. Four years later, he became the first Aborigine to be knighted, attending the investiture at Buckingham Palace in November 1972. Nicholls was also the first Aborigine to be appointed to a viceregal position, when he became governor of South Australia in December 1976. Illness forced his retirement five months later, but in 1977, he received yet another royal appointment in the form of Knight Commander of the Royal Victorian Order. In declining **health**, Nicholls spent the last years of his life at Nathalia in northern Victoria. After his death in June 1988, Nicholls was granted a state funeral and interred at Cummeragunja.

NOONUCCAL, OODGEROO (1920–93). Indigenous activist, poet, and educator. Oodgeroo Noonuccal, sometimes known as Kath Walker, was born on North Stradbroke Island near Brisbane as Kathleen Ruska. After leaving school at 13 years of age, she entered domestic service in Brisbane. With the outbreak of World War II, Oodgeroo joined the Women's Land Army and became a telephonist, before illness forced her return to domestic service. A short-lived **marriage** to Bruce Walker resulted in the birth of two boys, one of whom predeceased her. Oodgeroo joined the Communist Party of Australia, which at that time was the only political organization concerned with Aboriginal issues. By 1961, she was Queensland secretary of the Federal Council for Aboriginal Advancement (later the **Federal Council for the Advancement of Aborigines and Torres Strait Islanders**) and played a major role in the successful 1967 **referendum**.

Oodgeroo had joined a Brisbane writer's group in 1954, and 10 years later, she published her first book of verse, *We Are Going*. This was the first volume of poetry to be published by an Aboriginal writer, and it brought widespread acclaim. It was followed two years later by a second volume of verse, *The Dawn Is At Hand*. In 1972, Oodgeroo published a collection of childhood and traditional Aboriginal stories as *Stradbroke Dreamtime*, with subsequent publications including two children's books, one of which, *Father Sky and Mother Earth* (1981), was illustrated with her own artwork.

Appointed a Member of the Order of the British Empire (MBE) in 1970, Oodgeroo remained prominent in Aboriginal affairs. During the 1970s, she was chairperson of the National Tribal Council, the Aboriginal Arts Board, the Aboriginal Housing Committee, and the Queensland **Aboriginal Advancement League**. Annoyed by the federal government's failure to legislate nationally for Aboriginal **land rights** and in protest over the 1988 bicentennial celebrations, Oodgeroo returned her MBE and assumed her Aboriginal name. At her home on North Stradbroke Island, she ran a series of educational programs for both Aboriginal and non-Aboriginal children aimed at effecting **reconciliation** through an appreciation of the natural environment and Aboriginal culture until shortly before her death from cancer in September 1993. *See also* LITERATURE; WOMEN.

NORTHERN DEVELOPMENT AND MINING (NODOM). *See* BLACK EUREKA.

NORTHERN TERRITORY EMERGENCY RESPONSE. On 8 August 2006, a Board of Inquiry into the Protection of Children from Sexual Abuse was established in the Northern Territory. The following year (15 June 2007), the report *Little Children Are Sacred*, a catalog of physical and sexual abuse of children in remote Northern Territory Aboriginal communities, was officially released. This served as the catalyst for the federal government's direct intervention into 73 communities and 45 town camps. As a special measure, the emergency response was exempted from the 1975 Commonwealth Racial Discrimination Act, and after invoking Section 122 of the Australian Constitution, the federal government was able to override the powers of the Northern Territory government. Five pieces of legislation were passed by the federal government, the most important of which was the Northern Territory National Emergency Response Act.

A taskforce led by Major General Dave Chambers was formed, with the entire operation to be carried out in three stages over five years. The initial stabilization period involved Commonwealth, territory, and interstate police moving into the communities with **health** workers and government officials. Military personnel provided logistical support.

A general ban was implemented in regard to the possession, consumption, transportation, and sale of **alcohol** in prescribed areas. Pornography was similarly banned, with all publicly funded computers audited and the results forwarded to the Australian Crime Commission. The legislation also gave the federal government the power to acquire five-year leaseholds over townships on **land rights** land, community living areas, and other specified districts. Although it did not affect the actual ownership, provisions were made for compensation to be paid if that was found to be necessary. The idea was to gain unlimited access to Aboriginal land and assets so that buildings could be repaired and the general infrastructure overhauled.

Stage two was intended to provide essential services where they were needed most, with the overall aim being to commit $AUD1 billion in funding over five years to completely reform the Northern Territory's remote Aboriginal communities. At the end of the stipulated period, it is expected that the emergency response teams will be withdrawn.

NUNGA. This term is used by Aborigines of South Australia to collectively identify themselves. *See also* KOORI; MURRI; NYUNGAR.

NYUNGAR. Also spelt "Nyoongah," this term is used by Aborigines of southwestern Western Australia to collectively identify themselves. *See also* KOORI; MURRI; NUNGA.

O

O'DONOGHUE, LOWITJA ("LOIS") (1932–). Indigenous advocate. Born in Indulkana, South Australia, Lowitja O'Donoghue is a member of the Yankunjatjara people. She grew up during the era of the **assimilation policy**, and at the age of two, she was taken into care away from her mother. She was later taken to the Colebrook Home for Half Caste Children, where missionaries sought to Christianize Aboriginal children. She fought racism and discrimination to become the first Aboriginal nurse in South Australia. Throughout her early years, she was encouraged by the **protector** of Aborigines to apply for exemption from the application of protectionist legislation and obtain what was colloquially and disparagingly known as a **dog tag**. O'Donoghue refused to do so. In 1967, she joined the Department of Aboriginal Affairs, rising to become its regional director in South Australia in 1975.

In 1976, she was the first Aboriginal **woman** to become a Member of the Order of Australia (AM). She became a Commander of the Order of the British Empire (CBE) in 1982 and, in 1984, was named Australian of the Year. She was a member of the Aboriginal negotiation team that negotiated with the federal government to establish the Commonwealth **Native Title** Act 1993. She was the inaugural and respected chairperson of the **Aboriginal and Torres Strait Islanders Commission** from 1990 to 1996. In 1998, she was named one of Australia's Living National Treasures, and in 1999, she was awarded the Companion of the Order of Australia (AC) for her public service to, and leadership of, Indigenous and non-Indigenous people in the area of human rights and social justice.

OLGAS, THE. *See* ULURU.

ONE PEOPLE OF AUSTRALIAN LEAGUE. *See* BONNER, NEVILLE.

ONUS, LIN (1948–96). Artist. Lin Onus was one of Australia's foremost artists, working in both sculpture and painting. Based in Melbourne, Onus left school at 14 and worked as a carver in his father's business (Aboriginal Enterprises), which sold an array of arts and crafts, including **boomerang**s and some of Onus's early paintings. He also worked as a panel beater and mechanic. First drawing inspiration from a number of Aboriginal and non-Aboriginal artists, in 1986, Onus established enduring relationships with a number of traditional artists in central northern **Arnhem Land**, an association that profoundly influenced his artwork. He exhibited both in Australia and overseas, and his artwork is represented in the major public galleries. *See also* ART.

ORAL HISTORY. As the source of much historical data pertaining to Aboriginal subjects, oral history comprises the information contained in stories that have been transmitted from generation to generation. Because there are few early records of Aboriginal voices in textual archives and other repositories, oral history is sometimes the only avenue to Aboriginal perspectives. From the 1970s, many historians have turned to Aboriginal testimony as a way of including Aboriginal voices, particularly in respect to revealing Aboriginal agency in Aboriginal–settler contact history. Many Aborigines argue that oral histories reveal truths that are elided in archive-based historical analysis. Yet oral histories, too, are contingent and can similarly reflect contemporary concerns, needs, and interests. Nevertheless, oral histories have contributed greatly to our understanding of Aboriginal Australia and the history of Aboriginal–settler contact.

O'SHANE, PATRICIA (PAT) (1941–). Controversial barrister, magistrate, and Aboriginal spokesperson, Patricia (Pat) O'Shane was born into poor circumstances at Mossman, northern Queensland, in 1941. Her father was of Irish descent and her mother an Aboriginal woman. Educated at Cairns, O'Shane won a teacher's scholarship and, after completing her studies in Brisbane, returned to Cairns where she worked as a secondary school teacher. In 1973, however, she received a Commonwealth grant to study law at the University of New South Wales. O'Shane graduated in 1975 and became a barrister the following year. From 1981 to 1986, she served as permanent head of the New South Wales Department of Aboriginal Affairs. Appointed a magistrate in 1986, O'Shane's subsequent legal career has been marked by a number of controversial decisions. On the other hand, she has worked tirelessly to assist **women** and young Aboriginal people and has played a prominent role in debates on Aboriginal issues. Between 1993 and 2003, O'Shane was chancellor of the University of New England, and in 1998, she was named by the National Trust as one of Australia's Living National Treasures.

OUTSTATIONS. These very small and isolated Aboriginal settlements have been created, for the most part, by kinfolk leaving larger administrative centers/communities to return to live on their traditional lands. Starting in the late

1960s, the movement gathered apace throughout the 1970s and 1980s. There were numerous reasons for this. Many of the larger communities have a suite of problems arising from a complex mix of impoverishment, reliance on welfare, and historical injustices, among other problems. **Alcohol**ism, domestic violence, unemployment, poor educational standards, inadequate **housing**, and very poor **health** are some of the disadvantages and social dysfunction characteristic of Aboriginal communities. Many Aborigines wanted to escape these conditions and live on their traditional lands or lands otherwise of significance. Some sought a more autonomous existence, with less day-to-day intervention in their lives. Some wished to practice more traditional forms of living not possible in large communities. Others sought to return to their homelands so as to care for their country in the proper way, ensuring its appropriate spiritual and physical management.

While initially supported by governments, who aided this movement by providing water bores and other facilities, a number of serious problems threaten their ongoing viability. There is limited access to **education**, employment, medical assistance, and the benefits of participating more fully in the broader community. Additionally, the outstations are expensive to maintain. *See also* PAPUNYA TULA.

P

PAGE, WALTER. *See* FERGUSON, WILLIAM.

PALAWA KANI LANGUAGES PROGRAM. *See* LANGUAGE.

PALM ISLAND. *See* ROYAL COMMISSION INTO ABORIGINAL DEATHS IN CUSTODY (RCIADIC).

PAPUNYA TULA. This small hill and important honey ant **Dreaming** site is situated beside the Aboriginal community of Papunya, a small government-established township (1959) approximately 241 kilometers northwest of Alice Springs in central Australia. It was here that the renowned Western Desert acrylic **art** movement arose, before extending across central Australia and beyond. In 1972, the Papunya artists formed their own company, Papunya Tula Artists. Papunya Tula is also the name used to describe the distinctive **Western Desert art** movement (in which there are a number of different "schools").

The catalyst for what became the Western Desert art movement occurred in 1971 when Aboriginal elders expressed a desire to commit their Dreamings to paint. An art and craft teacher at the local school, Geoffrey Bardon, provided encouragement and assistance. The first paintings appeared as murals on the school walls, including a honey ant Dreaming mural. The work attracted more artists, and soon paintings were being produced on any available surface, including tiles, boards, discarded packing boxes, and the like. With limited available funds, Bardon purchased boards and paints so as to enable the artists to continue their work.

This early work, though often innovative, was steeped in the traditions, imagery, and symbolism associated with the Dreaming and with country. Symbols used in ground sculptures and body designs and those incised in tools and ritual paraphernalia were incorporated into the paintings. Many paintings served as maps, indicating the path and passage of **ancestral beings** and their various activities. Together, the paintings served to reinvigorate traditions that were under enormous pressure. As the **outstation** movement gathered impetus, a number of artists returned to their traditional country to live and paint, extending the reach and influence of what was to become a most significant contemporary art movement. While Western Desert art is now recognized internationally and its leading artists are dynamic and innovative, it continues to be informed by cultural heritage and traditions. It is from this region that the so-called **dot paintings** originate. *See also* KNGWARREYE, EMILY KAME; TJAPALTJARRI, CLIFFORD POSSUM.

PATTEN, JOHN (JACK) (1905–57). Indigenous activist. Jack Patten was born at Moama, New South Wales, in 1905. After receiving an elementary **education**, he worked at laboring jobs, supplementing his income by boxing. Settling near Sydney in 1930, Patten began organizing Aboriginal political groups along the New South Wales coast. In 1937, he began receiving assistance from P. R. Stephensen, a nationalist publicist and leader of the neofascist Australia First Movement. Patten also impressed **William Ferguson**, who made him president of the Aborigines Progressive Association (APA), which vigorously protested against the policies of the government's Aborigines Protection Board.

Patten assisted Ferguson in organizing the **Day of Mourning** in January 1938 and, shortly afterwards, headed the deputation that met with Prime Minister Joseph Lyons in an unsuccessful bid to improve the conditions of the Aboriginal people. Again with Stephensen's support, Patten founded and edited a short-lived Aboriginal journal, the *Australian Abo Call*, editorial comments in which led to a disagreement with Ferguson and a split in the APA. In 1939, Patten attempted to assist relatives living on the Cummeragunja Aboriginal reserve in southern New South Wales and was expelled by the European manager. This resulted in many of the residents leaving the reserve which, in turn, led to Patten's arrest. He was bailed by Stephensen and bound over to keep the peace.

Patten and Ferguson finally reconciled their differences at an APA conference held in Dubbo, New South Wales, in January 1940. The following month, Patten enlisted in the Second Australian Imperial Force and saw action in the Middle East as a member of the 6th Division. He was discharged in April 1942 after suffering a serious knee wound and spent the remainder of the war years working in the Civil Construction Corps in the Northern Territory. Settling in Melbourne in 1946, Patten worked in a number of clerical positions while undertaking voluntary work for the **Australian Aborigines' League**. He died in October 1957 from injuries sustained in a motor vehicle accident. *See also* ABORIGINAL PROTECTION BOARDS.

PEARSON, NOEL (1965–). Indigenous lawyer and activist. Born in Cooktown in northern Queensland, Noel Pearson grew up on the Lutheran

mission at Hopevale on southern **Cape York** Peninsula. After completing primary school, he boarded at the prestigious St. Peters College in Brisbane and later graduated from the University of Sydney with a degree in history and law. Until the late 1990s, he was active in **land rights** campaigns, playing a key role in negotiations that resulted in the 1993 Commonwealth Native Title Act. In 1990, Pearson cofounded the Cape York Land Council, and in 2004, he became director of the **Cape York Institute for Policy and Leadership**. With support from both the Commonwealth and Queensland governments, Pearson implemented a number of controversial social reforms in Cape York Aboriginal communities aimed at ending the welfare dependence of Aboriginal people, promoting economic self-sufficiency, and improving school attendance rates. An eloquent speaker, Pearson has also published widely on Aboriginal issues. In April 2009, he briefly stepped down from his directorship to challenge the Queensland government's Wild Rivers Act, which Pearson believed would stifle Aboriginal economic development on Cape York.

PEMULWUY (?–1802). First identified Indigenous resistance fighter. Pemulwuy (also spelt Pemulwoy) was probably born in the Botany Bay district immediately south of Sydney, New South Wales. He first came to the notice of British settlers in December 1790, after he fatally speared Governor Arthur Phillip's gamekeeper, John McIntyre, in retribution for past offenses committed against local Aboriginal people. From 1792, Pemulwuy organized a series of raids on British farms and settlements on the western outskirts of Sydney. In 1797, he was wounded and captured, but he managed to escape from the hospital and resumed his campaign against the settlers. In November 1801, Governor Philip Gidley King proclaimed Pemulwuy an outlaw and offered a reward for his capture dead or alive. He was shot dead in June 1802, and his severed head was sent to England, where it remains. Pemulwuy's son, Tedbury, continued to oppose the British settlers until his own violent death in 1810.

PEOPLE'S WALK FOR RECONCILIATION. *See* NATIONAL SORRY DAY.

PERKINS, CHARLES NELSON (1936–2000). Indigenous sportsman, activist, and government bureaucrat. Born in Alice Springs in the Northern Territory, Charles Perkins was of Arrernte and Kalkadoon descent. He was educated in Alice Springs, Adelaide, and Sydney and became the first Indigenous Australian to be awarded a university degree, after completing a bachelor of arts in 1965.

A talented soccer player, Perkins began his sporting career at Adelaide in 1950 before making his way to England in 1957, where he played first-grade soccer with the Everton and Wigan football clubs. Returning to Australia in 1959, Perkins continued to play first-grade soccer with clubs in Adelaide and Sydney until his retirement from **sport** in 1965.

Perkins first came to national attention in February 1965 after co-organizing the **Freedom Ride**, which exposed widespread discrimination against Aborigines in northern New South Wales. Later the same year, he became manager of the Foundation for Aboriginal Affairs, a position he relinquished four years later when he moved to Canberra and joined the federal government's Office of Aboriginal Affairs.

In the early 1970s, Perkins played a key role in establishing the National Aboriginal Consultative Committee (*see* FEDERAL COUNCIL FOR THE ADVANCEMENT OF ABORIGINES AND TORRES STRAIT ISLANDERS), and in 1981, he was appointed chairperson of the newly formed Aboriginal Development Commission. In 1984, Perkins was appointed secretary of the Department of Aboriginal Affairs, at that time, the highest official position held by an Aboriginal person. He remained with the department for almost four years, during which time he became increasingly outspoken in his condemnation of government policies. Resigning from the public service in 1989, Perkins served as chairperson of the Arrernte Council of central Australia in his hometown of Alice Springs. Before his death from kidney failure in October 2000, concerns had been raised about the legality of his private business dealings, a shadowy affair that did not prevent Perkins from being accorded a state funeral in Sydney.

PETROGLYPHS. *See* ENGRAVINGS.

PIGEON. *See* JANDAMARRA.

PILKINGTON, DORIS. *See* FILM.

PLOMLEY, BRIAN. *See* FRIENDLY MISSION.

POPULATION. *See* DEMOGRAPHICS.

PROTECTORS. Beginning with Governor Lachlan Macquarie's 1814 Native Institution at Parramatta in New South Wales, run by former missionary William Shelley, the use of individual officials to oversee government policies aimed at institutionalizing, segregating, and controling the Aboriginal population was steadily strengthened during the 19th and 20th centuries. One of the first official protectors was George Augustus Robinson, whose superintendence of exiled **Tasmanian Aborigines** at **Wybalenna** on Flinders Island in Bass Strait between 1835 and 1839 was an abject failure. Robinson fared little better in Victoria, where he served as chief protector of Aborigines from 1839 to 1849.

Nor did the appointment of William Moorhouse as protector of Aborigines in South Australia in 1836 improve the plight of Aboriginal people in that colony, as European settlement rapidly overwhelmed them on distant frontiers. In 1832, there was little pretense of humanitarian concern in Western Australia, where Lieutenant Governor James Stirling merged the duties of the superintendent of Aborigines with the Mounted Police, whose primary task was to destroy Aboriginal opposition.

A major turning point in the role of official protectors came in 1897, when Queensland passed the Aboriginals Protection and Restriction of the Sale of Opium Act—legislation that became the blueprint for acts subsequently passed in Western Australia, South Australia, and, later, the Northern Territory. Heavily influenced by Archibald Meston, a self-proclaimed authority on Aborigines, the Queensland legislation gave the government power to physically remove Aboriginal people to centralized reserves, where their lives were rigidly controlled by subordinate protectors. Queensland initially appointed two senior protectors owing to its geographic size: Meston in the south and a medical practitioner and ethnologist, Walter Roth, in the north. Notwithstanding the abolition of his position when Roth was appointed Chief Protector of Aborigines in 1904, Meston defined the future role of protectors with his insistence on having complete authority over the lives of his charges.

With subsequent legislative amendments, Aborigines were stripped of all basic civil and legal rights, their situation exacerbated by the lengthy terms of powerful protectors who were heavily influenced by either eugenicist or progressivist beliefs. John Bleakley served as Queensland's chief protector of Aborigines from 1914 to 1942, though there was a subtle title change in 1939, when he was officially designated director of Native affairs. Auber Octavius Neville was Western Australia's chief protector of Aborigines from 1915 to 1940, during which time he conducted a strict policy of removing part-Aboriginal children to institutions. Similar, though slightly more benign, policies were implemented in the Northern Territory, where the chief medical officer, Cecil Cook, was also appointed chief protector of Aborigines in 1927. While harsh government policies were to continue until as late as the 1980s in Queensland, the supreme authority of individual protectors had largely been eroded throughout Australia by the mid-1960s.

PUKUMANI POLES. The most distinctive creative expression of the **Tiwi**, *pukumani* poles are named after the *pukumani* ceremony, a component of the Tiwi mortuary rituals. The ceremony commemorates the deceased subject's life. Following a death and during an extended period of mourning, relatives of the deceased commission the manufacture of tall ironwood grave posts that are sculpted and painted. These posts invigorate the ancestral story concerning the coming of death to the Tiwi. Figures, prongs, and birds are sometimes sculpted at the top of the post. Figures represent the **ancestral beings** associated with the *pukumani* story; forks or prongs, the clubs used by the two protagonists in the fight that precipitated the ceremony; and birds, the birdlife present at the inaugural funeral ceremony. The posts can take weeks or even months to complete. A year or so after the deceased's death, they are stood around the grave. It is then that the full *pukumani* ceremony begins. At the end of the period of mourning, the posts are left to tumble and rot away.

As with much Aboriginal ceremonial and ritual **art**, *pukumani* poles have now entered the fine art market, are represented in major national art galleries, and are manufactured for sale and collection. *See also* BURIAL.

R

RAMINGINING DANCE GROUP. *See* GULPILIL, DAVID.

RAWLINGS, WILLIAM. *See* MILITARY SERVICE.

RECONCILIATION. This term is applied to the journey of healing through an acknowledgment of past injustices experienced by Indigenous people, understanding how these continue to impact upon their lives, and recognizing the necessity of redressing the disadvantages and injustices Indigenous people continue to experience. Reconciliation involves both symbolic reconciliation, such as a national apology to the **Stolen Generations**, and practical reconciliation, such as remedying infrastructure problems like inadequate **housing**. *See also* COUNCIL FOR ABORIGINAL RECONCILIATION (CAR); NATIONAL SORRY DAY.

RECONCILIATION AUSTRALIA. *See* COUNCIL FOR ABORIGINAL RECONCILIATION (CAR); RECONCILIATION.

REFERENDUM 1967. On 27 May 1967, a national referendum was held to alter two clauses concerning Aborigines in the Australian Constitution, resulting not only in a rare vote for change through a referendum but also in the highest "yes" vote for change ever recorded (90.77 percent). (Because the changes sought enjoyed majority support among all federal parliamentarians, a "no" case was not officially presented during the campaign.)

The referendum related to sections 51 and 127 of the Constitution, which before the referendum, read as follows:

> 51. The Parliament shall, subject to this Constitution, have power to make laws for the peace, order, and good government of the Commonwealth with respect to:-
> (xxvi) The people of any race, other than the aboriginal people in any State, for whom it is necessary to make special laws.
> 127. In reckoning the numbers of the people of the Commonwealth, or of a State or other part of the Commonwealth, aboriginal natives should not be counted.

The referendum secured the removal of the phrase "other than the aboriginal people in any State" from section 51 and the deletion of section 127. These changes enabled the Commonwealth to pass "special laws" for Aborigines. While it was possible for the Commonwealth to wield considerable influence in Aboriginal affairs under other sections of the Constitution, it was hoped that amending section 51 would facilitate a greater Commonwealth role in the management of Aboriginal affairs. The deletion of section 127 allowed for Aborigines to be counted in national censuses.

The 1967 referendum is popularly remembered and celebrated for enacting changes that in a formal sense it did not make. It is widely regarded as heralding Aboriginal enfranchisement, both in terms of giving Aborigines the right to vote and granting them citizenship, among other matters. Aborigines, however, were already enfranchised. Nevertheless, national advocacy for the "yes" vote, and the nature of this advocacy in respect to focusing on rights, alerted many Aborigines and settlers to these issues. Hence, in a practical sense, the referendum facilitated changes that, in a formal sense, it did not enact.

RELIGION. The early European observers of Aboriginal societies following colonization in 1788 and subsequent settlement were ill-prepared to find religion revealed in the corpus of Aboriginal beliefs and myths. At the most basic level, the familiar theistic structures and personnel appeared absent. There were no apparent religious edifices—imposing or otherwise—and no obvious priestly or pastoral role or an equivalent. In the late 19th century, attempting to trace the evolution of humankind's major social institutions, the nascent discipline of anthropology found in Aboriginal societies what they conjectured to be earlier, less developed institutional forms. In respect to religion, whereas the Western world was in the process of moving from a religious phase to the realm of science, Aborigines had not yet made the transition from magic to religion. At best, customary practices, not religion, bound Aborigines. This understanding persisted until the late 19th to early 20th century, at which point it was rapidly revised, and the richness and complexity of Aboriginal spiritual and sacred life began to be acknowledged.

One of the first attempts to include Aboriginal beliefs in the category of religion assumed they were a form of animism. This was based on increasing knowledge of the **Dreaming**, in which animate and inanimate forms harbor the spiritual essence of the creator **ancestral beings**. Others postulated that totemism described the nature of Aboriginal religions. **Totems** were common across Australia. Although they took a plethora of forms and their significance and deployment varied from the mundane to the spiritually profound, they did serve to bind social groupings and natural species and link both to the spiritual realm. However, neither animism nor totemism adequately describes Aboriginal religions.

Aboriginal belief systems did incorporate responses to those fundamental human questions as to the nature and origin of the universe, of life, and of what happened upon death. Many Dreaming stories, either in whole or in part, address elements of these questions, as do many rituals and ceremonies that typically have nonempirical referents and are richly symbolic. The quality of sanctity was known and extensively applied. **Sacred sites**, of varying importance and significance and subject to varying controls and prohibitions, are widely distributed, and all were (some still are) attended to and cared for in ways prescribed by the ancestral beings by those appropriately ritually qualified. Although nowhere in Australia was a single all-powerful god envisaged, Aborigines of southeast Australia did believe in a sky god called Baiame, who had created the earth and culture and who still announced his presence through thunder. In Tasmania, the creator spirit and progenitor of humankind was an ancestral kangaroo known as Tarner. It needs to be noted that in southern Australia, including Tasmania, the rate of dispossession and the destruction of Aboriginal societies was so rapid that much ethnographic information was lost, and hence, a great deal of knowledge is fragmentary. However, throughout Australia, the corpus of Aboriginal beliefs was engaged in the ontological quest that is a characteristic of religion, and through the fruits of that quest, Aborigines articulated their underpinning reality.

Today, very few Aborigines report adherence to a traditional Aboriginal religion. In the 2006 census, it was 1 percent only. In the remote regions of Australia, it was 6 percent but less than 1 percent everywhere else. Many, however, describe themselves as Christian and reported their affiliation with Christianity in the census (in 2006, this was 73 percent, comprising one-third Catholic and one-third Anglican). This does not necessarily mean an abandonment of traditional beliefs. Individuals are able to rationalize in ways that make compatible the elements of traditional beliefs they hold and their Christian faith. There are a number of Aboriginal ministers and lay preachers of various denominations. There are also a very few Aboriginal Muslims. Some, like the boxer Anthony Mundine, are relatively recent converts, but others trace their Muslim faith through several generations. In the second half of the 19th century, a number of individuals and groups of Islamic faith from what are now India, Afghanistan, and Pakistan came to Australia as cameleers. Known as "Afghans," they played a crucial role in the exploration and infrastructure development of the arid interior, as well as transporting mail and essential supplies to those living in the region. They enjoyed mostly cordial relations with the Aborigines they encountered, with some marrying Aboriginal **women**. *See also* DEATH; MISSIONS.

REPORT OF THE NATIONAL INQUIRY INTO THE SEPARATION OF ABORIGINAL AND TORRES STRAIT ISLANDER CHILDREN FROM THEIR FAMILIES. *See BRINGING THEM HOME.*

RESERVES. *See* GOVERNMENT RESERVES.

ROACH, ARCHIBALD (ARCHIE) (1955–). Singer-songwriter. Born at Mooroopna in northern Victoria in 1955, Archie Roach has been described as Australia's first true soul singer. Roach and his siblings were forcibly removed from their parents, and he grew up in government institutions and foster homes. At the age of 14, he ran away to Sydney in search of a lost sister, only to end up living on the streets and becoming addicted to **alcohol**. For years, he drifted aimlessly, spending time in Melbourne and Adelaide, where he met his future partner, **Ruby Hunter**. A few years after Hunter joined Roach in Melbourne, the pair underwent rehabilitation for their alcoholism and worked as counselors before forming a band in the late 1980s. Encouraged by singer-songwriter Paul Kelly, Roach recorded a solo album, *Charcoal Lane*, in 1990, that received two Australian Record Industry Association awards. A single from the album, "Took the Children Away," also received the inaugural Human Rights Achievement Award in 1991. More albums followed in 1993, 1997, and 2002, by which time Roach was firmly established on the Australian **music** scene and recognized internationally.

ROBINSON, GEORGE AUGUSTUS. *See* ABORIGINAL MEDIA; BLACK LINE; FRIENDLY MISSION; PROTECTORS; TASMANIAN ABORIGINES; TRUGANINI; WYBALENNA.

ROCK ART. *See* ART.

ROSE, LIONEL (1948–). Sportsman. The first Aboriginal boxer to win a world title, Lionel Rose was born in Victoria at Jackson's Track near Drouin, east of Melbourne. The son of a professional boxer, he won the Australian amateur flyweight title in 1963, before turning professional and defeating Noel Kunde for the Australian Bantamweight crown in 1966. He successfully defended the title nine times, before challenging Japanese boxer, Fighting Harada, for the world bantamweight title in Tokyo on 26 February 1968. Rose won the 15-round bout on points and became an overnight celebrity in Australia. He was named Australian of the Year, was appointed a Member of the Order of the British Empire (MBE), and became an inspiration to young Aboriginal people across the continent.

Rose successfully defended his title three times, before being defeated by Ruben Olivares at Inglewood, California, in August 1969. Moving into the lightweight division, his performances were mediocre until October 1970, when he defeated future world champion Itshimatsu Suzuki. In May 1971, Rose lost on points to Yoshiaki Munata for the world lightweight title and announced his retirement. He briefly returned to the ring in 1975, but after losing four of his next six fights, he retired permanently to concentrate on his business interests. During his entire boxing career, Rose had 64 fights for 53 wins (12 by knockout) and 11 losses. *See also* SPORT.

ROYAL COMMISSION INTO ABORIGINAL DEATHS IN CUSTODY (RCIADIC). In October 1987, the RCIADIC was formally established to investigate whether a disproportionate number of Aborigines and Torres Strait Islanders were dying in police custody and whether there were any precipitating social, cultural, and/or legal factors. It was also to examine how any recent Indigenous deaths in custody had in fact occurred. The commission examined 99 deaths that had occurred between 1 January 1980 and 31 May 1989. A **death** in custody is defined broadly and includes a death that takes place in prison, police custody, or detention; a death that takes place when an individual is detained or attempting to be detained by police or prison officers; or a death that takes place when an individual is escaping or attempting to escape police, prison, custody, or juvenile detention.

The commission produced a number of reports, including an individual report for each death in custody it investigated. Its final report was tabled with federal, state, and territory governments on 15 April 1991. It concluded that the overrepresentation of Indigenous people in the criminal justice system explained, in part, the disproportionate number of Indigenous deaths in custody. It found there was no evidence to suggest that deaths had resulted from deliberate violence or brutality by police and prison officers. The report did find, however, that police and prison officers did not properly understand the duty of care owed to those in their care and that a complex set of exacerbating factors contributed to the occurrence of deaths in custody. In order to address these concerns, the commission made 339 recommendations, many of which remain unimplemented. Nevertheless, in 1992, in accordance with one of the commission's recommendations, the Australian Institute of Criminology's National Death in Custody Program was established to monitor and report on all deaths in custody.

The issue of Aboriginal deaths in custody reemerged in 2004 with the death of Mulrunji Doomadgee (also known as Cameron Doomadgee) while in police custody on Palm Island, Queensland. He was arrested for creating a public nuisance and being intoxicated. Doomadgee died shortly after being detained. The arresting officer was later tried for manslaughter and found not guilty. On 11 July 2007, it was announced that the Palm Island watch-house would be among the first to receive a closed-circuit television facility upgrade.

RUGBY LEAGUE. *See* SPORT.

RUGBY UNION. *See* SPORT.

S

SACRED SITE. One's country, and all topographical features, is held to have been formed or created by **ancestral beings** and their activities. The ancestral beings remain present, though usually not in the form or forms they appeared in during the period of creation. Their power and essences continue to resonate throughout the landscape. In certain places, for example, the intersecting tracks of different ancestral beings, or particular sites where a significant event happened in the **Dreaming**, are held to be of crucial importance. Many such sites are deemed sacred. A range of prohibitions can attend such sites. **Women** and children might be banned from approaching, or if it is a women's site, men might be subject to prohibition. Some sites have an additional restriction in that they are secret. Knowledge of them and their significance is restricted to a select few of appropriate initiatory and **kinship** status. Other sites are publicly revealed and open to approach by all. Frequently, sacred sites need maintaining, whether by ceremony and song from afar or through physically tending to the site or both. The function of a site, and its maintenance, can serve a variety of purposes.

Knowledge of *sacred sites*, and evidence of their continuing maintenance and influence, is one way that **land rights** and **native title** claimants can demonstrate their traditional and unbroken connection to country and their exercise of primary spiritual responsibility for it.

The term *sacred site* is being applied more widely today than it was in the past. Sociohistorical association with place, even when not within a people's former or current traditional lands, is sufficient reason for that place to be referred to as sacred. This is particularly so when a specific place (for example, somewhere to which Aborigines were forcibly moved) has been a site of great hardship, illness, and **death** and harbors the graves of those who died. *See also* RELIGION.

SAUNDERS, REGINALD (REG) WALTER (1920–90). Indigenous soldier. The first Aborigine to be commissioned as an officer in the Australian Army, Reg Saunders was born at the Framlingham Aboriginal Reserve in Victoria. His father, Chris, was a veteran soldier of World War I. Following the **death** of his mother when Saunders was four years of age, he and his younger brother Harry were largely raised by their grandmother at Lake Condah. After an elementary **education**, Reg and Harry Saunders left school to establish their own timber-cutting business in the aftermath of the disastrous 1939 Victorian bushfires.

Both brothers enlisted in the Australian Army in April 1940, with Reg Saunders joining the 6th Division in Palestine, where he was promoted to sergeant. He saw action in Greece and Crete, from where he was evacuated 11 months after the German occupation. Recalled to Australia when Japan entered the war, Reg Saunders underwent jungle training before being sent to Papua New Guinea, where he fought in the Salamaua-Lae campaign. Harry Saunders was killed in the fighting around Gona. In early 1944, Reg Saunders was commissioned as a lieutenant, a precedent that required the personal endorsement of Australian Commander-in-Chief General (later Field Marshal) Thomas Blamey. Returning to Papua New Guinea, Saunders commanded a platoon in the Aitape-Wewak area.

Despite volunteering for service in Japan with the British Commonwealth Occupation Forces, Saunders was discharged from the army in October 1945. He spent almost five years working as a shipping clerk and builder's laborer before reenlisting with the outbreak of the Korean War in 1950. Saunders took part in a number of major actions and was promoted to captain, but after returning to Australia when a truce was declared in 1953, he became dissatisfied with routine training and was discharged the following year.

Saunders briefly returned to the timber industry in Victoria before moving to Sydney. Due to his high profile, he was appointed a liaison and public relations officer in the Office of Aboriginal Affairs in 1967 and, four years later, was honored as a Member of the Order of the British Empire (MBE) in recognition of his work in the community. Saunders died in March 1990. *See also* MILITARY SERVICE.

SAVE THE ABORIGINES COMMITTEE. *See* ABORIGINES ADVANCEMENT LEAGUE (AAL).

SCOTT, KIM (1957–). Indigenous writer. An award-winning novelist of the **Nyungar** people, Kim Scott is best known for *Benang: From the Heart* (1999), which won the prestigious Miles Franklin Award in 2000, and his first novel, *True Country* (1993). Scott was formerly a teacher. *See also* LITERATURE.

SECRETARIAT OF NATIONAL ABORIGINAL AND ISLANDER CHILD CARE (SNAICC). *See* ABORIGINAL AND ISLANDER CHILD CARE AGENCY (AICCA).

SECRET WOMEN'S BUSINESS. *See* HINDMARSH ISLAND.

SEGREGATION. Notwithstanding a number of failed attempts to assimilate Aboriginal people during the first half of the 19th century, their dramatic **demographic** collapse appeared to confirm the widely held view among Europeans that the Aborigines were doomed to extinction. By the mid-19th century, government intervention was, therefore, largely limited to the provision of rations to the young, the aged, and infirm. By the final decades of the 19th century, however, it was becoming increasingly apparent that rather than heading rapidly toward extinction, the Aboriginal population was beginning to undergo a resurgence.

Ostensibly to avoid the harmful influences of Europeans, Queensland became the first colony in Australia to implement a policy of segregation in 1897, which, *inter alia*, resulted in the establishment of centralized reserves where Aborigines could be forcibly removed on the slightest pretext. It is clear that the majority of Aboriginal people removed to reserves were those who were no longer able to contribute economically, particularly to the pastoral industry. Protectors were granted enormous powers over their charges. Under their direction, Aborigines could be transferred from one reserve to another, and under a myriad of draconian rules and regulations, the Aboriginal people became totally dependent on reserve superintendents. They required permission to marry and to temporarily leave the reserve. They lost any property they had acquired, and all written communication to or from the reserve was censored. Many reserves established their own courts, with punishments being inflicted for the most trivial offenses. These policies were adopted in all other areas of Australia except Tasmania, where authorities refused to accept that the descendants of the original inhabitants were Aborigines. Segregation effectively prevented Aboriginal people from achieving any measure of independence, and it was not until the shift toward **assimilation** from the 1930s that their basic human rights slowly began to be restored. *See also* FREEDOM RIDE; GOVERNMENT RESERVES.

SELF-DETERMINATION. This policy was introduced by the federal Labor government in 1972, when Indigenous peoples were increasingly vocal in their demands not only to have the right to implement policies that impacted upon them but also the right to make and shape policy. Under the policy, there was a rapid burgeoning of Indigenous institutions, organizations, and services, including the **Aboriginal Health Service** and the **Aboriginal Legal Service**. *See also* ASSIMILATION POLICY; PROTECTORS; SELF-MANAGEMENT.

SELF-MANAGEMENT. Indigenous Australians are yet to realize **self-determination** in its broadest sense. Governments have been reluctant to cede full decision-making powers to Aborigines. Instead, varying degrees of self-management, usually under the auspices of broader legislation and auditing requirements, is the extent of granted authority. Nevertheless, considerable autonomy has been achieved under self-management, with a range of institutions and organizations managing their programs and constituencies and some communities enjoying a high level of autonomy, with the devolution of authority to local decision-making councils. The **Northern Territory Emergency Response**, for which the Racial Discrimination Act 1975 was suspended, demonstrated the limits of Indigenous autonomy. *See also* ASSIMILATION POLICY; PROTECTORS.

SMALLPOX. Aboriginal people in southeastern Australia were exposed to two catastrophic epidemics of smallpox: in 1789 and 1828–29. The first outbreak, in Sydney in April 1789, has never been satisfactorily explained. A number of historians have contended that smallpox may have been introduced by the **Macassans** and spread south. Others have suggested that it emanated from the "variolous matter" carried on the First Fleet in 1788 as a precaution against smallpox infection. It is believed that this first outbreak spread as far north as southeastern Queensland, south to the present site of Melbourne, and west to Adelaide. The **death** toll was almost certainly considerable. The second major outbreak occurred in 1828, when ineffective quarantine measures were undertaken following the arrival in Sydney of an infected convict transport, the *Bussorah Merchant*. From the accounts of European settlers, it appears that this epidemic was no less devastating across a wide swath of southeastern Australia. Later in the century, further outbreaks of smallpox occurred in northern, western, and central Australia, with largely unknown consequences for the Aboriginal people. *See also* HEALTH.

SOCCER. *See* PERKINS, CHARLES; SPORT.

SOCIAL ORGANIZATION. The rules and strictures governing Aboriginal social organization were left by the **ancestral beings** in the **Dreaming**. They determined the patterns to be followed by all Aborigines forever more. And the major structural social force in Aboriginal societies was the **kinship** system. This system cleaved Aboriginal **tribe**s into two fundamental exogamous halves. Most Aboriginal societies further organized their social groupings into a number of additional (mainly endogamous) divisions, based on descent, gender, and age groupings (generations). Through the complex assignation of social **identity**, an individual was brought into relationship with everyone else in a particular society, and the nature of that relationship determined the quality and type of relations possible with every other individual and what responsibilities one carried. For example, who one could marry, with whom one could enjoy a relaxed or more circumspect relationship, who one was to avoid (typically a mother- or son-in-law, among others), what role one was to play in **initiation** rites, and to whom one was obligated and in what ways, among much else. Given that one's social status and category were all determining in respect to relations with everyone else, Aboriginal societies traditionally had no capacity for accommodating an alien in their midst. Instead, a long-term visitor would be assigned a position within the kinship system and a social category, and he or she would be expected to adhere to the social behaviors inherent in his or her newly acquired status. Any breach of expected behavior aligned with one's social category attracted sanction, mild or harsh depending on the nature of the breach, except in the very young where innocent mistakes were usually indulged tolerantly. This quality of relatedness governed an individual's social behavior and etiquette throughout his or her entire life.

The sexes also formed a major organizational division in Aboriginal societies. Women's and men's labor were oriented to different tasks, with **women** responsible for the majority of sustenance through gathering flora, such as fruits, nuts, and tubers, and collecting smaller game, and men responsible for hunting the less reliably obtained larger animals. Women's and men's ceremonial and ritual lives were distinctive though mostly complementary, but it was the men who held the most sacred knowledge, which they kept secret from women and children.

Age, too, conferred status, with older men and women having authority and rights over those younger, and older, fully initiated men generally had some authority over all women. Although there were no chiefdoms, chiefs, "bigmen," or nobles with vested power, and the organizational social structure as mediated through the kinship system and assigned social categories was very flat, leading to observations that Aboriginal societies were egalitarian, hierarchies based on age and sex were sturdy. The apparent authority of the older, fully initiated men and the deference in which they were held led to an understanding that governance in Aboriginal societies was exercised through a council of male elders, or headmen. However, ultimate authority was the Dreaming and the laws laid down by the ancestral beings. The old men's authority was circumscribed, not all encompassing. It could only be exercised over those areas for which they had responsibility, as determined by place of birth, position in the kinship system, and social category. Their prominence was most evident in the production of ceremonies in which they had primary responsibility and for which they were the holders of religious esotery.

Different ceremonies, or even the same ceremony where different roles were assigned, would privilege the authority of different elders. There was no council of elders exercising overarching political authority.

Occasionally, senior men and women would exercise authority in areas beyond the religious domain, but again, that authority would be circumscribed by the boundaries of the country to which they were affiliated. For example, in some societies, any serious breach of law would attract the interest of elders. For the most part, disputes and grievances were settled locally and publicly, and it would involve both the aggrieved and the accused and often their kin. The number of individuals involved and who depended on the severity of the dispute. The aim was not to find fault but to come to a resolution that ensured harmony prevailed. Some quarrels were settled through elaborate, cathartic, carefully choreographed ceremonies, with the roles of "punisher" and "punished" alternating each performance. There was no separate agency or personnel assigned the role of law enforcement.

Another common organizational form was the division of rights and responsibilities through patrilineal and matrilineal descent. This division created a system of "owners" (the *patriclan*) and "managers" (the *matriclan*). Owners enjoyed primary spiritual responsibility for the land to which they were affiliated, but this responsibility could only be exercised with the aid and guidance of the managers, who ensured, among other duties and obligations, its proper discharge. For example, they ensured **sacred sites** were maintained, that ceremonies and rituals were performed correctly, and that symbols and motifs were used appropriately. For different tracts of country, the role of owners and managers would be reversed.

The family, comprising a father and one or more wives and children, was at the heart of social and economic organization of Aboriginal societies. If conditions allowed, however, the tendency was for a number of families to form a band that lived, hunted, gathered, and moved as a group, waxing and waning according to conditions and whim. These constellations were remarkably fluid. Bands were subsidiaries of a larger land-owning collective, now usually known as clans. A clan held primary spiritual responsibility for the land, the sacred sites it contained, and all associated mythology. Clans were a subsidiary of the much broader **language** group in any given region.

To greater or lesser extent, elements of traditional social organization exist today, with greater adherence in Australia's northern and remote regions. In all societies, there has been modification, reflecting historical and current exigencies. Nevertheless, despite a more settled life in "communities," which often house formerly disparate and sometimes disputant tribal groupings, vestiges of traditional social organization adapted to current circumstances remain, and are vigorously upheld. In southern Australia, capital cities, and large regional centers, the nuclear household is increasingly the norm, particularly when sufficient affluence affords this lifestyle. Many urban dwellers, however, retain links to their "homelands" and accept certain accompanying responsibilities.

SPEAR-THROWER. A wooden implement that has a projection peg either carved into or secured to the butt, the spear-thrower greatly increased the range and accuracy of spears hurled by Aboriginal hunters. It could also be used for a number of other purposes: as a friction stick for making fire, for digging out small animals, and as a **clapstick** during ceremonial performances.

Once widely used by Indigenous people throughout the world, the spear-thrower may have been a relatively late introduction to Australia. There is no evidence that it was used in Tasmania, on the **Tiwi Islands** off the Northern Territory coast, on the central coast of Queensland, or in certain parts of southern Queensland and northern New South Wales. In many other areas of southern Australia, it did not entirely supersede hand-thrown spears.

SPORT. Despite an obvious history of discrimination, Aborigines and **Torres Strait** Islanders have featured prominently in many fields of sporting endeavor, though it is noticeable that they have been distinctly underrepresented in the more elite sports. From the early 1860s, Aboriginal men were in demand as **cricket** players in the western districts of Victoria, and in 1868, an all-Aboriginal cricket team became the first representative side to tour England. Since then, players of the caliber of Jack Marsh, **Eddie Gilbert**, Ian King, Roger Brown, and Jack McGuire have all had distinguished first-class cricketing careers.

Aborigines have been especially notable in amateur and professional athletics, champion runners including the likes of Tom Dancey, Bobby Kinnear, Bobby McDonald (credited with inventing the crouch start), and Charles (Charlie) Samuels, who is often said to have been the greatest runner Australia has ever produced. It is a claim not to be taken lightly. In May 2003, Patrick Johnson became the first Australian runner to break the 10-second barrier for 100 meters, while on the other side of the gender divide, 400-meter specialist **Cathy Freeman** won one gold and one silver Olympic medal, two gold and one bronze World Championship medals, and four gold and one silver Commonwealth Games medals.

There has also been considerable debate as to whether an Aboriginal game played with a round ball made from possum skin may have been the origin of Australian Rules football. One thing is certain: Aboriginal players have been, and remain, well-represented in this and all other football codes.

During the 1950s and early 1960s, **Charles Perkins** played first-class soccer in Australia and England, while in 1980, Arthur Beetson, just one of many talented Aboriginal rugby league players, led Queensland to victory over New South Wales in the inaugural State of Origin competition. In rugby union, the Ella brothers, Mark, Glen, and Gary, all represented New South Wales and Australia during their careers.

It is no surprise that Aborigines have also made their mark in rural sports such as wood-chopping and rough-riding. Tasmanian-born Greg Lovell held 16 wood-chopping world titles, and in 1980, he accomplished the remarkable feat of breaking four world records in one event. Rodeo circles still revere the likes of Alec Hayden, who won the Australian saddle bronc championship in 1936, 1938, and 1939, before going on to take out the Australian bull-riding title in 1941. Hayden and his cousin Jimmy Williams also represented Australia in a tri-test against the United States and Canada.

There can be no doubt that the one sport in which Aborigines have dominated is boxing. Champion fighters still remembered among the boxing fraternity include Jerry Jerome, Elley Bennett, Alby Roberts, George Bracken, Jack Hassen, Ron Richards, Hector Thompson, and Tony Mundine. Two Aboriginal fighters, **Lionel Rose** and Anthony Mundine, have won world boxing titles, and it is quite likely that if he had not been killed in a truck accident in 1952, Dave Sands would have secured a world title. Along with Dave, all six Sands brothers held state, Australian, Australasian, and Empire boxing titles.

Aboriginal and Islander **women** have proved no less competitive than their male counterparts. When the Aboriginal and Islander Sports Hall of Fame was inaugurated in 1993, it included such female luminaries as Mabel Campbell and Edna Crouch (cricket), May Chalker (golf), Phynea Clark, Lorelle Morissey, and Nova Peris (hockey), Nicole Cusack (basketball), Marcia Ella and Sharon Finnan (netball), Kayleen Janssen and Karen Menzies (soccer), Cheryle Mullett (badminton), and **Evonne Goolagong-Cawley** (tennis).

STOLEN GENERATIONS. First coined by historian Peter Read, this term describes the removal of part-Aboriginal children from their families between the 1860s and the 1970s. Reasons for the policies implemented by Australian governments over more than a century ranged from perceived neglect to fear of miscegenation and a deliberate attempt at **assimilation**. Children were sent to government institutions and church **missions** and frequently fostered out to European families. Owing to incomplete documentation, the total number of removals may never be known, but it is believed to have been in the region of 100,000. Despite the pioneering work of Read and others, it was not until the release of the report *Bringing Them Home* in 1997 that the extent of Aboriginal child removals became widely known among the general Australian community. In the wake of the report, formal apologies for past practices were offered by the governments of Tasmania, Victoria, South Australia, the Northern Territory, and New South Wales, but it was not until 13 February 2008 that Prime Minister Kevin Rudd issued an apology on behalf of the federal government, endorsed by both houses of parliament. While compensation remains a contentious issue, in 2006, the Tasmanian state government set aside $AU5 million to be paid to Stolen Generations members and their children.

T

TABOO. The most widely recognized taboo today is that of not mentioning the name or showing the image of a recently deceased person. **Film**s, television programs, and radio broadcasts containing names, images, or the voices of Aboriginal people carry a general warning for **Torres Strait** Islanders and Aborigines that names or images of those now deceased might be included. Traditionally, a taboo on using the name of the recently deceased was practiced across most of Australia. The form this particular taboo took and its duration varied from group to group and from circumstance to circumstance. It also formed part of a complex set of taboos associated with funerary rites, which also were practiced across Australia, with considerable variation.

A multiplicity of other taboos and assorted prohibitions were practiced Australia-wide. Depending on region, group, and circumstance, there were food taboos based on age and initiatory status; taboos on hunting, gathering, and eating particular foodstuffs at particular times; taboos related to **sacred sites**, objects, **totems**, and the organization of campsites; a range of restrictive practices exercised during a **woman**'s menses and pregnancy; and various **kinship** avoidance rules that regulated restrictions and prohibitions between relationship groups. The most widely practiced of these was that between son-in-law and mother-in-law.

The above list is not exhaustive. Traditionally, across Australia, numerous taboos were practiced. When, where, what, and how varied considerably. Some taboos are still followed.

TALGAI SKULL. Unearthed on a grazing property in southeastern Queensland during 1886, the Talgai skull was the first physical evidence suggesting that the Aboriginal occupation of Australia occurred as early as the Pleistocene epoch. The skull languished as a curio until 1896, when a preliminary examination of the cranium was undertaken, though it was not until 1914 that the results were presented to the British Association for the Advancement of Science in Sydney. The announcement that the cranium was of unprecedented antiquity generated considerable debate, which did not fully subside until more advanced dating techniques confirmed that it belonged to an Aboriginal youth who died between 18,000 and 11,000 years ago.

TANGENTYERE. *See* ALICE SPRINGS TOWN CAMPS.

TASMANIAN ABORIGINES. An occupation site at Warreen Cave in the Maxwell River valley has revealed that Aboriginal people inhabited present-day Tasmania at least 35,000 years ago, making them the most southerly people in the world at that time. Between 12,000 to 8,000 years BP, the Bassian Plain was submerged by rising seas, leaving the Tasmanians completely isolated from mainland Australia. Over that vast time period, the Tasmanian Aborigines became generally shorter in stature with thick coiled hair in response to the cooler climatic conditions. While there is no evidence that **boomerangs** or **spear-throwers** were ever part of their toolkit, stone tools became markedly smaller in size, largely owing to the use of raw materials such as chert, spongolite, and breccia, all of which had superior flaking qualities. Around 4,000 years ago, the Tasmanians also stopped manufacturing bone tools, an event that closely coincided with the disappearance of scale fish bones from coastal **middens**.

It is believed that between 4,000 and 5,000 Aborigines lived in Tasmania prior to the arrival of Europeans. They were divided into perhaps as many as nine distinct **political** groups, each of which comprised bands of up to 80 individuals who were territorially based. The basic social unit was the extended family, and with few exceptions, **marriage**s were monogamous. Despite the cooler climate, the Tasmanians were able to exploit a wide range of plant and animal foods, resulting in a semisedentary existence. On the west coast of Tasmania, the Aboriginal people constructed solid huts shaped somewhat like a beehive, which they decorated with feathers and shells. Tasmanian Aborigines coated themselves with ochre for ceremonies and wore shell necklaces, the making of which is a craft that continues to the present day. **Religion** was closely linked to celestial bodies, and many of their songs and **dance**s had spiritual significance.

The arrival of Europeans from 1803 had devastating consequences. The introduction of disease, raids by sealers and other seafarers, and the brutal **Black War**—particularly during the years 1828–31—drastically reduced the **population**. The outcome of George Augustus Robinson's **Friendly Mission** was exile at **Wybalenna** on Flinders Island, from where the few survivors were transferred to Oyster Cove, south of Hobart, in 1847. A number of Tasmanian Aboriginal **women** nevertheless managed to avoid being segregated during the 1830s and 1840s and continued to live with Europeans on the islands of Bass Strait. Their descendants comprise Tasmania's modern Aboriginal community. *See also* ARTHUR, WALTER GEORGE.

TEDBURY. *See* PEMULWUY.

TENNIS. *See* GOOLAGONG-CAWLEY, EVONNE; SPORT.

TERRA NULLIUS. Under international law as it existed in 1788, territory could be acquired by occupying uninhabited land or through conquest, cession, or where the inhabitants did not have a form of government recognizable by a European power. Largely based on erroneous reports from James Cook and Joseph Banks in 1770, the British government believed that the eastern coast of Australia was only sparsely inhabited, with the Aboriginal people lacking any political organization. As they did not cultivate the soil in the European fashion, the land, in effect, was deemed "desert and uncultivated." Moreover, as Banks reiterated before a select committee in 1785, if the British established a settlement, the Aborigines would hastily abandon the country. When the First Fleet arrived in Sydney Harbour in January 1788 and realized the considerable size of the Aboriginal population and, later, that they occupied defined territories, it was already too late to halt British colonization.

Although the British still had no legal basis to claim sovereignty over the entire continent, it was not until the 1830s that the legality of the British occupation was first seriously questioned by James Stephen, Under Secretary of the British Colonial Office. In 1836, a legal challenge in *Rex v. Jack Congo Murrell* that the British could not claim sovereignty over the Aboriginal people was dismissed by a court in Sydney. By then, the belief that the continent was "desert and uncultivated" was too well entrenched and the spread of settlement too rapid to alter the existing situation, and with self-government less than two decades away, the concerns of conscience-stricken colonials and distant British officials were easily ignored.

The Latin term *terra nullius* has been used to explain how Aboriginal Australians were dispossessed of their land as well as being stripped of their sovereignty. It has two definitions, both of which are drawn from Roman law. On one hand, *terra nullius* refers to land that is uninhabited and essentially belongs to no one, but it also means that where land is inhabited, the people do not have a form of government recognizable by a European power. While both concepts were understood by the British in 1788, the term itself only entered legal discourse in 1975, first being applied in the Australian context four years later, when Paul Coe of the **Aboriginal Legal Service** in Sydney pursued a compensation claim for Aboriginal people in the High Court of Australia. Coe argued that the British government had wrongly treated the Australian continent as *terra nullius* in 1788, and although his case was unsuccessful, the term began to gain wider usage. As a modern equivalent for "desert and uncultivated," *terra nullius* was finally overturned by the High Court of Australia in the 1992 **Mabo Decision**.

See also ABORIGINAL LAND RIGHTS COMMISSION; ABORIGINAL LAND RIGHTS (NORTHERN TERRITORY) ACT 1976 (COMMONWEALTH) (ALRA); AUSTRALIANS FOR NATIVE TITLE AND RECONCILIATION (ANTaR); GOVE LAND RIGHTS CASE; INDIGENOUS LAND USE AGREEMENTS; LAND CLAIMS; LAND OWNERSHIP; LAND RIGHTS; LINGIARI, VINCENT; MABO DECISION; MABO, EDDIE ("KOIKI"); NATIONAL NATIVE TITLE TRIBUNAL (NNTT); NATIVE TITLE; WAVE HILL; WIK DECISION; WOODWARD INQUIRY.

THANCOUPIE (1937–). Indigenous artist. A leading Australian ceramist, Thancoupie was born on **Cape York** Peninsula, and while she now lives and has her studio elsewhere, she retains strong ties to her country, which she frequently visits. Thancoupie initially sought training in Sydney as a painter, but lacking the formal entry requisites, she gained entry into a pottery school instead. Excelling as a ceramist, she sought further inspiration overseas, traveling to both South and North America and India. Her deeply incised and/or dark line drawings on her spherical, sculptured pots are drawn from her traditional heritage and invoke the local **Dreaming** stories and creator **ancestral beings**. She has held many solo exhibitions and is represented in all major Australian galleries. Thancoupie is an adopted professional name, taken from her totemic name meaning "wattle flower."

THOMAS, HAROLD. *See* ABORIGINAL FLAG.

THOMAS, ROVER (c. 1926–98). Indigenous artist. Rover Thomas was a preeminent artist of the East **Kimberley** region and one of the founders of the distinctive artwork produced there. As with so many Aboriginal artists, he took up painting later in life. He lived in the bush as a child, underwent **initiation** according to traditional law, and then worked as an itinerant laborer and stockman on various pastoral stations and communities. In 1975, following the **death** of an old **woman** from injuries received in a car accident, Thomas received through a dream the songs and paintings for the *gurrir gurrir* ceremony. This ceremony commemorated the woman's life, and the paintings represented the country through which the woman passed en route to medical attention and helped her spirit return to her country. For the ceremony, the images were painted on boards, which were held aloft facing forward across the participant's shoulders. At first Thomas did not paint any of these boards but instructed others on how to do so. He only began painting himself in 1981. Although he maintained the same distinctive style as that used in the *gurrir gurrir* ceremony—the apparently simple depiction of figures and/or country, the freedom of clutter, and the solid banks of color for which the region is now known—he did not only paint for ceremonial purposes but also for the wider **art** market and galleries. His work was quickly respected, and in 1990, it was chosen to represent Australia at the 1990 Venice Biennale.

THURSDAY ISLAND (TI). Also known as Waiben, TI is the administrative and commercial center of the **Torres Strait** Islands. A small island of only about 3.5 square kilometers, it was established as an administrative center in 1877 by the Queensland government.

TIWI ISLANDS. Comprising both Bathurst and Melville islands, the Tiwi Islands lie in the Arafura Sea, some 128 kilometers north of Darwin in the Northern Territory and some 40 kilometers from the mainland coast at the narrowest point. Separated from the mainland by rising sea levels approximately 4,000 BP and with contact between mainland Aborigines and the Tiwi infrequent, Tiwi **language** and culture developed in distinctive ways. It is not known conclusively if Tiwi is related to mainland Aboriginal languages. Iconographic tools of many mainland Aborigines, such as the **spear-thrower** and returning **boomerang**, were not used by the Tiwi. Nor did their male **initiation** ceremonies include circumcision or subincision, one or both of which are characteristic of many mainland groups. Further, no females on the Tiwi Islands, irrespective of age, were unbetrothed. The intricately designed, painted, and carved grave posts, or **pukumani poles**, are unique to the Tiwi Islands. Currently, the Tiwi are moving toward establishing regional self-government over their islands and are engaged in a number of enterprises aimed at achieving greater economic autonomy.

TJAPALTJARRI, CLIFFORD POSSUM (1932–2002). Indigenous artist. One of Australia's most celebrated artists, Tjapaltjarri was born on a pastoral station in central Australia, some 170 kilometers to the northwest of Alice Springs. After a childhood spent in the bush, he worked as a stockman on a number of stations throughout the region. In the 1970s and 1980s, he lived mostly at Papunya and was one of three individuals already painting prior to the arrival of Geoffrey Bardon. It is the major works produced in the late 1970s and 1980s for which Tjapaltjarri is best known. Derived from his **Dreaming**s, they recorded the country to which he was traditionally affiliated. His *Warlugulong*, painted in 1977, is considered one of Australia's most significant paintings. Tjapaltjarri was a key member of the **Papunya Tula** artists cooperative and served as its chairperson in the early 1980s. *See also* ART; KNGWARREYE, EMILY KAME; WESTERN DESERT ART.

TJAPUKAI ABORIGINAL DANCE THEATRE. *See* CORROBOREE.

TJAPUKAI CULTURAL CENTRE. *See* TOURISM.

TOAS. These curious artifacts were produced by the Diyari people from the Lake Eyre region. They are small, carved, painted wooden objects frequently coated with an overlay of gypsum. They sometimes have grass and other natural and/or manmade adornments stuck to them with clay. They were collected in the late 19th and very early 20th century by Johann Reuther, a Lutheran missionary from Killalpaninna Mission, and it has long been debated whether the objects represented a brief flourishing of a new creative output or were recent examples of a long and continuing tradition that ceased around the time the objects were collected. Reuther described the objects as signposts used by traveling groups of Diyari to indicate to those following their intended destination. By molding *toas* to either directly or obliquely reference a site associated with the relevant **Dreaming** story, specific destinations could be indicated to those who shared the requisite knowledge. Recent research suggests that while the *toas* are unmistakably connected to the Dreaming and Aboriginal understanding of their landscape, they were a newly produced artifact arising from Reuther's interest in place and its mythological representation.

TORRES STRAIT. This is an expanse of water linking the Coral and Arafura seas and separating **Cape York** from Papua New Guinea. At its narrowest point, it is 150 kilometers wide. Named after Luis Vaez de Torres, a Spanish navigator who was the first European to enter this region in 1606, Torres Strait is marked by strong currents that thread their way among some 274 islands. Although only 18 islands are permanently inhabited, all are utilized by the Torres Strait Islanders, a Melanesian people closely related to the Papuan New Guineans who settled permanently in Torres Strait around 2,000 years ago. Australia's second Indigenous people, the Torres Strait Islanders, developed three distinct cultures, which are linked to their respective island topographies.

The eastern islands have rich red volcanic soils suitable for cultivation. The main crop was initially taro, but around 1600 AD, sweet potatoes were introduced and subsequently became the main staple. Other crops grown include sugar cane, bananas, and yams. By contrast, the western islands are largely barren. Cultivation is carried out where good patches of soil do exist, but it is largely slash-and-burn agriculture rather than methodical tillage. The life of the western islanders traditionally revolved around hunting, particularly maritime resources such as dugongs, turtles, and fish. The central islands are mostly sandy cays, where the inhabitants rely heavily on fishing. Despite these differences, all three groups developed complex hierarchical societies based on trade and warfare.

TORRES STRAIT ISLANDER FLAG. Designed by Bernard Namok, the flag is a symbol of unity and **identity** for **Torres Strait** Islanders. The flag was selected in January 1992 from a range of competing designs by the Island Co-ordinating Council to represent Torres Strait Islanders. It was recognized, together with the **Aboriginal flag**, as an official "flag of Australia" under the Commonwealth Flags Act 1953.

The flag features a green band at the top and bottom representing land. Narrow black bands representing Torres Strait peoples separate the green from the wide, blue central band, representing the sea. A white five-point star, representing the five major island groups that comprise the region and the stars' importance in traditional navigation methods, is positioned centrally. A *dhari* (traditional headdress), symbolizing the Islanders, surrounds the star.

TORRES STRAIT REGIONAL AUTHORITY (TSRA). The TSRA is a Commonwealth statutory authority established in 1994 by the Commonwealth Aboriginal and Torres Strait Islander Act 2005. It works to recognize, respect, and foster the diverse *ailan kastom* (island custom) throughout the **Torres Strait**. It is responsible for formulating and implementing programs for Torres Strait Islanders and Aboriginal people living in the Torres Strait and monitoring the implementation of these programs. The TSRA is also responsible for reporting to the minister for Indigenous affairs on matters that impact upon Torres Strait Islanders. The authority is working toward **self-determination** for the Torres Strait through initiatives aimed at strengthening the regional **economy**. *See also* TORRES STRAIT ISLANDER FLAG.

TOTEM. A relationship between individuals or groups who share the same totem—usually a plant or animal—that represents a mythical **Dreaming** being is called a totem. Totems can also be inanimate objects or natural phenomena, in which case they still relate to specific ancestral places or acts of Dreaming beings. Either way, totemism maintains a strong spiritual connection with the distant past. Where a totem is a plant or animal, it also links people in a mutually dependent ecological web, and where, in certain circumstances, that particular resource is denied to the individual or group, it can serve as an important conservation measure.

TOURISM. Aboriginal people have been involved in the tourist industry since the 1840s, when they organized public **corroborees** to cater for European audiences in Adelaide and Melbourne. By the late 19th century, the concept had spread north to New South Wales and southern Queensland, occasionally involving a business association with non-Aboriginal entrepreneurs. It was the latter who were at the forefront when the promotion of Aboriginal culture took a new turn during the following century. In 1928, a European settler named James English opened a section of tropical rainforest on his property near Malanda in northern Queensland as the "Malanda Jungle" and began employing local Aboriginal people as guides for tourists. The Aboriginal employees, some of whom still lived in the rainforest, showed visitors local fauna and flora, entertained them with **boomerang**-throwing demonstrations and traditional **dances**, and recited local **Dreaming** stories. The highlight of the attraction was a demonstration of tree-climbing, in which Aboriginal men used a loop of lawyer cane to ascend trees more than 30 meters high. While the Malanda Jungle became one of Australia's foremost tourist attractions, by the mid-1970s, the opening of alternative attractions in northern Queensland resulted in a decline in visitor numbers and its subsequent closure. By then, Aboriginal tourism had expanded into a number of different areas and was once again largely in the hands of Aboriginal people themselves.

One of the most common means of tapping into the lucrative tourist trade was through the establishment of small-scale enterprises based on the manufacture and sale of cultural artifacts. The majority required only minimal capital, but with an increase in government funding from the early 1970s, Aboriginal people were provided with the opportunity to considerably expand their tourism enterprises. In many rural areas and remote communities, there was an emphasis on developing cultural keeping places for the preservation of historic photographs and cultural artifacts focusing on the local area. They operate as small museums, but at the other end of the scale, Aboriginal people have been heavily involved in the creation of medium or large cultural centers specifically built to cater to tourists. The majority have a close association with Aboriginal land, and they serve a number of different functions.

At one level, they display local Aboriginal culture, with income generated through arts and crafts retail outlets that also stock the usual run of souvenirs. The majority also operate as cultural locations for guided tours to nearby natural attractions and cultural sites. A few of the larger centers, such as Brambuck Cultural Centre in Victoria's Grampian National Park, Yarrawarra Cultural Centre at Corindi in northern New South Wales, and Tjapukai Cultural Park at Cairns in Queensland have expanded into virtual theme parks. By so doing, they combine a variety of experiences and entertainment for tourists, while remaining heavily focused on local Aboriginal culture. *See also* ECONOMY.

TREVORROW, BRUCE. *See BRINGING THEM HOME.*

TRIBE. Although this term is used to describe Aboriginal groups, particularly those based on pre- and early-colonial formations, its usefulness in accurately describing Aboriginal organizational forms is limited. Nevertheless, at the time of European colonization in 1788, it is estimated that between 300 and 700 tribal units existed, with membership varying between 100 and 1,500. A tribe usually comprises a group sharing a number of features. Among these is a descent group that distinguishes itself from other groupings, shares a common **language** or dialect, occupies a particular tract of land, and enjoys rights based on **religion** to exploit its resources. **Marriage** is usually endogamous, occurring within the tribe. (Subgroups within tribes are usually exogamous.) The notion of a tribe does not adequately capture many Aboriginal and **Torres Strait Islander** social, political, economic, and religious forms. Some practices occur within tribal subgroups, whereas others reach beyond postulated tribal boundaries. A range of terms is used to more accurately describe particular clusters. Terms include linguistic group, estate group, horde, clan, community, **kinship** grouping, and band. For example, a group utilizing a particular tract of land is often described as a band, whereas a clan or estate group is a land-owning group.

TRUGANINI (1812?–76). Indigenous mediator. Also known as Trugenernanner and Trukanini, Truganini was the daughter of Mangerner, leader of the Bruny Island people in southeastern Tasmania, who experienced great brutality from Europeans. A highly intelligent woman, Truganini was renowned for her promiscuity, good looks, and sharp sense of humor. She married five times, her last husband being Woorrady, in 1829. Between 1829 and 1835, the pair played prominent roles in George Augustus Robinson's **Friendly Mission**, which brought the **Black War** to an end with the exile of the **Tasmanian Aborigines** to **Wybalenna** on Flinders Island. While there are suspicions that Robinson and Truganini may have had a love affair, Truganini became increasingly bitter about the fate of the Aboriginal people. In 1839, she was one of 14 Tasmanian Aborigines who accompanied Robinson to Port Phillip after his appointment as Chief **Protector**, but she absconded with two other **women** and two men. The group raided isolated huts and killed two European whalers before being captured. The men were executed and the women returned to Flinders Island.

When **Wybalenna** closed down in 1847, Truganini was among the remnant population transferred to Oyster Cove, south of Hobart. In 1873, she was the sole survivor and moved to Hobart, where she was cared for by the Dandridge family until her **death** in May 1876. In December 1878, Truganini's remains were exhumed by the Royal Society of Tasmania, and in 1904, her skeleton was displayed in the Tasmanian Museum. It remained on display until 1947, when it was placed in storage following complaints from the public. In the late 1960s, the Tasmanian Aboriginal community, led by mainland activist **Burnum Burnum**, began a successful campaign for Truganini's remains to be given a decent burial. Her bones were finally cremated in April 1976 and the ashes spread in the D'Entrecasteaux Channel close to her homeland of Bruny Island.

U

ULURU. One of Australia's best-known and most distinctive landmarks, Uluru is a large reddish sandstone monolith in central Australia situated approximately 335 kilometers southwest of Alice Springs in the Northern Territory. Standing some 347 meters high above the semiarid surrounds and with a circumference of 9.3 kilometers, it is an imposing sight. Following an increase in **tourism** to what was then known as Ayers Rock in the 1940s, an area comprising Uluru and Kata Tjuta (the Olgas) was excised from the South West Aboriginal Reserve in 1958 to establish a national park. *See* GOVERNMENT RESERVES. In 1979, the traditional owners, collectively known as Anangu, lodged a land claim to an area that included the national park. In addition to the land already granted to the Anangu, in 1985, the park itself was granted as Aboriginal land, and under a comanagement arrangement, the park was leased back to the Commonwealth for a period of 99 years. Under terms of the agreement, the park's Board of Management comprises an Anangu majority. Now known as the Uluru–Kata Tjuta National Park, it covers 1,326 square kilometers (132,550 hectares) and is on the World Heritage List. **Kakadu National Park** and Nitmiluk (Katherine Gorge) National Park in the Northern Territory are two other major tourist destinations that have been returned to the traditional owners under a similar management scheme.

Uluru–Kata Tjuta is of considerable symbolic importance to the Anangu (comprising Pitjantjatjara and Yankunjatjara people) as well as to settler Australians. It is also a site of pilgrimage for various so-called New Age devotees and is one of Australia's premier tourist destinations. A popular activity is to watch "the rock" at sunrise and sunset, when it dramatically changes color through a range of reddish-purplish hues. Another popular activity is undertaking the steep climb to the summit, from where a commanding view is gained. The traditional owners, for various reasons, currently discourage this activity, and a growing number of tourists are respecting their concerns. The Anangu believe features in the park—both the readily apparent and the nondescript—were formed during the **Dreaming**, or *Tjukurpa* in their **language**. The features of the park indicate the activities of the **ancestral beings**. Further cultural heritage of the Anangu is evident in the many paintings and engraving sites round the base of Uluru. There are a number of caves and overhangs where this artwork can be readily viewed.

Kata Tjuta, a Pitjantjatjara word meaning "many heads," lies some 32 kilometers to the west of Uluru. Thirty-six dome-shaped red rocks that have been smoothed through weathering rise from the plain. Mount Olga, the highest of these domes is, at 500 meters, considerably higher than Uluru. Kata Tjuta is an important sacred site of particular significance under Anangu men's law. Much knowledge pertaining to the site is restricted and not disseminated.

UNAIPON, DAVID (1872–1967). The first published Indigenous writer, inventor, and musician. A member of the Ngarrindjeri people, Unaipon was born in Raukkan (Point McLeay Mission), South Australia. He was awarded patents for mechanical designs, including a patent in 1909 that modified existing mechanical sheep shearers so that the motion of the shearers changed from a circular motion to a straight motion, thus considerably improving its efficiency. From 1924 to 1925, he wrote what became the *Legendary Tales of the Australian Aborigines*. When it was published in 1930, it was wrongly credited to William Ramsey Smith, an anthropologist.

After his **death**, in 1985, Unaipon was awarded the FAW Patricia Weickhardt Award for Aboriginal writers. In 1988, an annual David Unaipon Award was established to recognize and promote unpublished Indigenous writers. In 1995, Unaipon was selected to feature on the new $50 Australian note.

UNITED NATIONS INTERNATIONAL WORK GROUP FOR INDIGENOUS AFFAIRS. *See* LANGTON, MARCIA.

UNITED NATIONS SUB-COMMISSION ON THE PREVENTION OF DISCRIMINATION AND PROTECTION OF MINORITIES. *See* IDENTITY.

UNITED NATIONS WORKING GROUP ON INDIGENOUS POPULATIONS. *See* DODSON, MICHAEL (MICK).

W

WAIBEN. *See* THURSDAY ISLAND (TI).

WALKER, KATH. *See* NOONUCCAL, OODGEROO.

WANDJINA. This distinctive rock **art** featuring human-like figures of comparatively recent origin is found in the **Kimberley**, Western Australia. Dating from around 1500 BP, the images were regularly repainted—a practice that continued into the 20th century—ensuring their continued vibrancy and freshness. The figures themselves are the Wandjina—creator ancestral beings that took to the rock shelters and caves after their landscape forming and other activities. Generally comprising a white background, features resembling a head, shoulders, and torso facing forward are delineated in red ochre. Large black "eyes," an outline of a nose but no mouth, and a halo usually feature. Up to seven meters in length, their size contributes to their impressive appearance. The Wandjina played a crucial role in the region, regulating, among other things, the flooding rains of the monsoon season. Today, Wandjina are painted on bark, canvas, and the nuts of the boab tree. A 35-meter-high Wandjina figure designed by Donny Woolagoodja featured in the Sydney Olympic Games opening ceremony (2000). *See also* BRADSHAW ART.

WATERCRAFT. Aboriginal people across the Australian continent constructed a wide variety of watercraft ranging from wood, reed, and bark rafts to highly sophisticated outrigger canoes. Around much of the coast and on inland waterways, one of the most common were canoes made from a large sheet of eucalypt or she-oak bark, which was heated and stretched into the required shape. Both ends were bound with vine rope, and scarred canoe trees from which the bark was removed are still to be found in eastern Australia. An alternative craft, mostly found along the inland river systems, consisted of layers of reeds bound together to form a platform. A type of punt, it was propelled by a single pole.

On the western and southern coasts of Tasmania, canoes were made from three separate bundles of ti tree bark bound together. The center bundle provided most of the buoyancy, while the outer bundles acted as stabilizers. They were either propelled by a pole or pushed ahead by swimmers, and although they rapidly became waterlogged, as did the bark and other mainland craft, such as reed rafts, these craft were capable of reaching islands up to 15 kilometers off the coast. Less well documented are the bark catamarans from southern Tasmania mentioned by early European explorers. **Tasmanian Aborigines** also made use of driftwood logs for crossing rivers, as did some mainland groups.

While rafts made from mangrove logs lashed together with a splayed bow were used right across northern Australia, the Yanyuwa people from the southwestern shores of the Gulf of Carpentaria and the Sir Edward Pellew Islands were once renowned for their sewn-bark canoes. These were superseded to some extent by the dugout canoes introduced by the **Macassans**—solid and stable craft up to six meters long that enjoyed a wide distribution in far northern Australia.

In northeastern Queensland, outrigger canoes were known as far south as the Whitsunday Islands. They may have been an introduction from **Torres Strait**, where large seagoing canoes up to 20 meters in length and equipped with woven pandanus sails traveled regularly among the islands as far north as Papua New Guinea and south to the shores of **Cape York** and the Gulf of Carpentaria.

WATERS, LEONARD. *See* MILITARY SERVICE.

WAVE HILL. The name of one of the largest pastoral leasehold stations in the world came to prominence when, in August 1966, Aboriginal stockmen and domestic workers—mostly Gurindji people—walked off their camp and established a settlement at Wattie Creek, approximately 13 kilometers away. The strike, led by **Vincent Lingiari**, was first assumed to be for better wages and conditions, and these were contributing factors. In 1965, the Arbitration Commission granted Aboriginal pastoral workers uniform wage awards, which were to be phased in over three years. Previously, Aboriginal workers in this industry received scant wages. In return, however, they were largely left to their own devices when there was no work to be done. This arrangement enabled traditional cultural practices to continue with little interruption, providing these activities were organized around the seasonal stock work. The equal wage decision led many pastoral companies to declare that they could not afford to keep Aboriginal employees, and they sought to exclude them from their leases.

While pay and conditions were factors underlying the Gurindji strike, the more fundamental request was for the return of their traditional land, a request formalized in a petition. Ultimately, the Gurindji were successful, with the first portion of their traditional land and adjacent Crown land being returned to them in 1975. The return was rendered symbolically by Prime Minister Gough Whitlam pouring a handful of soil into the hands of Vincent Lingiari, creating a potent image. The Gurindji strike, or walk-off as it is more popularly known, served as both inspiration and catalyst for further Aboriginal activism. *See also* ABORIGINAL LAND RIGHTS COMMISSION; ABORIGINAL LAND RIGHTS (NORTHERN TERRITORY) ACT 1976 (COMMONWEALTH) (ALRA); GOVE LAND RIGHTS CASE; LAND CLAIMS; LAND OWNERSHIP; LAND RIGHTS; MABO DECISION; MABO, EDDIE ("KOIKI"); NATIONAL NATIVE TITLE TRIBUNAL (NNTT); NATIVE TITLE; *TERRA NULLIUS*; WIK DECISION; WOODWARD INQUIRY.

WESTERN DESERT ART. The acrylic **art** of the Western Desert is one of the most recognizable contemporary Aboriginal art forms. While derivative of traditional aesthetic expression, such as body painting and ground or sand sculptures, it is a dynamic and innovative art form dating from the 1970s. The early canvasses (although many of the early works were simply painted on whatever material was available) were usually small and often featured figures (both human and animal) and sacred paraphernalia. The palette was largely restricted to red, yellow, black, and white, the colors most readily available traditionally.

As the nascent art movement reached beyond **Papunya**, it rapidly developed into the more familiar style of today. The canvasses substantially increased in size, more vibrant colors were used, figures were omitted (though animal tracks continue to feature), and dots were increasingly used as infill. Although ostensibly appearing more abstract, the paintings are frequently and accurately described as representing "maps of country." Line and circle motifs dominate, signifying sites of significance, which might include where a particular activity took place in the **Dreaming**, and the links between these sites. The lines linking sites, as with the sites themselves, often contain multiple meanings. A circle can indicate a waterhole and the place where a particular **ancestral being** rested, among other things. The meandering lines joining such sites can represent a watercourse and the track taken by particular ancestral beings during the period of creation. In this way, Western Desert acrylics can represent vast tracts of country, and while not recognizable as conventional maps, they can and do function as conceptual maps.

The meaning one gleans from a particular painting is dependent upon one's status. Gender, initiatory status, age, and classificatory position in the **kinship** system are key determinants in what detailed information a painting reveals (*see* SOCIAL ORGANIZATION).

Art from the Western Desert continues to develop, partly in response to market forces but also in response to internal dynamism and painterly interests, skills, and desires. *See also* DOT PAINTINGS; KNGWARREYE, EMILY KAME; NAMATJIRA, ALBERT; TJAPALTJARRI, CLIFFORD POSSUM.

WIK DECISION. The **Mabo decision** of the High Court of Australia and the subsequent Native Title Act did not clarify whether or not pastoral leases extinguished **native title** by way of conferring exclusive possession to the lessees. The Wik and Thayorre peoples of Cape York Peninsula in far northern Queensland sought resolution of this issue before the High Court. They were claiming native title to two pastoral leases. In December 1996, by a 4–3 majority, the High Court found that pastoral leases did not necessarily confer exclusive possession to the lessee and that such leases did not necessarily extinguish native title. It was possible, therefore, for pastoral leases and native title rights to coexist. The High Court's decision was contrary to widely held beliefs, particularly within the pastoral lobby, which held that pastoral leases must extinguish native title. Significantly, the High Court decision did not determine the Wik and Thayorre claims of native title: it simply determined that their native title rights had not necessarily been extinguished through the granting of pastoral leases. *See also* ABORIGINAL LAND RIGHTS COMMISSION; ABORIGINAL LAND RIGHTS (NORTHERN TERRITORY) ACT 1976 (COMMONWEALTH) (ALRA); GOVE LAND RIGHTS CASE; LAND CLAIMS; LAND OWNERSHIP; LAND RIGHTS; MABO, EDDIE ("KOIKI"); NATIONAL NATIVE TITLE TRIBUNAL (NNTT); *TERRA NULLIUS*.

WILD RIVERS ACT. *See* CAPE YORK INSTITUTE FOR POLICY AND LEADERSHIP; PEARSON, NOEL.

WITCHETTY GRUBS. *See* BUSH FOOD.

WOMEN. The role of women in Aboriginal societies was often marginalized. Early anthropological work, with notable exceptions, focused on the role of men. It was assumed that women were men's subordinates and that their sacred and ritual affairs and social and ceremonial roles were of lesser importance. In respect to **land ownership**, it was thought to be vested in *patriclans*. This understanding impacted upon the capacity of women to demonstrate rights to land in early **land rights** claims. Further anthropological studies—particularly those undertaken by female anthropologists—and the representations of Aboriginal women themselves through literature, paintings, and other media have demonstrated that while women's social and cultural roles can be distinguished from men's, they were more complementary than subordinate. It is now recognized that women did and do maintain, and in some areas of Australia still perform, their own complex ceremonies and rituals and enjoy a rich and discrete sacred life. It is also now recognized that women can be the principal holders of rights to land.

Nevertheless, while many see in traditional Aboriginal societies an enviable egalitarianism and equality between the sexes, there is considerable historical and archaeological evidence that a high level of violence against women was a feature of traditional societies. Also, only senior initiated men were privy to the most exclusive religious esotery.

As with most hunter-gatherer societies, there was a marked division of labor in Aboriginal society. While there was variation across cultural groups, men were primarily responsible for hunting larger game, and women provided the bulk of day-to-day foodstuffs—primarily vegetables, fruit, and seeds—through their gathering activities. They also captured smaller game, including assorted reptiles, and shellfish (both salt and freshwater). Vegetable foodstuffs comprised the bulk of foods collected by women, and they constituted a more reliable source than the larger animals provided by the men.

The abuse of Aboriginal women exacerbated early frontier conflict and continued well into the 20th century. Few European women ventured beyond the settled districts, and Aboriginal women were vulnerable. Conflict over the abuse of women, however, was not in all instances generated by rape or other deprivations. Aboriginal men, seeking to establish relations of reciprocity with the Europeans occupying Aboriginal lands, sometimes lent their wives for sexual purposes. Failure to recognize the nature of the relationship this established and one's reciprocal obligations was a significant source of conflict.

There is some debate that disruption to Aboriginal societies and dispossession of land has impacted more adversely on the traditional role of men than that of women. Through their role of giving birth to and raising children and maintaining the domestic space, it is argued that women have been able to more readily adapt their traditional ceremonial and ritual roles to the changed conditions. The realms in which they enjoyed authority have not been challenged to the same extent by the secular authority of the imposed political **economy** of the nation state or by the religious authority of the Church, which clearly undermined the status of senior initiated men who previously enjoyed primacy in these matters. For these reasons, some argue that women's social and ceremonial role in certain communities is now stronger than men's.

However, Aboriginal women did suffer considerably. As noted, they were not immune to the deprivations of the frontier. They, too, witnessed the loss of their lands, the often violent bloodshed, and the loss of a great many kin through disease. They experienced the removal of their children under welfare measures and, during the period of the **assimilation policy**, their children's removal for the purposes of separating them from their Aboriginal heritage. Nevertheless, throughout this, they demonstrated strength and resilience, and many emerged as spokespeople for their communities and as activists championing for better conditions. **Pearl Gibbs** was an important Indigenous activist throughout the mid- to late-20th century. **Lowitja O'Donoghue** rose to become the inaugural and respected chairperson of the **Aboriginal and Torres Strait Islanders Commission**, a position she held from 1990 to 1996. A number of women turned to writing, particularly in memoir form but also poetry, as a means of telling history from an Aboriginal perspective, expressing **identity**, and critiquing the dominant society. **Oodgeroo Noonuccal**, then known as Kath Walker, published the first book by an Aboriginal woman, a collection of poetry entitled *We Are Going* (1964). Oodgeroo went on to achieve widespread acclaim for her poetry and for her unrelenting advocacy for all Aborigines. Best known of the memoirs is *My Place* by **Sally Morgan** (1987), a best-seller now published in many languages. Sport is another arena in which Aboriginal women have excelled. **Evonne Goolagong-Cawley** won three of tennis's grand slam singles events, twice at Wimbledon (1971 and 1980) and the French open (1971). The track athlete **Cathy Freeman** is a world champion and Olympic gold medalist and is tireless in her support of helping Indigenous children in setting and achieving their goals. In **art**, the late **Emily Kngwarreye** achieved international renown with her traditionally oriented canvases. The anthropologist **Marcia Langton** contributes to contemporary policy debates concerning Aboriginal affairs from her position as a respected intellectual. *See also* CONCEPTION; FILM; HEISS, ANITA; HINDMARSH ISLAND; HUNTER, RUBY; LUCASHENKO, MELISSA; O'SHANE, PATRICIA (PAT); SOCIAL ORGANIZATION; SPORT; THANCOUPIE; TRUGANINI; WRIGHT, ALEXIS.

WOODWARD INQUIRY. Justice A. E. Woodward was appointed in 1973 by Prime Minister Gough Whitlam's Labor government to lead a commission of inquiry into how Aboriginal **land rights** could be realized in the Northern Territory. As it was a territory and not a state, the federal government could impose legislation without fear of state opposition. Woodward's second and final report, handed down in early 1974, formed the basis of what became the **Aboriginal Land Rights (Northern Territory) Act 1976**, which was introduced by Prime Minister Malcolm Fraser's Coalition government in 1976.

See also ABORIGINAL LAND RIGHTS COMMISSION; GOVE LAND RIGHTS CASE; LAND CLAIMS; LAND OWNERSHIP; LINGIARI, VINCENT; MABO DECISION; MABO, EDDIE ("KOIKI"); NATIONAL NATIVE TITLE TRIBUNAL (NNTT); NATIVE TITLE; *TERRA NULLIUS*; WAVE HILL; WIK DECISION.

WOOMERA. *See* SPEAR-THROWER.

WORLD HERITAGE AREAS. *See* KAKADU NATIONAL PARK; LAKE MUNGO; NEIDJIE, BILL ("BIG BILL"); ULURU.

WRIGHT, ALEXIS (1950–). Indigenous writer and advocate. An acclaimed novelist, Alexis Wright's first novel, *Plains of Promise* (1997), was published to critical commendation, while the novel *Carpentaria* (2006) has won many awards, including, in 2007, the prestigious Miles Franklin Award. Of the Wannji people from southeastern Queensland, Wright has worked diligently as an advocate for Aboriginal rights and in numerous government positions and Aboriginal organizations. *See also* LITERATURE.

WYBALENNA. An Aboriginal word meaning "black man's house," in 1834, the name was given to the "Aboriginal Establishment" on Flinders Island in Bass Strait to which nearly all remaining **Tasmanian Aborigines** were removed from the Tasmanian mainland following George Augustus Robinson's **Friendly Mission**. The intention was to "Christianise and civilise" the 134 Aborigines initially housed there. However, conditions were atrocious and the infrastructure woefully inadequate, and the Aborigines quickly succumbed. In 1847, the 47 surviving Aborigines were transferred to Oyster Cove to the south of Hobart on the Tasmanian mainland.

WYLIE (mid-19th century). Indigenous guide. A young Aboriginal man from King George Sound in Western Australia, Wylie is remembered today as the loyal companion of the European explorer, Edward John Eyre. Eyre took Wylie to Adelaide in May 1840, but the latter did not accompany Eyre on any of his northern explorations. It was not until Eyre abandoned his search for grazing land in the interior of South Australia and determined on finding an overland route to King George Sound that he was again joined by Wylie at Fowler's Bay in January 1841. Along with Eyre and Wylie, the expedition consisted of Eyre's former overseer, John Baxter, and two South Australian Aborigines, Neramberein (Joey) and Cootachah (Yarry). On the night of 29 April 1841, Neramberein and Cootachah killed Baxter when he disturbed them plundering the stores, and although Wylie raised the alarm,

Eyre believed that he had intended returning to the settled districts with his South Australian companions.

For reasons known only to himself, Wylie remained with Eyre, and the pair continued west, with Wylie largely responsible for finding food and water when their remaining supplies were exhausted. After undergoing great privations, they were fortunate to fall in with the crew of a French whaler near present-day Esperance, and after being reprovisioned, they finally reached Albany on 7 July 1841.

For his loyalty to Eyre, Wylie was rewarded by the government of Western Australia with £2 and a weekly ration of flour and meat; he received a medal from the Perth Agricultural Society. Apart from his brief service as a police constable, nothing certain is known of Wylie's later life.

X

X-RAY ART. In this striking style of artwork from western **Arnhem Land**, elements of an animal's skeletal structure are often depicted—particularly the backbone and, often, internal organs, such as the heart, lungs, and liver. In Aboriginal artistic history, x-ray **art** emerged comparatively recently, becoming a major feature of rock art some 3,000 years BP. Today, x-ray-style art appears on bark, board, and canvas, with a great deal produced for sale. Typically, one or two figures (animal and/or vegetable) appear in outline on a monochrome background, with some internal organs, backbones, or structures depicted. Finely detailed cross-hatching often fills the interior of the figure outside of any organs shown. The monochrome background surrounding the figure also often brims with assorted implements associated with the figure and other mythical beings. As with most Aboriginal art, and notwithstanding the aesthetic pleasure experienced and desired by artists, it is produced within strict controls over which individuals have the appropriate authority, connections to country, and **Dreaming** to paint specific symbols, motifs, and figures. *See also* BARK PAINTING.

Y

YAGAN (?–1833). Indigenous resistance fighter. Yagan's father, Midgigoroo, was an influential member of the Aboriginal clan residing immediately south of Perth in Western Australia. Reprisals against European settlers began nine months after a colony was established on the Swan River in 1829, though it was not until 1831 that Midgigoroo and Yagan were identified as the killers of a European farm servant. In May 1832, Yagan was held responsible for the **death** of a European laborer named William Gaze. Captured four months later, Yagan and other members of his clan were sentenced to temporary detention on Carnac Island. They escaped after six weeks, and, for a brief period, Yagan frequented the European settlement, where he occasionally entertained the settlers. Aboriginal raids on European stores soon recommenced, and in April 1833, Midgigoroo and Yagan ambushed a supply cart between Fremantle and the Canning River, killing two farm workers. They were proclaimed outlaws the following day, with a reward being offered for their capture, dead or alive. Midgigoroo was taken two weeks later and executed. Yagan was finally shot dead on 11 July 1833. He was decapitated, and after being smoke-dried, his head was sent to England, where it was publicly exhibited until 1964, when it was buried in a cemetery with two Maori heads and a Peruvian mummy. It was exhumed in 1997 and returned to the Western Australian Aboriginal community.

YARRAWARRA CULTURAL CENTRE. *See* TOURISM.

YIDAKI. *See* DIDGERIDOO.

YIRRKALA BARK PETITIONS. *See* BARK PETITIONS; GOVE LAND RIGHTS CASE.

YOTHU YINDI. Taking their name from a Yolngu Aboriginal term meaning child-mother, Yothu Yindi arose from a combination of the non-Aboriginal band Swamp Jockeys and a loose-knit Yolngu musical group that together toured **Arnhem Land** in 1986. While the line-up has changed considerably, Yothu Yindi has intentionally remained a mixture of Aboriginal and non-Aboriginal musicians. The band's repertoire ranges from traditional Yolngu songs to Western pop and rock, backed by European and traditional Yolngu musical instruments, including the **didgeridoo**. As enshrined in its name, the band's broader aim is to actively promote recognition, respect, and collaboration of different cultures.

Members of the Yunupingu family, including lead vocalist Mandawuy Yunupingu, have been heavily represented in the band, which has toured extensively both within Australia and overseas. Yothu Yindi's debut album in May 1989, *Homeland Movement*, initially aroused little attention, but in 1990, the band had a hit single with "Treaty," a song that lamented the lack of progress since Prime Minister Robert Hawke had responded to the **Barunga Statement** two years earlier. The follow-up album, *Tribal Voice*, reached number four on the Australian Record Industry Association charts. Subsequent albums are *Freedom* (1993), *Birrkuta-Wild Honey* (1996), *One Blood* (1999), and *Garma* (2000).

Yothu Yindi has undoubtedly been Australia's most successful Aboriginal band, with its unique blend of musical genres raising appreciation of Aboriginal culture around Australia and on the global stage. It has also inspired the Yolngu people, five clans of whom came together in 1990 to form the Yothu Yindi Foundation to promote Yolngu culture. *See also* MUSIC.

YUNUPINGU, JAMES GALARRWUY (1948–). Indigenous activist. Former **land rights** activist and one of the most influential Aboriginal community leaders in Australia, James Galarrwuy Yunupingu was born near Yirrkala in northeastern **Arnhem Land**. Educated at Yirrkala Methodist **Mission** and the Methodist Bible College in Brisbane, Yunupingu assisted his father and other Yolngu elders to prepare the Yirrkala **bark petitions** in 1963. In 1971, he played a prominent role in the unsuccessful **Gove land rights case**, the first time powerful mining interests had been challenged in the courts by Aboriginal people. In 1976, he joined the Northern **Land Council**, which had been established in the wake of the Commonwealth **Aboriginal Land Rights Act**, serving as chairperson from 1977 to 1980 and subsequently reelected on numerous occasions.

In 1978, Yunupingu was jointly named Australian of the Year in recognition of his exceptional negotiating skills, which permitted an agreement to be reached over the Ranger uranium mine (*see* JABILUKA). In 1985, he was honored with Membership of the Order of Australia (AM) and was later named one of the country's Living National Treasures by the National Trust of Australia. Yunupingu is on the Council for Aboriginal **Reconciliation** and continues to be heavily involved in organizations aimed at protecting and promoting the interests of the Yolngu people.

YUNUPINGU, MANDAWUY. *See* YOTHU YINDI.

Bibliography

Introduction
I. REFERENCE WORKS
   1. Encyclopedias and Dictionaries
   2. Bibliographies
   3. Internet Resources
II. ETHNOGRAPHY AND ANTHROPOLOGY
   1. Colonial Ethnography and Anthropology
   2. Modern Ethnography and Anthropology
III. THEMATIC WORKS
   1. Prehistory and Archeology
   2. Historiography
   3. Frontier Conflict
   4. The Stolen Generations
   5. Politics, Activism, and Race Relations
   6. Legal and Judicial Matters Including Land Rights and Native Title
   7. Health and Welfare
   8. Aborigines and Military Service
   9. Film and Media
   10. Art and Photography
   11. Education
   12. Literature
   13. Demographics
IV. Works by Indigenous Writers
   1. Memoirs
   2. Anthologies
   3. Fiction, Plays, and Poetry
   4. Non-Fiction

INTRODUCTION

European explorers and merchants visiting the coasts of Australia from the early 17th century provided the first fragmentary accounts of Aboriginal society. They were men of their time and usually left unflattering accounts of people they saw only briefly and often at a distance. By the late 18th century, the number of visiting ships increased, sojourns ashore grew more common, and the attitudes of the time shaped more sympathetic observations. The French expeditions of D'Entrecasteaux in 1796 and Baudin in 1802 produced both important ethnographic information and admiring art work.

With the establishment of the first British colonies at Sydney in 1788 and Hobart in 1803–04, the written accounts of Aborigines proliferated, both in official reports sent to the Colonial Office and in works produced for the reading public in Great Britain. No book about the Australian colonies was thought complete without some reference to, and often at least a chapter about, the Aborigines. The most valuable ethnographic observations were provided by the explorers who pushed out well beyond the frontiers of settlement—men like Sturt, Mitchell, Eyre, Leichhardt, and Grey.

Missionaries worked in the colonies from the 1820s without much success. But they often spent much time with the people they sought to convert, talked to them at length, and tried to understand their society and their psyches. They also wrote reports and letters back to their mission societies and kept journals tracing their difficulties in the world outside and their struggles with turmoil within. The writings of men like Threlkeld in New South Wales, Thomas in Victoria, and Robinson in Tasmania contain large amounts of important information, although the reader learns more about European prejudices and perceptions than about the ostensible subject under consideration.

The recurring conflict on the frontiers of settlement produced an extensive literature that took many forms: letters to the proliferating newspapers, petitions and appeals to government, polemical pamphlets, and books. Such material was often lacking in ethnographic sophistication, but it allows us to understand a good deal about the contact and conflict on the ragged fringes of European settlement. By the end of the 19th century, the colonial governments were feeling the pressure of mounting criticism of the abject condition of remnant Aboriginal populations and concern about continuing conflict. Parliaments set up select committees and appointed royal commissions to investigate the problems of dealing with what was universally thought to be a dying race.

Such foreboding helped stimulate a generation of amateur ethnographers—men like Curr, Roth, and Howitt, who sought to recover what they could before it was too late. More systematic anthropology was undertaken at the turn of the 19th century by the Cambridge expedition led by A. C. Haddon in the Torres Strait and by Baldwin Spencer in central Australia.

The 20th century saw a proliferation of written material about Aborigines. As in the colonial period, most visitors who wrote travel books or articles included an obligatory section about Aborigines, rarely original and often sensational. Professional anthropology took root with the establishment of the first chair in the discipline in Sydney in 1926. Much of the resulting literature was hidden away in scholarly journals, but several anthropologists, Elkin, Stanner, and Thompson, for instance, wrote widely in the popular press. Political and polemical literature appeared with increasing frequency after World War II as Australia came under international scrutiny in a decolonizing world totally unsympathetic with the racial ideas of the prewar period, which Australia had eagerly embraced. Growing understanding of and interest in traditional and tribal societies saw a proliferation of books and articles about Aborigines still living at least partly traditional lives in the remote parts of the country.

Australian historiography underwent dramatic changes in the 1970s with the appearance of large numbers of books and articles that rewrote Aborigines back into the national story, dramatically changing the way many Australians saw the past. Interest in Aboriginal history peaked in 1988, at the time of the bicentenary of the settlement of New South Wales. The momentum continued in the 1990s, with the federal government setting in train a 10-year period of reconciliation, which provided a stimulus to historical research all over the continent, often resulting in many local communities exploring their local history with new eyes. In this period, many settler Australians came to agree with the cogency of the common, contemporaneous Aboriginal slogan: "White Australia has a Black History." The 1990s also saw the dramatic decisions of the High Court to recognize native title on public or Crown Land and, even more contentiously, on the vast tracts of land held under pastoral lease. A large volume of legal commentary, both technical and popular, resulted. A controversial report of the Human Rights and Equal Opportunity Commission into the practice of removing Aboriginal children from their families, which had been common throughout the 20th century, produced another stream of commentary, memoir, and polemic. Growing resistance to the revisionist historiography among conservative scholars and commentators resulted in attack and counterattack in a series of skirmishes given the title of the "history wars," which have persisted in one form or another to the present day. However, the controversies will work their way out, it is obvious that the Aborigines who were once neglected and overlooked have become a central constituent of the cultural life of contemporary Australia. There are now many indigenous writers working successfully in many genres: history, education, anthropology, politics, law, novels, memoir, poetry, plays, lyrics, and film scripts.

I. REFERENCE WORKS

1. Encyclopedias and Dictionaries

The single most important work of general reference is:

Horton, David, ed. *The Encyclopaedia of Aboriginal Australia: Aboriginal and Torres Strait Islander History, Society and Culture.* 2 vols. Canberra: Aboriginal Studies, 1994.

On Tasmania, see:

Alexander, Alison, ed. *The Companion to Tasmanian History.* Hobart: Centre for Tasmanian Historical Studies, University of Tasmania, 2005.

On art and culture, see also:

Kleinert, Sylvia, and Margo Neale, eds. *The Oxford Companion to Aboriginal Art and Culture.* South Melbourne: Oxford University Press, 2000.

For people, see also:
Pike, Douglas, ed. *Australian Dictionary of Biography*. Melbourne: Melbourne University Press, 1966.

2. Bibliographies

For a comprehensive survey of printed material, see the early but still valuable work:
Greenway, John. *Bibliography of the Australian Aborigines and the Native Peoples of Torres Strait to 1959*. Sydney: Angus & Robertson, 1963.

For a listing of academic theses, see:
Coppell, William George. *World Catalogue of Theses and Dissertations about the Australian Aborigines and Torres Strait Islanders*. Sydney: Sydney University Press, 1977.

Similar information can be found in:
Barwick, Diane, James Urry, and D. Bennett. "A Select Bibliography of Aboriginal History and Social Change." *Aboriginal History* 1 (1977): 111–69.

The large number of assorted bibliographies are listed in:
Arthur, Bill, and Frances Morphy, eds. *Macquarie Atlas of Indigenous Australia: Culture and Society through Space and Time*. Sydney: Macquarie University, 2005.
Barwick, Diane, and Michael Mace, eds. *Handbook for Aboriginal and Islander History*. Canberra: Aboriginal History, 1979.
Thawley, John, and Sarah Gauci. *Bibliographies on the Australian Aborigine: An Annotated Listing*. Bundoora: LaTrobe University, 1987.

3. Internet Resources

Australian Dictionary of Biography Online Edition. http://www.adb.online.anu.edu.au/adbonline.htm.
Australian Human Rights Commission. "Aboriginal and Torres Strait Islander Social Justice." http://www.humanrights.gov.au/social_justice/native_title/index.html.
Australian Institute of Aboriginal and Torres Strait Islander Studies. http://www.aiatsis.gov.au/.
Dictionary of Australian Artists Online. http://www.daao.org.au/.
National Native Title Tribunal. http://www.nntt.gov.au/Pages/default.aspx.

On demographics, see the Australian Bureau of Statistics:
Australian Bureau of Statistics. "3301.0—Births, Australia, 2008." http://www.abs.gov.au/ausstats/abs@.nsf/mf/3301.0.
———. "4704.0—The Health and Welfare of Australia's Aboriginal and Torres Strait Islander Peoples, 2008." http://abs.gov.au/ausstats/abs@.nsf/mf/4704.0/.

———. "4714.0—National Aboriginal and Torres Strait Islander Social Survey, 2008." http://abs.gov.au/AUSSTATS/abs@.nsf/mf/4714.0/.
———. "Statistics." http://www.abs.gov.au/AUSSTATS.

II. ETHNOGRAPHY AND ANTHROPOLOGY

1. Colonial Ethnography and Anthropology

Much of what we know about Aboriginal society in the parts of Australia settled in the 19th century was provided by explorers, surveyors, pioneer settlers, and missionaries. The same people provided us with valuable testimony about the impact of European colonization. There is a vast amount of material. Almost every book about Australia published in the 19th century contained comments about the indigenous people. The material varied widely in value, perception, and originality. The officers of the first settlement in 1788 and early explorers provided the first accounts of traditional society. The most extensive material on Tasmania is found in the journals and letters of George Augustus Robinson.

Collins, David. *An Account of the English Colony in New South Wales*. 2 vols. London: Cadell and Davies, 1798, 1802.
Eyre, Edward John. *Journals of Expeditions of Discovery into Central Australia, and Overland from Adelaide to King George's Sound, in the Years 1840–1*. London: T. & W. Boone, 1845.
Grey, George. *Journals of Two Expeditions of Discovery in North-Western and Western Australia*. 2 vols. London: T. & W. Boone, 1841.
Leichhardt, Ludwig. *Journal of an Overland Expedition from Moreton Bay to Port Essington, a Distance of Upwards of 3000 Miles, During the Years 1844–1845*. London: T. & W. Boone, 1847.
Mitchell, Thomas. *Three Expeditions into the Interior of Eastern Australia: With Descriptions of the Recently Explored Region of Australia Felix, and of the Present Colony of New South Wales*. 2 vols. London: T. & W. Boone, 1838.
Plomley, N. J. B., ed. *Friendly Mission; The Tasmanian Journals and Papers of George Augustus Robinson, 1829–1834*. Launceston: Queen Victoria Museum and Art Gallery and Quintus, 2008.
———. *Weep in Silence: A History of the Flinders Island Aboriginal Settlement*. Hobart: Blubber Head, 1987.
Sturt, Charles. *Two Expeditions into the Interior of Southern Australia, During the Years 1828, 1829, 1830, and 1831*. 2 vols. London: Smith, Elder, & Co., 1834.
Tench, Watkin. *Sydney's First Four Years: Being a Reprint of* A Narrative of the Expedition to Botany Bay [1788] *and* A Complete Account of the Settlement at Port Jackson [1793]. Sydney: Angus & Robertson, 1961.

Missionaries also wrote numerous accounts of varying value about their contact with Aborigines in differing parts of the continent.

Backhouse, James. *A Narrative of a Visit to the Australian Colonies*. London: Hamilton, Adams & Co., 1843.

Dredge, James. *Brief Notices of the Aborigines of New South Wales*. Geelong: James Harrison, 1845.

Gribble, John Brown. *Black but Comely, or, Glimpses of Aboriginal Life in Australia*. London: Morgan & Scott, 1884.

Gunson, Niel, ed. *Australian Reminiscences & Papers of L. E. Threlkeld*. Canberra: AIATSIS, 1974.

Hale, Mathew B. *The Aborigines of Australia: Being an Account of the Institution for Their Education at Poonindie*. London: Society for Promoting Christian Knowledge, 1889.

Parker, Edward S. *The Aborigines of Australia: A Lecture*. Melbourne: Hugh McColl, 1854.

Smyth, Robert Brough. *The Aborigines of Victoria: With Notes Relating to the Habits of the Natives of Other Parts of Australia and Tasmania*. 2 vols. Melbourne: Govt. Printer, 1878.

Taplin, George, ed. *The Folklore, Manners, Customs and Languages of the South Australian Aborigines*. Adelaide: E. Spiller, 1879.

There were many amateur ethnographers and anthropologists in the Australian colonies. Some of the books they wrote are still worth reading.

Bonwick, James. *Daily Life and Origins of the Tasmanians*. London: Sampson Low, Son & Marston, 1870.

Curr, Edward. *The Australian Race: Its Origins, Languages, Customs, Place of Landing in Australia, and the Routes by Which it Spread Itself over that Continent*. 4 vols. Melbourne: John Farnes, 1886–87.

Fison, Lorimer, and A. W. Howitt. *Kamilaroi and Kurnai*. Melbourne: George Robertson, 1880.

Fraser, John. *The Aborigines of New South Wales*. Sydney: Charles Potter, 1892.

Howitt, A. W. *The Native Tribes of South-East Australia*. London: Macmillan, 1904.

Roth, H. Ling. *The Aborigines of Tasmania*. Halifax: F. King and Sons, 1890.

Roth, Walter. *Ethnological Studies among the North-West-Central Queensland Aborigines*. Brisbane: Edmund Gregory, 1897.

Sadlier, Richard. *The Aborigines of Australia*. Sydney: Thomas Richards, 1883.

Woods, J., ed. *The Native Tribes of South Australia*. Adelaide: E. S. Wigg & Son, 1879.

2. Modern Ethnography and Anthropology

The first professional anthropology was carried out by the Cambridge University Expedition to Torres Strait in 1898 led by A. C. Haddon. The official reports were published serially but not in sequence over many years. See the following:

Haddon, A. C., ed. *Reports of the Cambridge Anthropological Expedition to Torres Strait*. 6 vols. Cambridge: Cambridge University Press, 1903–35.

———. *Reports of the Cambridge Anthropological Expedition to Torres Strait.* Vol. 1, *General Ethnography.* Cambridge: Cambridge University Press, 1935.
———. *Reports of the Cambridge Anthropological Expedition to Torres Strait.* Vol. 2, *Physiology and Psychology.* Cambridge: Cambridge University Press, 1903.
———. *Reports of the Cambridge Anthropological Expedition to Torres Strait.* Vol. 3, *The Languages of Torres Strait.* Cambridge: Cambridge University Press, 1907.
———. *Reports of the Cambridge Anthropological Expedition to Torres Strait.* Vol. 4, *Arts and Crafts.* Cambridge: Cambridge University Press, 1912.
———. *Reports of the Cambridge Anthropological Expedition to Torres Strait.* Vol. 5, *Magic and Religion of the Western Islanders.* Cambridge: Cambridge University Press, 1904.
———. *Reports of the Cambridge Anthropological Expedition to Torres Strait.* Vol. 6, *Sociology, Magic and Religion of the Eastern Islanders.* Cambridge: Cambridge University Press, 1908.

While the Cambridge expedition was in the far north, Baldwin Spencer was working in Central Australia. See his texts:
Spencer, W. Baldwin, ed. *Report on the Work of the Horn Scientific Expedition to Central Australia.* London: Dulau, 1896.
Spencer, W. Baldwin, and Francis James Gillen. *Across Australia.* 2 vols. London: Macmillan, 1912.
———. *Native Tribes of Central Australia.* London: Macmillan, 1938.
———. *The Northern Tribes of Central Australia.* London: Macmillan, 1904.

Numerous anthropologists worked in Australia during the first half of the 20th century. For some of the best known work, see:
Elkin, Adolphus Peter. *Aboriginal Men of High Degree.* Sydney: Australasian, 1945.
———. *The Australian Aborigines: How to Understand Them.* Sydney: Angus & Robertson, 1938.
Kaberry, Phyllis. *Aboriginal Women: Sacred and Profane.* London: G. Routledge, 1939.
Strehlow, Theodor. *Aranda Traditions.* Melbourne: Melbourne University Press, 1947.
Thomson, Donald. *Economic Structure and the Ceremonial Exchange Cycle in Arnhem Land.* Melbourne: Macmillan, 1949.
Warner, W. Lloyd. *A Black Civilization.* New York: Harper & Brothers, 1937.

Several authors have written books of synthesis for the general reader. See:
Beckett, Jeremy. *Torres Strait Islanders: Custom and Colonialism.* Cambridge: Cambridge University Press, 1987.
Berndt, Catherine, and Ronald Berndt. *The Aboriginal Australians: The First Pioneers.* Melbourne: Pitman, 1985.
———. *The World of the First Australians.* Sydney: Ure Smith, 1964.
Edwards, W. H. *An Introduction to Aboriginal Societies.* Wentworth Falls: Social Science, 1988.

———, ed. *Traditional Aboriginal Society: A Reader*. South Melbourne: Macmillan, 1987.

Maddock, Kenneth. *The Australian Aborigines: A Portrait of Their Society*. London: Allen Lane, 1972.

Among a very large, more specialist anthropological literatures, see:

Akerman, Kim. "Shoes in Invisibility and Invisible Shoes: Australian Hunters and Gatherers and Ideas on the Origins of Footwear." *Australian Aboriginal Studies*, no. 2 (2005): 55–64.

Beckett, Jeremy R., ed. *Past and Present: The Construction of Aboriginality*. Canberra: Aboriginal Studies, 1988.

Bell, Diane. *Daughters of the Dreaming*. Sydney: Allen & Unwin, 1983.

Burbank, Victoria Katherine. *Fighting Women: Anger and Aggression in Aboriginal Australia*. Berkley: University of California Press, 1994.

Cahir, David, and Ian Clark. "'An Edifying Spectacle': A History of 'Tourist Corroborees' in Victoria, Australia, 1835–1870." *Tourism Management* 30 (2009): 1–9.

Charlesworth, Max, ed. *Religious Business: Essays on Australian Aboriginal Spirituality*. Melbourne: Cambridge University Press, 1998.

Charlesworth, Max, Dussart, Françoise, and Howard Morphy, eds. *Aboriginal Religions in Australia: An Anthology of Recent Writings*. Hants: Ashgate, 2005.

Dixon, Robert. *The Languages of Australia*. Cambridge: Cambridge University Press, 1980.

Enright, Walter. "The Initiation Ceremonies of the Aborigines of Port Stephens, N.S. Wales." *Journal of the Royal Society of New South Wales* 33 (1899): 115–24.

Hiatt, Lester. *Arguments about Aborigines: Australia and the Evolution of Social Anthropology*. New York: Cambridge University Press, 1996.

———, ed. *Australian Aboriginal Concepts*. Canberra: AIATSIS, 1978.

———. *Kinship and Conflict: A Study of an Aboriginal Community in Northern Arnhem Land*. Canberra: Australian National University Press, 1965.

Keen, Ian, ed. *Being Black: Aboriginal Cultures in "Settled" Australia*. Canberra: Aboriginal Studies, 1988.

Kirk, Robert. *Aboriginal Man Adapting: The Human Biology of Australian Aborigines*. Melbourne: Oxford University Press, 1983.

Kitching, H. S. "Observation of Customs Associated with Kadaitja Practices in Central Australia." *Oceania* 31, no. 3 (March 1961): 210–14.

Matthews, Robert Hamilton. "The Aboriginal Bora at Gundabloui in 1894." *Journal and Proceedings of the Royal Society of New South Wales* 28 (1894): 98–129.

———. "The Bora, or Initiation Ceremonies of the Kamilaroi Tribes." *Journal of the Anthropological Institute* 24 (1895): 411–27.

———. "The Keeparra Ceremony of Initiation." *Journal of the Royal Anthropological Institute* 26 (1886): 320–40.

McConnel, Ursula. *Myths of the Munkan*. Melbourne: Melbourne University Press, 1957.

Meggitt, Mervyn J. *Desert People: A Study of the Walbiri Aborigines of Central Australia*. Chicago: University of Chicago Press, 1962.

Munn, Nancy. *Walbiri Iconography: Graphic Representation and Cultural Symbolism in a Central Australian Society*. Ithaca, NY: Cornell University Press, 1973.

Myers, Fred. *Pintupi Country, Pintupi Self: Sentiment, Place and Politics among Western Desert Aborigines*. Canberra: Australian Institute of Aboriginal Studies, 1986.

Nakata, Martin. *Disciplining the Savages, Savaging the Disciplines*. Canberra: Aboriginal Studies, 2007.

Peterson, Nicolas, ed. *Tribes and Boundaries in Australia*. Canberra: AIATSIS, 1976.

Plomley, N. J. B. *A Word-List of the Tasmanian Aboriginal Languages*. Hobart: Plomley and Government of Tasmania, 1976.

Pounder, Derrick. "A New Perspective on Kadaitja Killings." *Oceania* 56, no. 1 (September 1985): 77–82.

Rose, Frederick. *The Traditional Mode of Production of the Australian Aborigines*. Sydney: Angus & Robertson, 1987.

Sharp, Nonie. *Stars of Tagai: The Torres Strait Islanders*. Canberra: Aboriginal Studies, 1993.

Stanner, W. E. H. *On Aboriginal Religion*. Sydney: Sydney University Press, 1989.

Strehlow, Theodor. *Songs of Central Australia*. Sydney: Angus & Robertson, 1971.

Tindale, Norman. *Aboriginal Tribes of Australia: Their Terrain, Environmental Controls, Distribution, Limits, and Proper Names*. Canberra: Australian National University Press, 1974.

Tonkinson, Robert. *The Mardu Aborigines: Living the Dream in Australia's Desert*. Fort Worth, TX: Holt, Rinehart & Winston, 1991.

Warner, W. Lloyd. "Malay Influence on the Aboriginal Cultures of North-Eastern Arnhem Land." *Oceania* 11, no. 4 (June 1932): 476–95.

Williams, Nancy. *Two Laws: Managing Disputes in a Contemporary Aboriginal Community*. Canberra: Australian Institute of Aboriginal Studies, 1987.

II. THEMATIC WORKS

1. Prehistory and Archaeology

Professional archaeology was not practiced in Australia until the 1960s. For a general survey of the field, see:

Blainey, Geoffrey. *Triumph of the Nomads: A History of Ancient Australia*. South Melbourne: Macmillan, 1976.

Cosgrove, Richard. "Forty-Two Degrees South: The Archaeology of Late Pleistocene Tasmania." *Journal of World Prehistory* 13, no. 4 (December 1999): 357–402.

Flannery, Tim. *The Future Eaters: An Ecological History of the Australasian Lands and People*. Melbourne: Reed, 1995.

Flood, Josephine. *Archaeology of the Dreamtime: The Story of Prehistoric Australia and its People*. Marleston: JB, 2004.

———. *The Original Australians: Story of the Aboriginal people*. Sydney: Allen & Unwin, 2006.

Horton, David. *Recovering the Tracks: The Story of Australian Archaeology.* Canberra: Aboriginal Studies, 1991.
Johnson, Murray. "'Cranial Connections': Queensland's 'Talgai Skull' Debate of 1918 and Custodianship of the Past." *Aboriginal History* 24 (2000): 117–31.
Jones, Rhys. "Tasmanian Archaeology: Establishing the Sequences." *Annual Review of Archaeology* 24 (October 1995): 423–46.
Lourandas, Harry. *Continent of Hunter-Gatherers: New Perspectives in Australian Prehistory.* Melbourne: Cambridge University Press, 1997.
Macintosh, N. W. G. "The Talgai Cranium: The Value of Archives." *Australian Natural History* 16, no. 6 (June 1967): 189–95.
Mulvaney, John, and Johan Kamminga. *A Prehistory of Australia.* Sydney: Allen & Unwin, 1999.
Prentis, Malcolm. "From Lemuria to Kow Swamp: The Rise and Fall of Tri-Hybrid Theories of Aboriginal Origins." *Journal of Australian Studies* 45 (June 1995): 79–91.
Schultz, Dennis. "Backdating the Clock: Were There Humans in Australia 60,000 Years Ago?" *Bulletin* 4 (July 1995): 36–37.
Smith, Stewart Arthur. "The Fossil Human Skull Found at Talgai, Queensland." *Philosophical Transactions of the Royal Society of London* 208, series B (1918): 351–87.
Tunitz, Claudio, Richard Gillespie, and Cheryl Jones. *The Bone Readers: Atoms, Genes and the Politics of Australia's Deep Past.* Sydney: Allen & Unwin, 2009.
Urry, James. "Old Questions: New Answers? Some Thoughts on the Origin and Antiquity of Man in Australia." *Aboriginal History* 2, pt. 2 (1978): 149–66.
White, J. Peter, and James F. O'Connell. *A Prehistory of Australia, New Guinea, and Sahul.* Sydney: Academic, 1982.
Wright, R. V. S., ed. *Stone Tools as Cultural Markers: Change, Evolution and Complexity.* Canberra: Australian Institute of Aboriginal Studies, 1977.

2. Historiography

Many of the books written about Australia in the 19th century contained historical accounts of the Aborigines. Few of these accounts were original or had any lasting value. But see the following:

Bonwick, James. *The Last of the Tasmanians; or, the Black War of Van Diemen's Land.* London: Sampson Low, Son & Marston, 1870.
Rusden, George William. *History of Australia.* 3 vols. Melbourne: Melville, 1897.
West, John. *The History of Tasmania.* 2 vols. Launceston: Henry Dowling, 1852.

Interest in the history of the Aborigines declined during the first half of the 20th century. A few works are still worth the reader's attention. See, for instance:
Berndt, Ronald, and Catherine Berndt. *From Black to White in South Australia.* Melbourne: Chesire, 1951.

Hasluck, Paul. *Black Australians: A Survey of Native Policy in Western Australia, 1829–1897.* Melbourne: Melbourne University Press, 1942.
Turnbull, Clive. *Black War: The Extermination of the Tasmanian Aborigines.* Melbourne: Cheshire, 1948.

The modern efflorescence of history about race relations in Australia can be conveniently dated from the publication of a lecture series by W. E. H. Stanner, originally broadcast in 1968 on what was then the Australian Broadcasting Commission.
Stanner, William Edward. *After the Dreaming: Black and White Australians—an Anthropologist's View.* Sydney: Australian Broadcasting Commission, 1969.

This work was followed by an important trilogy commissioned by the Academy of Social Sciences:
Rowley, Charles D. *The Destruction of Aboriginal Society.* Canberra: Australian National University, 1970.
———. *Outcasts in White Australia.* Canberra: Australian National University Press, 1971.
———. *The Remote Aborigines.* Canberra: Australian National University Press, 1971.

During the 1970s, a number of historians produced collections of documents. They are still useful. See:
Franklin, Margaret, ed. *Black and White Australians: An Inter-Racial History, 1788–1975.* Melbourne: Heinemann, 1976.
Reynolds, Henry, ed. *Aborigines and Settlers: The Australian Experience, 1788–1939.* Melbourne: Cassell, 1972.
Stone, Sharman, ed. *Aborigines in White Australia: A Documentary History.* Melbourne: Heinemann, 1974.
Woolmington, Jean, ed. *Aborigines in Colonial Society, 1788–1850: From "Noble Savage" to "Rural Pest."* Melbourne: Cassell, 1973.

Over the last generation, many historical works have been published covering many aspects of Aboriginal history. Among them, see the following:
Attwood, Bain. *The Making of the Aborigines.* North Sydney: Allen & Unwin, 1989.
———. *Possession: Batman's Treaty and the Matter of History.* Carlton: Miegunyah, 2009.
Attwood, Bain, and Fiona Magowan, eds. *Telling Stories: Indigenous History and Memory in Australia and New Zealand.* Crows Nest: Allen & Unwin, 2001.
Attwood, Bain, and Andrew Markus. *The 1967 Referendum: Race, Power and the Australian Constitution.* Canberra: Aboriginal Studies, 2007.
Biskup, Peter. *Not Slaves, Not Citizens: The Aboriginal Problem in Western Australia, 1898–1954.* St. Lucia: University of Queensland Press, 1973.
Bonwick, James. *John Batman: The Founder of Victoria.* Edited by C. E. Sayers. Melbourne: Wren, 1973.

Borch, Merete. "Rethinking the Origins of *Terra Nullius.*" *Australian Historical Studies* 32, no. 117 (October 2001): 222–39.
Broome, Richard. *Aboriginal Australians: Black Responses to White Dominance 1788–2001.* Sydney: Allen & Unwin, 2001.
Campbell, Alastair. *John Batman and the Aborigines.* Malmsbury: Kibble, 1987.
Christie, Michael. *Aborigines in Colonial Victoria, 1835–86.* Sydney: Sydney University Press, 1979.
Clendinnen, Inga. *Dancing with Strangers.* Melbourne: Text, 2003.
Curthoys, Ann. *Freedom Ride: A Freedom Rider Remembers.* Crows Nest: Allen & Unwin, 2002.
Evans, Raymond, Kay Saunders, and Kathryn Cronin. *Exclusion, Exploitation, and Extermination: Race Relations in Colonial Queensland.* Sydney: Australia & New Zealand Book Co., 1975.
Griffiths, Max. *Aboriginal Affairs: A Short History, 1788–1995.* Kenthurst: Kangaroo, 1995.
Janson, Susan, and Stuart Macintyre, eds. *Through White Eyes.* Sydney: Allen & Unwin, 1990.
McGrath, Ann. *Contested Ground: Australian Aborigines under the British Crown.* Sydney: Allen & Unwin, 1995.
McGregor, Russell. *Imagined Destinies: Aboriginal Australians and the Doomed Race Theory, 1880–1939.* Melbourne: Melbourne University Press, 1997.
Mulvaney, Derek John. *Encounters in Place: Outsiders and Aboriginal Australians, 1606–1985.* St. Lucia: University of Queensland Press, 1989.
Reece, Robert. *Aborigines and Colonists: Aborigines and Colonists in New South Wales in the 1830s and 1840s.* Sydney: Sydney University Press, 1974.
Reynolds, Henry. *Frontier: Aborigines, Settlers, and Land.* Sydney: Allen & Unwin, 1987.
———. *Nowhere People.* Camberwell: Penguin, 2005.
———. *The Other Side of the Frontier: An Interpretation of the Aboriginal Response to the Invasion and Settlement of Australia.* Townsville: James Cook University, 1981.
———. *With the White People.* Ringwood: Penguin, 1990.

Many important recent books have had a regional or a state focus.

For New South Wales, see:
Goodall, Heather. *Invasion to Embassy: Land in Aboriginal Politics in New South Wales, 1770–1972.* Sydney: Allen & Unwin, 1996.
Milliss, Roger. *Waterloo Creek: The Australia Day Massacre of 1838, George Gipps and the British Conquest of New South Wales.* Ringwood: McPhee Gribble, 1992.
Ramsland, John. *Custodians of the Soil: The History of Aboriginal-European Relations in the Manning Valley of New South Wales.* Kempsey: Taree City Council, 2001.
Read, Peter. *A Hundred Years War: The Wiradjuri People and the State.* Canberra: Australian National University Press, 1988.

For Queensland, see:

Bottoms, Timothy. *Djabugay Country: An Aboriginal History of Tropical North Queensland.* Sydney: Allen & Unwin, 1999.

French, Maurice. *Conflict on the Condamine: Aborigines and the European Invasion.* Toowoomba: Darling Downs Institute, 1989.

Ganter, Regina. *The Pearl-Shellers of Torres Strait: Resource Use, Development and Decline, 1860s–1960s.* Melbourne: Melbourne University Press, 1994.

Kidd, Rosalind. *The Way We Civilise: Aboriginal Affairs—The Untold Story.* St. Lucia: University of Queensland Press, 1997.

May, Dawn. *Aboriginal Labour and the Cattle Industry: Queensland from White Settlement to the Present.* Melbourne: Cambridge University Press, 1994.

Mullins, Steve. *Torres Strait: A History of Colonial Occupation and Culture, 1864–1897.* Rockhampton: Central Queensland, 1995.

Loos, Noel. *Invasion and Resistance: Aboriginal-European Relations on the North Queensland Frontier, 1861–1897.* Canberra: Australian National University Press, 1982.

Reid, Gordon. *A Nest of Hornets: The Massacre of the Fraser Family at Hornet Bank Station, Central Queensland, 1857.* Melbourne: Oxford University Press, 1982.

Richards, Jonathan. *The Secret War: A True History of Queensland's Police.* St. Lucia: University of Queensland Press, 2008.

Singe, John. *The Torres Strait: People and History.* St. Lucia: University of Queensland Press, 1989 [1979].

Thorpe, Bill. *Colonial Queensland: Perspectives on a Frontier Society.* St. Lucia: University of Queensland Press, 1996.

Trigger, David. *Whitefella Comin': Aboriginal Responses to Colonialism in Northern Australia.* Cambridge: Cambridge University Press, 1992.

Watson, Pamela L. *Frontier Lands and Pioneer Legends: How Pastoralists Gained Karuwali Land.* Sydney: Allen & Unwin, 1998.

Wright, Judith. *The Cry for the Dead.* Melbourne: Oxford University Press, 1981.

For the Northern Territory, see:

Austin, Tony. *Never Trust a Government Man: Northern Territory Aboriginal Policy, 1911–1939.* Darwin: Northern Territory University Press, 1997.

Baker, Richard. *Land is Life: From Bush to Town: The Story of the Yanyuwa People.* Sydney: Allen & Unwin, 1999.

Markus, Andrew. *Governing Savages.* North Sydney: Allen & Unwin, 1990.

McGrath, Ann. *Born in the Cattle: Aborigines in Cattle Country.* Sydney: Allen & Unwin, 1987.

Reid, Gordon. *A Picnic with the Natives: Aboriginal-European Relations in the Northern Territory to 1910.* Melbourne: Melbourne University Press, 1990.

Roberts, Tony. *Frontier Justice: A History of the Gulf Country to 1900.* St. Lucia: University of Queensland Press, 2005.

Vallee, Peter. *God, Guns, and Government on the Central Australian Frontier.* Canberra: Restoration, 2007.

Williams, Nancy. *The Yolngu and Their Land: A System of Land Tenure and the Fight for Its Recognition.* Canberra: AIATSIS, 1986.

For Western Australia, see:

Forrest, Kay. *The Challenge and the Change: The Colonisation and Settlement of North West Australia, 1861–1914*. Perth: Hesperian, 1996.

Haebich, Anna. *For Their Own Good: Aborigines and Government in the Southwest of Western Australia, 1900–1940*. Perth: University of Western Australia, 1988.

Jebb, Mary. *Blood, Sweat and Welfare: A History of White Bosses and Aboriginal Pastoral Workers*. Perth: University of Western Australia, 2002.

McLeod, Don. *How the West Was Lost: The Native Question in the Development of Western Australia*. Port Hedland: D. W. McLeod, 1984.

Pedersen, Howard, and Banjo Woorunmurra. *Jandamarra and the Bunuba Resistance*. Broome: Magabala Books, 1995.

For Victoria, see:

Broome, Richard. *Aboriginal Victorians: A History since 1800*. Sydney: Allen & Unwin, 2005.

Cannon, Michael. *Who Killed the Koories?* Port Melbourne: William Heinemann, 1990.

Critchett, Jan. *A Distant Field of Murder: Western District Frontiers, 1834–1848*. Melbourne: Melbourne University Press, 1990.

Fels, Marie. *Good Men and True: The Aboriginal Police of the Port Phillip District, 1837–1853*. Carlton: Melbourne University Press, 1988.

For Tasmania, refer to:

Johnston, Anna, and Mitchell Rolls, eds. *Reading Robinson: Companion Essays to Friendly Mission*. Hobart: Quintus, 2008.

McFarlane, Ian. *Beyond Awakening: The Aboriginal Tribes of North West Tasmania*. Hobart: Fullers, 2008.

Plomley, N. J. B., ed. *Friendly Mission: The Tasmanian Journals and Papers of George Augustus Robinson, 1829–1834*. Launceston: Queen Victoria Museum and Art Gallery and Quintus, 2008.

———. *Weep in Silence: A History of the Flinders Island Aboriginal Settlement*. Hobart: Blubber Head, 1987.

Pybus, Cassandra. *Community of Thieves*. Melbourne: Heinemann, 1991.

Reynolds, Henry. *Fate of a Free People*. Camberwell: Penguin, 1995.

Ryan, Lyndall. *The Aboriginal Tasmanians*. St. Leonards: Allen & Unwin, 1996.

3. Frontier Conflict

Much of the controversy about Aboriginal history in recent years has centered on the question of frontier conflict. This issue has been at the center of the so-called history wars. For some of the most important literature, see the following:

Attwood, Bain. *Telling the Truth about Aboriginal History*. Crows Nest: Allen & Unwin, 2005.

Attwood, Bain, and S. G. Foster, eds. *Frontier Conflict: The Australian Experience*. Canberra: National Museum of Australia, 2003.

Clark, Ian D. *Scars in the Landscape: A Register of Massacre Sites in Western Victoria, 1803–1859*. Canberra: AIATSIS, 1995.
Connor, John. *The Australian Frontier Wars, 1788–1838*. Sydney: University of New South Wales Press, 2002.
Foster, Robert, Amanda Nettelbeck, and Rick Hosking. *Fatal Collisions: The South Australian Frontier and the Violence of Memory*. Adelaide: Wakefield, 2001.
Macintyre, Stuart, and Anna Clark. *The History Wars*. Carlton South: Melbourne University Press, 2003.
Manne, Robert, ed. *Whitewash: On Keith Windschuttle's Fabrication of Aboriginal History*. Melbourne: Black, 2003.
Moran, Rod. *Massacre Myth: An Investigation into Allegations Concerning the Mass Murder of Aborigines at Forrest River, 1926*. Perth: Access, 1999.
Windschuttle, Keith. *The Fabrication of Aboriginal History: Vol. 1, Van Dieman's Land 1803–1847*. Sydney: Macleay, 2002.

4. The Stolen Generations

Bird, Carmel, ed. *The Stolen Children: Their Stories*. Sydney: Random House, 1998.
Choo, Christine. *Mission Girls: Aboriginal Women on Catholic Missions in the Kimberley, Western Australia, 1900–1950*. Perth: University of Western Australia Press, 2001.
Edwards, Coral, and Peter Read, eds. *The Lost Children: Thirteen Australians Taken from Their Aboriginal Families Tell of the Struggle to Find Their Natural Parents*. Sydney: Doubleday, 1989.
Haebich, Anna. *Broken Circles: Fragmenting Aboriginal Families, 1800–2000*. Fremantle: Freemantle Arts Centre, 2000.
Human Rights and Equal Opportunities Commission. *Bringing Them Home: Report of the Inquiry into the Separation of Aboriginal and Torres Strait Islander Children from Their Families*. Sydney: Human Rights and Equal Opportunities Commission, 1997.
Mellor, Doreen, and Anna Haebich, eds. *Many Voices*. Canberra: Australian National Library, 2002.
Read, Peter. *A Rape of the Soul So Profound: The Return of the Stolen Generations*. Sydney: Allen & Unwin, 1999.
Windschuttle, Keith. *The Fabrication of Aboriginal History. Vol. 3, The Stolen Generations: 1881–2008*. Sydney: Mcleay, 2009.

5. Politics, Activism, and Race Relations

There were many people who attempted to improve the lot of the Aborigines during the 19th century. Some of them were featured in:
Reynolds, Henry. *This Whispering in Our Hearts*. Sydney: Allen & Unwin, 1998.

For activism in the first half of the 20th century, see:
Bennett, Mary. *The Australian Aboriginal as a Human Being*. London: Alston Rivers, 1930.

Elkin, Adolphus P. *Citizenship for the Aborigines: A National Aboriginal Policy.* Sydney: Australasian, 1944.
Horner, Jack. *Bill Ferguson: Fighter for Aboriginal Freedom.* Canberra: J. Horner, 1994.
Markus, Andrew. *Blood from a Stone: William Cooper and the Australian Aborigines' League.* Sydney: Allen & Unwin, 1988.
Paisley, Fiona. *Loving Protection? Feminism and Women's Rights, 1919–1939.* Melbourne: Melbourne University Press, 2000.
Wright, Thomas. *New Deal for the Aborigines.* Sydney: NSW Labour Council, 1939.

For the struggle for civil rights, see:
Attwood, Bain. *Rights for Aborigines.* Sydney: Allen & Unwin, 2003.
Attwood, Bain, and Andrew Markus. *The Struggle for Aboriginal Rights: A Documentary History.* Sydney: Allen & Unwin, 1999.
Chesterman, John. *Civil Rights: How Indigenous Australians Won Formal Equality.* St. Lucia: University of Queensland Press, 2005.
Chesterman, John, and Brian Galligan. *Citizens without Rights: Aborigines and Australian Citizenship.* Melbourne: Cambridge University Press, 1997.
Taffe, Susan. *Black and White Together FCAATSI: The Federal Council for the Advancement of Aborigines and Torres Strait Islanders, 1958–1973.* St. Lucia: University of Queensland Press, 2005.

There are biographies of some of the leading Indigenous and non-Indigenous activists:
Attwood, Bain, and Andrew Markus. *Thinking Black: William Cooper and the Australian Aborigines' League.* Canberra: Aboriginal Studies, 2004.
Beresford, Quentin. *Rob Riley: An Aboriginal Leader's Quest for Justice.* Canberra: Aboriginal Studies, 2006.
Clark, Mavis Thorpe. *Pastor Doug: The Story of Sir Douglas Nicholls, Aboriginal Leader.* Melbourne: Lansdowne, 1972.
Cochrane, Kathie. *Oodgeroo.* Brisbane: University of Queensland Press, 1994.
Horner, Jack. *Vote Ferguson for Aboriginal Freedom: A Biography.* Sydney: Australia & New Zealand Book Company, 1974.
Lake, Marilyn. *Faith: Faith Bandler, Gentle Activist.* Sydney: Allen & Unwin, 2002.
Norst, Marlene. *Burnum Burnum: A Warrior for Peace.* Sydney: Simon & Schuster, 1999.
Read, Peter. *Charles Perkins: A Biography.* Camberwell: Viking, 1990.
Rowse, Tim. *Obliged to be Difficult: Nugget Coombs' Legacy in Indigenous Affairs.* Melbourne: Cambridge University Press, 1998.
Sekuless, Peter. *Jessie Street, a Rewarding but Unrewarded Life.* St. Lucia: University of Queensland Press, 1978.
Wilmott, Eric. *Pemulwuy: The Rainbow Warrior.* Sydney: Weldon, 1987.

For more general books on indigenous politics and race relations, see:
Behrendt, Larissa. *Achieving Social Justice: Indigenous Rights and Australia's Future.* Sydney: Federation, 2003.

Bennett, Scott. *White Politics and Black Australians.* Sydney: Allen & Unwin, 1999.
Coombs, Herbert. *Kulinma: Listening to Aboriginal Australians.* Canberra: Australian National University Press, 1978.
Cowlishaw, Gillian. *Black, White or Brindle: Race in Rural Australia.* Cambridge: Cambridge University Press, 1988.
——. *Blackfellas, Whitefellas, and the Hidden Injuries of Race.* Carlton: Blackwell, 2005.
——. *Rednecks, Eggheads, and Blackfellas: A Study of Racial Power and Intimacy in Australia.* St. Leonards: Allen & Unwin, 1999.
Fletcher, Christine. *Aboriginal Politics: Intergovernmental Relations.* Melbourne: Melbourne University Press, 1992.
Gale, F., and Alison Brookman, eds. *Race Relations in Australia: The Aborigines.* Sydney: McGraw Hill, 1975.
Lippmann, Lorna. *Words or Blows: Racial Attitudes in Australia.* Ringwood: Penguin, 1973.
Markus, Andrew. *Australian Race Relations, 1788–1993.* Sydney: Allen & Unwin, 1994.
McConnochie, Keith, and David Hollinsworth. *Race and Racism in Australia.* Sydney: Social Science, 1988.
Neville, Auber Octavius. *Australia's Coloured Minority: Its Place in the Community.* Sydney: Currawong, 1947.
Pittock, A. Barrie. *Toward a Multi-Racial Society.* Melbourne: Society of Friends, 1969.
Reay, Marie, ed. *Aborigines Now.* Sydney: Angus & Robertson, 1964.
Rowley, Charles. D. *A Matter of Justice.* Canberra: Australian National University Press, 1978.
——. *Recovery: The Politics of Aboriginal Reform.* Ringwood: Penguin, 1986.
Sutton, Peter. *The Politics of Suffering: Indigenous Australia and the End of the Liberal Consensus.* Melbourne: Melbourne University Press, 2009.

6. Legal and Judicial Matters Including Land Rights and Native Title

For general surveys see:
Australian Law Reform Commission. *Aboriginal Customary Law—Recognition?* Sydney: Australian Law Reform Commission, 1980.
Committee of Inquiry: Aboriginal Customary Law. *Report of the Committee of Inquiry into Aboriginal Customary Law.* Darwin: Northern Territory Law Reform Committee, 2003. http://www.nt.gov.au/justice/docs/lawmake/ntlrc_final_report.pdf.
Curthoys, Ann, Ann Genovese, and Alex Reilly. *Rights and Redemption: History, Law and Indigenous People.* Sydney: University of New South Wales Press, 2008.
Eggleston, Elizabeth. *Fear, Favour or Affection: Aborigines and the Criminal Law in Victoria, South Australia and Western Australia.* Canberra: Australian National University Press, 1976.
Hanks, Peter, and Brian Keon-Cohen, eds. *Aborigines and the Law: Essays in Memory of Elizabeth Eggleston.* Sydney: Allen & Unwin, 1984.

Law Reform Commission of Western Australia. *Aboriginal Customary Laws: The Interaction of Western Australia Law with Aboriginal Law and Culture, Final Report*. Perth: Government of Western Australia, September 2006.

McCorquodale, John. *Aborigines and the Law: A Digest*. Canberra: AIATSIS, 1987.

McRae, Heather, Garth Nettheim, and Laura Beacroft. *Indigenous Legal Issues: Commentary and Materials*. Pyrmont: Thomson Reuters, 2009.

Nettheim, Garth, ed. *Aborigines, Human Rights and the Law*. Sydney: ANZ Book, 1974.

Sutton, Peter. *Native Title in Australia: An Ethnographic Perspective*. Port Melbourne: Cambridge University Press, 2003.

Tatz, Colin. *Race Politics in Australia: Aborigines, Politics, and Law*. Armidale: University of New England, 1979.

Since the 1960s, land rights have been at the confluence of law and politics. This was particularly so in the 1990s, after several major decisions handed down by the High Court of Australia. For a selection of the extensive literature, see:

Attwood, Bain, ed. *In the Age of Mabo: History, Aborigines, and Australia*. Sydney: Allen & Unwin, 1996.

Bartlett, Richard. *The Mabo Decision*. Sydney: Butterworths, 1993.

———. *Native Title in Australia*. Sydney: Butterworths, 2000.

Brennan, Frank. *One Land, One Nation: Mabo—Towards 2001*. St. Lucia: University of Queensland Press, 1995.

Goot, Murray, and Tim Rowse. *Make a Better Offer: The Politics of Mabo*. Sydney: Pluto, 1994.

Havemann, Paul, ed. *Indigenous Peoples' Rights in Australia, Canada, and New Zealand*. Auckland: Oxford University Press, 1999.

Hiley, Graham, ed. *The Wik Case: Issues and Implications*. Sydney: Butterworths, 1997.

Keon-Cohen, Bryan, ed. *Native Title in the New Millennium: A Selection of Papers from the Native Title Representative Bodies Legal Conference, 16–20 April, 2000, Melbourne, Victoria*. Canberra: Aboriginal Studies, 2001.

Loos, Noel, and Koiki Mabo. *Edward Koiki Mabo: His Life and Struggle for Land Rights*. St. Lucia: University of Queensland Press, 1996.

Olbrei, Erik, ed. *Black Australians: The Prospects for Change*. Townsville: James Cook University, 1982.

Peterson, Nicholas, ed. *Aboriginal Land Rights: A Handbook*. Canberra: AIATSIS, 1981.

Sharp, Nonie. *No Ordinary Judgement: Mabo, the Murray Islanders' Land Case*. Canberra: Aboriginal Studies, 1996.

Stephenson, M. A., and Suri Ratnapala, eds. *Mabo: A Judicial Revolution*. St. Lucia: University of Queensland Press, 1993.

Sullivan, Patrick. *Regional Agreements in Australia*. Canberra: AIATSIS, 1997.

Tickner, Robert. *Taking a Stand: Land Rights to Reconciliation*. Sydney: Allen & Unwin, 2001.

Yunupingu, Galarrwuy, ed. *Our Land Is Our Life: Land Rights, Past, Present and Future*. St. Lucia: University of Queensland Press, 1997.

There have been a number of other issues that have brought together history, jurisprudence, and politics. The question of genocide is the most contentious. See:

Moses, A. Dirk, ed. *Genocide and Settler Society: Frontier Violence and Stolen Indigenous Children in Australian History.* New York: Berghahn Books, 2004.
Palmer, Alison. *Colonial Genocide.* Adelaide: Crawford House, 2000.
Reynolds, Henry. *The Question of Genocide in Australian History: An Indelible Stain?* Ringwood: Penguin, 2001.

Another question under debate in recent years is the matter of treaty making and indigenous sovereignty. See the following:

Fletcher, Christine, ed. *Aboriginal Self-Determination in Australia.* Canberra: AIATSIS, 1994.
Gilbert, Kevin. *Aboriginal Sovereignty: Justice, the Law and Land.* Canberra: Barrambunga Books, 1993.
Harris, Stewart. *It's Coming Yet—: An Aboriginal Treaty Within Australia Between Australians.* Canberra: Aboriginal Treaty Committee, 1979.
Langton, Marcia, ed. *Honour among Nations: Treaties and Agreements with Indigenous People.* Melbourne: Melbourne University Press, 2004.
Queensland Legislation Review Committee. *Towards Self-Government: A Discussion Paper.* Cairns: Queensland Legislative Review Committee, 1991.
Reynolds, Henry. *Aboriginal Sovereignty: Reflections on Race, State, and Nation.* Sydney: Allen & Unwin, 1996.
Wright, Judith. *We Call for a Treaty.* Sydney: Collins/Fontana, 1985.

7. Health and Welfare

Ah Kee, Margaret, and Clare Tilbury. "The Aboriginal and Torres Strait Islander Child Placement Principle Is About Self-Determination." *Children Australia* 24, no. 3 (1999): 4–8.
Blake, Thom. "'The Leper Shall Dwell Alone': A History of Peel Island Lazaret." In *Moreton Bay Matters*, edited by Murray Johnson, 72–86. Brisbane: Brisbane History Group, 2002.
Butlin, Noel. "Macassans and Aboriginal Smallpox: The '1789' and '1829' Epidemics." *Historical Studies* 21, no. 84 (April 1985): 315–35.
———. *Our Original Aggression: Aboriginal Populations of Southeastern Australia, 1788–1850.* Sydney: Allen & Unwin, 1983.
Byard, Roger. "Traditional Medicine of Aboriginal Australia." *Canadian Medical Association Journal* 139, no. 8 (15 October 1988): 792–94.
Campbell, Judy. *Invisible Invaders: Smallpox and Other Diseases in Aboriginal Australia, 1780–1988.* Melbourne: Melbourne University Press, 2002.
———. "Smallpox in Aboriginal Australia, 1829–31." *Historical Studies* 20, no. 81 (October 1983): 536–56.
Chisholm, Richard. "Destined Children: Aboriginal Child Welfare in Law and Policy," Pt 1. *Aboriginal Law Bulletin* 1, no. 14 (June 1985): 6.
Clarke, Philip. *Aboriginal People and Their Plants.* Sydney: Rosenberg, 2007.

Cripps, Kyllie. "Indigenous Family Violence: From Emergency Measures to Committed Long-Term Action." *Indigenous Law Centre* 11, no. 2 (2007): 6–18.
Davidson, W. S. *Havens of Refuge: A History of Leprosy in Western Australia*. Perth: University of Western Australia Press, 1978.
Genever, Geoffrey. "Queensland's Black Leper Colony." *Queensland Review* 15, no. 2 (August 2008): 59–68.
Isaacs, Jennifer. *Bush Food: Aboriginal Food and Herbal Medicine*. Sydney: Ure Smith, 1991.
Johnstone, Robert. "Spinifex and Wattle," Pt 6. *Queenslander* (13 June 1903): 10.
———. "Spinifex and Wattle," Pt 7. *Queenslander* (27 June 1903): 10.
Low, Tim. *Bush Tucker: Australia's Wild Food Harvest*. Sydney: Angus & Robertson, 1991.
Lush, Douglas, John Hargrave, and Angela Merianos. "Leprosy Control in the Northern Territory." *Australian and New Zealand Journal of Public Health* 22, no. 6 (October 1998): 709–13.
Maguire, John. "The Fantome Island Leprosarium." In *Health and Healing in Tropical Australia and Papua New Guinea*, edited by Roy Macleod and Donald Denoon, 142–48. Townsville: James Cook University, 1991.
Mak, Donna, Eleanor Platt, and Christopher Heath. "Leprosy Transmission in the Kimberley, Western Australia: Still a Reality in 21st-Century Australia." *Medical Journal of Australia* 179, no. 8 (20 October 2003): 452.
Mayers, N., and P. Fagan. "Medical Services." In *The Encyclopaedia of Aboriginal Australia*, vol. 2, edited by David Horton, 688–89. Canberra: Aboriginal Studies, 1994.
Parry, Suzanne. "'Of Vital Importance to the Community': The Control of Leprosy in the Northern Territory." *Health and History* 5, no. 1 (2003): 1–21.
Pearn, John. "Medical Ethnobotany in Australia: Past and Present." Paper read to the Linnean Society, London, 30 September 2004.
Reid, Janice, ed. *Body, Land and Spirit: Health and Healing in Aboriginal Society*. St. Lucia: University of Queensland Press, 1982.
Reid, Janice, and Peggy Trompf, eds. *The Health of Aboriginal Australia*. Sydney: Harcourt Brace Jovanovich, 1991.
Saggers, Sherry, and Dennis Gray. *Aboriginal Health & Society: The Traditional and Contemporary Aboriginal Struggle for Better Health*. North Sydney: Allen & Unwin, 1991.
Trudgen, Richard. *Why Warriors Lie Down and Die: Towards an Understanding of Why the Aboriginal People of Arnhem Land Face the Greatest Crisis in Health and Education since European Contact: Djambatj Mala*. Darwin: Aboriginal Resources and Development Services, 2000.
Webb, L. J. "The Use of Plant Medicines and Poisons by Australian Aborigines." *Mankind* 7, no. 2 (December 1969): 137–46.

8. Aborigines and Military Service

Anon. "Aboriginal War Veterans No Longer Forgotten." *Babana News* 1, no. 6 (February 2009): 1–10.

Hall, Robert. "Aborigines and Torres Strait Islanders in the Second World War." In *Aborigines in the Defence of Australia*, edited by Desmond Ball, 32–63. Sydney: Australian National University Press, 1991.

———. *The Black Diggers: Aborigines and Torres Strait Islanders in the Second World War*. Sydney: Allen & Unwin, 1989.

———. "Black Magic: Leonard Waters—Second World War Fighter Pilot." *Aboriginal History* 16 (1992): 73–80.

Huggonson, David. "The Dark Diggers of the AIF." *Australian Quarterly* 61, no. 3 (Spring 1989): 352–57.

Jones, Rhys, and Betty Meehan. "The Arnhem Salient." In *Aborigines in the Defence of Australia*, edited by Desmond Ball, 100–162. Sydney: Australian National University Press, 1991.

9. Film and Media

Anderson, Ian. "I, the 'Hybrid' Aborigine: Film and Representation." *Australian Aboriginal Studies* 1 (1997): 4–14.

Boyle, Anthony. "Two Images of the Aboriginal: *Walkabout*, the Novel and the Film." *Literature/Film Quarterly* 7, no. 1 (1997): 67–76.

Bryson, Ian, Margaret Burns, and Marcia Langton, eds. *Painting with Light: Australian Indigenous Cinema*. Melbourne: Oxford University Press, 2000.

Collins, Felicity, and Therese Davis. *Australian Cinema after Mabo*. Cambridge: Cambridge University Press, 2004.

de Brabander, Dallas. "Koori Radio." In *The Encyclopaedia of Aboriginal Australia*, vol. 1, edited by David Horton, 559. Canberra: Aboriginal Studies, 1994.

Dunlop, Ian. "Ethnographic Film-Making in Australia: The First Seventy Years (1898–1968)." *Aboriginal History* 3, pt. 2 (1979): 111–19.

Ginsburg, Faye. "Indigenous Media: Faustian Contract or Global Village?" *Cultural Anthropology* 6, no. 1 (February 1991): 92–112.

Hickling-Hudson, Anne. "White Construction of Black Identity in Australian Films about Aborigines." *Literature/Film Quarterly* 18, no. 4 (October 1990): 263–74.

Howie-Willis, Ian. "BRACS." In *The Encyclopaedia of Aboriginal Australia*, vol. 1, edited by David Horton, 148. Canberra: Aboriginal Studies, 1994.

———. "CAAMA." In *The Encyclopaedia of Aboriginal Australia*, vol. 1, edited by David Horton, 175. Canberra: Aboriginal Studies, 1994.

Jennings, Karen. *Sites of Difference: Cinematic Representations of Aboriginality and Gender*. Melbourne: Damned, 1993.

Langton, Marcia. *"Well I Heard It on the Radio, and I Saw It on the Television . . ."* Woolloomooloo: Australian Film Commission, 1993.

Langton, Marcia, and Brownlee Kirkpatrick. "A Listing of Aboriginal Periodicals." *Aboriginal History* 3, pt. 2 (1979): 120–27.

Lawson, Sylvia. "Along the 'Pot-Holed Track': Meditations on Mixed Inheritance in Recent Work by Ivan Sen and Dennis McDermott." *Aboriginal History* 30 (2006): 211–16.

Long, Chris. "Australia's First Films." Pt. 11, "Aborigines and Actors." *Cinema Papers* no. 102 (December 1994): 52–82.

Lydon, Jane. "A Strange Time Machine." *Australian Historical Studies* 35 no. 123 (2004): 137–48.

McCarthy, Greg. *Australian Cinema and the Spectres of Post-Coloniality: "Rabbit-Proof Fence," "Australian Rules," "The Tracker" and "Beneath Clouds."* London: Menzies Centre for Australian Studies, 2004.

McKee, Alan. "Films vs. Real Life: Communicating Aboriginality in Cinema and Television." *UTS Review* 3 no. 1 (1997): 160–82.

Moore, Catriona, and Stephen Muecke. "Racism and Representation of Aborigines in Film." *Australian Journal of Cultural Studies* 2, no. 1 (1984): 36–53.

Morris, Christine. "Framing the Future: Indigenous Communication in Australia." In *Contesting Media Power: Alternative Media in a Networked World*, edited by Nick Couldry and James Curran, 71–88. Lanham, MD: Rowan and Littlefield, 2003.

Probyn, Fiona. "An Ethics of Following and the No Road Film: Trackers, Followers and Fanatics." *Australian Humanities Review* 37 (2005).

Reckhari, Suneeti. "Myths and Absent Signifiers in Representations of Aboriginal Identity in Australian Cinema." *Journal of Australian Indigenous Issues* 10, no. 4 (2007): 3–13.

———. "The 'Other' in Film: Exclusions of Aboriginal Identity from Australian Cinema." *Visual Anthropology* 21, no. 2 (2008): 125–35.

———. "Return to Formula: Narrative Closures in Representations of Aboriginal Identity in Australian Cinema." *Australian Studies* 19, no. 2 (2004): 79–102.

Rose, Michael. *For the Record: 160 years of Aboriginal Print Journalism*. Sydney: Allen & Unwin, 1996.

Strange, Dorothy. "Walkabout . . . a 16-Week Safari through the Modern Dreamtime." *Walkabout* (August 1971): 8–15.

Turcotte, Gerry. "Spectrality in Indigenous Women's Cinema: Tracey Moffatt and Beck Cole." *Journal of Commonwealth Literature* 43, no. 1 (2008): 7–21.

10. Art and Photography

The global success of traditional Aboriginal painting in the last generation has been one of the most extraordinary developments in Australian cultural life. But urban Aborigines have also achieved prominence. For an introduction to the subject, see the following:

Bardon, Geoffrey, and James Bardon. *Papunya: A Place Made After the Story: The Beginnings of the Western Desert Painting Movement*. Melbourne: Melbourne University Press, 2004.

Batty, Joyce D. *Namatjira: Wanderer between Two Worlds*. Melbourne: Hodder and Stoughton, 1963.

Carrigan, Belinda, ed. *Rover Thomas: I Want to Paint*. Perth: Holmes à Court Gallery, 2003.
Flood, Josephine. *Rock Art of the Dreamtime: Images of Ancient Australia*. Pymble: Angus & Robertson, 1997.
French, Alison. *Seeing the Centre: The Art of Albert Namatjira 1902–1959*. Canberra: National Gallery of Australia, 2002.
Gellatly, Kelly. *Gordon Bennett*. Melbourne: National Gallery of Victoria, 2007.
Hardy, Jane, J.V.S. Megaw, and M. Ruth Megaw. *The Heritage of Namatjira: The Watercolourists of Central Australia*. Melbourne: Heinemann, 1992.
Hoorn, Jeanette. *Strange Fruit: Testimony and Memory in Julie Dowling's Portraits*. Melbourne: Ian Potter Museum of Art, 2007.
Jantjes, G., and E. Macgregor. *History and Memory in the Art of Gordon Bennett*. Birmingham: Ikon Gallery, 1993.
Johnson, Vivien. *Michael Jagamara Nelson*. Sydney: Craftsman House, 1997.
Murphy, Bernice, ed. *The Native Born: Objects and Representations from Ramingining, Arnhem Land*. Sydney: Museum of Contemporary Art, 1996.
Munn, Nancy. *Walbiri Iconography: Graphic Representation and Cultural Symbolism in a Central Australian Society*. New York: Cornell University Press, 1973.
Myers, Fred. *Painting Culture: The Making of an Aboriginal High Art*. Durham, NC: Duke University Press, 2002.
Neale, Margo. *Urban Dingo: The Art and Life of Lin Onus, 1948–1996*. South Brisane: Craftsman House, 2000.
Perkins, Hetti, and Hannah Fink, eds. *Papunya Tula: Genesis and Genius*. Sydney: Art Gallery of New South Wales, 2000.
Perkins, Hetti, and Margie West. *One Sun One Moon: Aboriginal Art in Australia*. Sydney: Art Gallery of New South Wales, 2007.
Sayers, Andrew. *Aboriginal Artists of the Nineteenth Century*. Melbourne: Oxford University Press, 1994.
Sutton, Peter, ed. *Dreamings: The Art of Aboriginal Australia*. Ringwood: Viking (in association with the Asia Society Galleries, New York), 1988.
Taylor, Luke, ed. *Painting the Land Story*. Canberra: National Museum of Australia, 1999.
Walsh, Grahame. *Australia's Greatest Rock Art*. Bathurst: E. J. Brill/Robert Brown & Associates, 1988.

For a general survey of the depiction of Aborigines in European painting, see:
Dutton, Geoffrey. *White on Black: The Australian Aborigine Portrayed in Art*. Melbourne: Macmillan, 1974.

Several Aboriginal photographers have developed successful careers:
Maggia, Filippo. *Tracey Moffat: Between Dreams and Reality*. Milan: Skira, 2006.
Munro, Keith. *Ricky Maynard: Portrait of a Distant Land*. Sydney: Museum of Contemporary Art, 2008.

11. Education

Beresford, Quentin, and Gary Partington, eds. *Reform and Resistance in Aboriginal Education: The Australian Experience.* Crawley: University of Western Australia Press, 2003.

Harris, Stephen. *Two-Way Schooling: Education and Cultural Survival.* Canberra: Aboriginal Studies, 1990.

Mills, John. *Bilingual Education and Australian Schools: A Review.* Melbourne: Australian Council for Educational Research, 1982.

12. Literature

For general reference work on literature about Aborigines (and some Aboriginal literature), see:

Healy, J. J. *Literature and the Aborigine in Australia.* St. Lucia: University of Queensland Press, 1989 [1978].

Shoemaker, Adam. *Black Words, White Page: Aboriginal Literature, 1929–1988.* St. Lucia: University of Queensland Press, 1989.

Toorn, Penny Van. *Writing Never Arrives Naked: Early Aboriginal Cultures of Writing in Australia.* Canberra: Aboriginal Studies, 2006.

13. Demographics

Birrell, B. "Intermix and Australia's Indigenous Population." *People and Place* 8, no. 1 (2000): 61–66.

Gardiner, G., and E. A. Bourke. "Indigenous Populations, 'Mixed' Discourses and Identities." *People and Place* 8, no. 2 (2000): 43–52.

Kinfu, Y., and J. Taylor. "Estimating the Components of Indigenous Population Change, 1996–2001." *Centre for Aboriginal Economic Policy Research Discussion Paper No. 240.* Canberra: Centre for Aboriginal Economic Policy Research/ Australian National University, 2002.

IV. WORKS BY INDIGENOUS WRITERS

1. Memoirs

One of the most striking features of the last generation has been the efflorescence of Aboriginal and Islander literature. Memoirs and other autobiographical/biographical writing has been the most prolific genre. Among a large literature, see the following:

Barker, Jimmie. *The Two Worlds of Jimmie Barker: The Life of an Aboriginal Australian, 1900–1972, as Told to Janet Mathews.* Canberra: AIATSIS, 1977.

Bropho, Robert. *Fringedweller.* Chippendale: APCOL, 1980.

Clarke, Banjo. *Wisdom Man.* Camberwell: Penguin, 2003.

Crawford, Evelyn. *Over My Tracks.* Ringwood: Penguin, 1993.

Gilbert, Kevin. *Because a White Man'll Never Do It*. Sydney: Angus & Robertson, 1973.
Huggins, Jackie. *Sister Girl*. St. Lucia: University of Queensland Press, 1988.
Huggins, Rita, and Jackie Huggins. *Auntie Rita*. Canberra: Aboriginal Studies, 1994.
Labumore [Elsie Roughsey]. *An Aboriginal Mother Tells of the Old and the New*. Edited by Paul Memmott and Robyn Horsman. Fitzroy: McPhee Gribble/Penguin, 1984.
Lamilami, Lazarus. *Lamilami Speaks, the Cry Went Up: A Story of the People of Goulburn Islands, North Australia*. Sydney: Ure Smith, 1974.
Langford, Ruby. *Don't Take Your Love to Town*. Ringwood: Penguin, 1988.
Lester, Yami. *Yami: The Autobiography of Yami Lester*. Alice Springs: Institute for Aboriginal Development, 1993.
Marika, Wandjuk. *Wandjuk Marika: Life Story*. St. Lucia: University of Queensland Press, 1995.
Morgan, Sally. *Mother and Daughter*. Fremantle: Fremantle Arts Centre, 1990.
———. *My Place*. Fremantle: Fremantle Arts Centre, 1987.
Neidjie, Bill. *Story about Feeling*. Broome: Magabala Books, 1999.
Ngabidji, Grant. *My Country of the Pelican Dreaming: The Life of an Australian Aborigine*. Canberra: AIATSIS, 1981.
Nunukul, Oodgeroo. *Stradbroke Dreamtime*. Sydney: Angus & Robertson, 1972.
Pepper, Phillip. *You Are What You Make Yourself to Be*. Melbourne: Hyland House, 1980.
Perkins, Charles. *A Bastard like Me*. Sydney: Ure Smith, 1975.
Pilkington, Doris [Nuri Gamimara]. *Follow the Rabbit-Proof Fence*. St. Lucia: University of Queensland Press, 2001.
Roughsey, Dick. *Moon and Rainbow: The Autobiography of an Aboriginal*. Sydney: Reed, 1971.
Scott, Kim, and Hazel Brown. *Kayang & Mme*. Fremantle: Fremantle Arts Centre, 2005.
Smith, Shirley, and Bobbi Sykes. *MumShirl: An Autobiography*. Richmond: Heinemann, 1985.
Summers, Ronnie. *Ronnie: Tasmanian Songman*. Broome: Magabala, 2009.
Tovey, Noel. *Little Black Bastard: A Story of Survival*. Sydney: Hodder Headline, 2004.
Tucker, Margaret. *If Everyone Cared*. Sydney: Ure Smith, 1977.
Ward, Glenyse. *Unna You Fullas*. Broome: Magabala Books, 1991.
———. *Wandering Girl*. Broome: Magabala, 1997.
West, Ida. *Pride against Prejudice*. Canberra: AIATSIS, 1984.

2. Anthologies

Davis, Jack, ed. *Paperbark: A Collection of Black Australian Writing*. St. Lucia: University of Queensland Press, 1990.
Heiss, Anita, and Peter Minter, eds. *Macquarie PEN Anthology of Aboriginal Literature*. Sydney: Allen & Unwin, 2008.

3. Fiction, Plays, and Poetry

Behrendt, Larissa. *Home*. St. Lucia: University of Queensland Press, 2004.
Lucashenko, Melissa. *Hard Yards*. St. Lucia: University of Queensland Press, 1999.
——. *Killing Darcy*. St. Lucia: University of Queensland Press, 1998.
Scott, Kim. *Benang: From the Heart*. Fremantle: Fremantle Arts Centre, 1999.
Watson, Sam. *The Kadaitcha Sung*. New York: Penguin, 1990.
Wright, Alexis. *Carpentaria*. Artarmon: Giramondo, 2006.
——. *Plains of Promise*. St. Lucia: University of Queensland Press, 1997.

There have been a number of successful Aboriginal playwrights. A collection of early works was published in 1989. See:
Davis, Jack, Eva Johnson, Richard Walley, and Bob Maza. *Plays from Black Australia*. Sydney: Currency, 1989.

Davis himself is the most successful playwright. Among his plays are:
Davis, Jack. *Honey Spot*. Sydney: Currency, 1987.
——. *Kullark (Home); The Dreamers*. Sydney: Currency, 1982.
——. *No Sugar*. Sydney: Currency, 1986.

The musical *Bran Nue Dae* (Sydney: Currency, 1991) by Jimmy Chi, was highly successful as a stage production and has recently been made into a feature film.

Numerous Aboriginal poets have been published in the last generation. A useful introduction is the anthology:
Gilbert, Kevin, ed. *Inside Black Australia: An Anthology of Aboriginal Poetry*. Ringwood: Penguin, 1988.

By far, the most successful poet is Kath Walker or, as she became known, Oodgeroo Noonuccal. Among her best known works are:
Noonuccal, Oodgeroo. *The Dawn Is at Hand*. Brisbane: Jacaranda, 1966.
——. *My People*. Brisbane: Jacaranda, 1970.
——. *We are Going*. Brisbane: Jacaranda, 1964.

4. Non-Fiction

There have been a number of collections of Aboriginal commentary.
Moores, Irene, comp. *Voices of Aboriginal Australia: Past, Present, Future*. Springwood: Butterfly Books, 1995.
Tatz, Colin, ed. *Black Viewpoints: The Aboriginal Experience*. Sydney: ANZ Book, 1975.

There have been fewer historical works than memoirs, but see the following:
Mattingley, Christobel, ed. *Survival in Our Own Land: "Aboriginal" Experiences in "South Australia" since 1836*. Adelaide: Wakefield, 1988.

Maynard, John. *Fight for Liberty and Freedom: The Origins of Australian Aboriginal Activism*. Canberra: Aboriginal Studies, 2007.

Miller, James. *Koori, a Will to Win: The Heroic Resistance, Survival and Triumph of Black Australia*. Sydney: Angus & Robertson, 1985.

A comprehensive historical work is the book based on a six-part television documentary series shown on SBS television in 2008:

Perkins, Rachel, and Marcia Langton. *First Australians: An Iillustrated History*. Carlton: Miegunyah, 2008.

About the Authors

Mitchell Rolls (BA, MA, PhD) is senior lecturer and codirector (academic) at Riawunna, Centre for Aboriginal Studies, University of Tasmania, and codirector of Colonialism and Its Aftermath, an interdisciplinary research center. His concurrent research interests include cultural identity, race and representation, cultural appropriation, and place-making in settler societies. He has published widely in these areas. With a colleague, he is currently working on an Australia Research Council Discovery Project, examining the popular Australian magazine *Walkabout*.

Murray Johnson (BA, PGBA, PhD) is a University Medal recipient from the University of Queensland. He has taught numerous undergraduate and postgraduate courses on Australian history, including Indigenous Australian history, at the University of Queensland, the Australian National University, and the University of Tasmania. He has published widely on various aspects of Australian history and has been involved in Aboriginal native title claims in Queensland. He is currently lecturer in Aboriginal studies at the Launceston Campus of Riawunna, Centre for Aboriginal Studies, University of Tasmania.

Henry Reynolds, the historian, holds an honorary position at the University of Tasmania. He has published widely on Aboriginal colonial relations. His publications include *The Law of the Land, The Other Side of the Frontier, Aboriginal Sovereignty*, and *Why Weren't We Told?*